REVIVAL
OF THE
RUNES

"*Revival of the Runes* is the most thorough presentation of the history and development of the runes, both historical and—most important—the magical esoteric side. This book provides various alternative theories regarding the origins of the runes and follows their trail from the 1500s onward (after a brief consideration of the earlier period), through the Middle Ages, the Enlightenment, and the 20th century. The author also dissects and discusses rationally the Nazi specter very effectively. This work is an intellectual heavyweight to drool over—very academic and rich in terms of source material referenced in the footnotes and bibliography. It is a must for serious students and practitioners."

FREYA ASWYNN, AUTHOR OF
NORTHERN MYSTERIES AND MAGICK

"Stephen Flowers's new book is a valuable chronological account that shows how the ancient wisdom of the runes has continued since ancient times and has been renewed throughout history by notable masters of the Northern tradition. This wide-ranging historical account of the runes is a comprehensive and erudite work that brings together many strands and historical currents into a coherent narrative. It is a valuable addition to the author's fine body of work on the history and practice of the runic tradition and deserves to be on the bookshelf of every person with an interest in the runes."

NIGEL PENNICK, AUTHOR OF
RUNIC LORE AND LEGEND

"Roughly two millennia ago, the ancient script of the runes was first codified, carved, and communicated by an unknown Germanic-speaking innovator whose vision absorbed elements of the neighboring Roman world. Although the traditional runestaves could later be employed for mundane purposes, their earliest associations were imbued with the sacred, and it is no wonder these stark and angular signs have exerted a fascination that continues right to the present day. The labyrinthian story of their decline and rediscovery, their use and abuse, is ably related in *Revival of the Runes* by Stephen Flowers, a trained runologist who is equally at home in the scholarly and spiritual domains. The results of his excavations are by turns exciting and disturbing but always culturally insightful and enriching."

MICHAEL MOYNIHAN, PH.D., COEDITOR OF *TYR: MYTH—CULTURE—TRADITION*

"The runes have enchanted people through the ages—the zeitgeist has been projected on these old signs from the Viking Age. In the 17th century Johannes Bureus combined runes with ideas from both folklore and Renaissance high magic. In the age of Enlightenment, runes and Viking myths were used for educational purposes in the Nordic countries. Most infamous is the Nazi regime's misuse of runes. In this book Stephen Flowers, today's foremost expert on rune magic, goes through different currents where runes are center. It is an invaluable contribution to both academic and practical esoteric knowledge of the mysteries of the runes."

THOMAS KARLSSON, PH.D., AUTHOR OF *NIGHTSIDE OF THE RUNES*

"An essential read for anyone who wishes to understand the runes as they relate to the reawakening of Germanic spirituality taking place today. *Revival of the Runes* provides a thorough and scholarly history of the runes, from their origins with the Older Futhark, the later development of the Younger Futhark, the runic resurgences that followed their decline in the Middle Ages, up to the present revival of which Stephen Flowers himself has been an essential part. This book examines runology from a scholarly as well as the magical standpoint of an accomplished runic practitioner. *Revival of the Runes* documents the survival of the runes over time and their repeated return to our awareness, showing that for us, like Allfather Odin himself, the mysteries of the runes are eternal, just waiting for us to take them up."

BERKELEY HARBIN, *DRIGHTEN* OF WODEN'S FOLK KINDRED

REVIVAL
OF THE
RUNES

The Modern Rediscovery
and Reinvention of the
Germanic Runes

STEPHEN EDRED FLOWERS, PH.D.

Inner Traditions
Rochester, Vermont

Inner Traditions
One Park Street
Rochester, Vermont 05767
www.InnerTraditions.com

SUSTAINABLE FORESTRY INITIATIVE
Certified Sourcing
www.sfiprogram.org
SFI-00854

Text stock is SFI certified

Cataloging-in-Publication Data for this title is available from the Library of Congress

ISBN 978-1-64411-178-9 (print)
ISBN 978-1-64411-179-6 (ebook)

Printed and bound in the United States by Lake Book Manufacturing, Inc. The text stock is SFI certified. The Sustainable Forestry Initiative® program promotes sustainable forest management.

10 9 8 7 6 5 4 3 2 1

Text design and layout by Virginia Scott Bowman
This book was typeset in Garamond Premier Pro, Gill Sans, and Futura with Highstories used as the display typeface

To send correspondence to the author of this book, mail a first-class letter to the author c/o Inner Traditions • Bear & Company, One Park Street, Rochester, VT 05767, and we will forward the communication, or contact the author directly at **runa@texas.net**.

✦ ✦ ✦

This book is dedicated to all those who have struggled to
understand the mysteries of the Germanic past

CONTENTS

ACKNOWLEDGMENTS

Thanks go to Jan Reimer, who supplied me with some of the materials that made this work possible, and to Peter Andersson for his corrections to some Swedish material. For various kinds of help in the process of writing the present book, a note of gratitude also goes to Mikael W. Gejel, Alice Karlsdottir, Thomas Karlsson, Michael Moynihan, Ralph Tegtmeier, and Don Webb.

Abbreviations

BCE   Before the Common Era (= BC)

CE   Common Era (= AD)

Gk.   Ancient Greek

Ger.   German

OE   Old English

OHG Old High German

ON   Old Norse

pl.   plural

pron. pronounced

sg.   singular

Sw.   Swedish

IK   Hauck, Karl, et al. *Die Goldbrakteaten der Völkerwanderungszeit.*

Note: Words that are directly preceded by an asterisk—for example, the noun *rūnō* or the name *Wōðanaz*—represent forms that have been reconstructed based on the principles of historical linguistics but which are unattested in the literary or epigraphical record.

STANDING ON THE SHOULDERS OF GIANTS

This book has roots that go back to a certain summer day in 1974 when I was suddenly inspired to seek the mysteries of the runes. At the time, I was an undergraduate student at the University of Texas at Austin with little motivation or direction, but I was interested in all things esoteric. This day changed everything and set me on a lifelong path. I was lucky enough to be enrolled at a university with the resources, teachers, and reference materials to make the scientific element of my journey possible, and ten years later I received a Ph.D. degree with a dissertation titled "Runes and Magic."

From its very beginnings, the study of the runes has been entwined with both the scientific and esoteric adventures of our culture, and this is all the more evident today. But academics do not like to be saddled with the baggage of modern-day would-be "rune magicians," and the average current "rune mystic" chafes under the rigor and historical accuracy demanded by the academic. To my thinking, however, these two impulses are not necessarily antagonistic. Indeed, my own experience was born of a synthesis of these two runological trends. This synthesis is also reflected in the contents of this book, which is an investigation of how the two trends have manifested historically and interacted culturally over the past half century.

Revival of the Runes constitutes the second book in a series of three thematically related works that I have been researching and writing over many years. The overarching goal of this project is to chronicle the most historically significant rune-using groups and individuals over the past two millennia. The first book in the series is a forthcoming study of the intertribal network—perhaps better described as gild—of runemasters that arose in ancient Germania (the latter term, which was originally used by ancient Roman writers such as Julius Caesar and Tacitus, refers to the areas of Europe traditionally and predominantly inhabited by Germanic-speaking peoples at the beginning of the first millennium of the Common Era). The second book in the series is the present volume, *Revival of the Runes,* which traces the general demise of ancient runic traditions during the latter Middle Ages in the wake of Christianization and also documents the resurgence of interest in the runes and the revival of their usage in the early modern and modern periods. The third and final book, written under my pen name, Edred Thorsson, is *History of the Rune-Gild: The Reawakening of the Gild 1980–2018* (Thorsson 2019), which documents the development of the modern Rune-Gild, an international confraternity dedicated to seeking out and prying into the runic mysteries—as expressed both esoterically and exoterically—for personal and cultural development, using the most rigorous intellectual and practical tools.

Revival of the Runes looks at the long struggle that took place on many levels to reawaken this particular aspect of ancient Germanic culture, myth, and intellectual life over five hundred years, from the outset of the sixteenth century through the end of the twentieth century. Those who today engage in inner or outer work with these mysterious signs from our collective past will benefit greatly from a deeper understanding of the scope and heroic dimension of our predecessors' efforts at reawakening the study of the runes. One will learn that indeed we do stand on the shoulders of giants—poets, magicians, warriors, scholars, mystics, and the occasional scoundrel—who were the rune-users of the past.

Although the present book begins its in-depth coverage at approximately 1500, I will first provide a brief consideration of the earlier period before 1500. The further back one goes in this study, the sparser the evidence becomes. But the runic inscriptions themselves stand as stark proof of the existence of such a gild of runemasters in various parts of Germania for approximately fifteen hundred years. Since those carving runes during this span of time were otherwise illiterate—and information about how to write in runes, and the lore of the system itself, was categorically a matter of oral tradition passed from master to pupil—they thus constituted the "gild."

For many reasons a book of this sort should be read and studied in conjunction with another multivolume project of mine called *The Northern Dawn,* which explores the general process of reawakening Germanic cultural values. For the reader who seeks to most fully understand the content of *Revival of the Runes,* it would also be of great benefit to absorb some general works on the histories of the various cultures we discuss—the Scandinavian, Icelandic, English, and German. Runes should always be seen as exponents of a much larger cultural base, of which they are weird and strange outcroppings of light and insight. For without a general grasp of the cultural matrix out of which these signs of light emerge, the information they can convey may become an instrument of delusion and unbridled mania.

STEPHEN E. FLOWERS,
WOODHARROW

BINDING TOGETHER THE IDEAS OF SCIENCE AND MAGIC

This book is mainly about the process of the revival, renewal, and reawakening of runic writing, ideology, and mythology from early modern times to the present day. When the earliest speakers of the Germanic dialects—which includes English—first wrote, they wrote in runes. The runic tradition lasted for about twelve hundred years before it began to fall into general decline in most regions where it had been practiced for all those centuries.

Over the past several decades the topic of "runes" has increasingly become a part of popular culture in the English-speaking world, but it has not always been that way. The runes constitute the original writing system used by a small, elite population who lived at one time or another among all of the ancient Germanic tribes, from Scandinavia to Germany and from the eastern steppes to England. In these ancient times, during the first centuries of the Common Era (ca. 100–800 CE), only about 1 percent of the population could ever be said to be literate in runes. Yet, to our imaginations at least, the runes seem to have embodied the essence of the soul of ancient Germanic culture. The use of runes more or less died out completely, except in very isolated pockets of the remotest parts of Sweden, by the dawn of the Modern Age, circa 1500.

The story of how and why this forgotten and rejected knowledge was revived and eventually popularized throughout the world shaped by the originators of this system is the subject of this study. This knowledge was largely suppressed due to a new cultural myth—that of Christianity—imported from southern Europe and Ireland, which was naturally threatened by the continuation of the pre-Christian myth and its structures. Our purpose or aim in telling this story is to clarify the process by which forgotten and hidden knowledge is revived and received. By examining the whole breadth of this process, it is hoped that greater clarity and insight can be gained by those who endeavor to awaken these slumbering mysteries in the future.

To understand any complex cultural phenomenon or movement, it is necessary to place it in its context within the history of ideas. One of the greatest causes of historical misunderstanding is the projection of contemporary values and mind-sets on other cultures, past or present. And indeed, in the study of the runic revival, we often find writers who have projected their own prejudices onto the runic data. This has been done as much from the so-called scientific side as it has from the esoteric one. Often the modern scientist will have no idea of how the ancients actually thought, and how that thought was different from their own modern ways of thinking. By the same token, the esotericist will often project entirely inappropriate models of esoteric thinking—models that are very unlikely to have been known to the original rune-users—onto the ancients. One of the ways to help avoid these problems of interpretation is by developing a more complete understanding of the various periods of intellectual history in which the revivals took place.

In this study, I will discuss the runic revival in the context of five periods: the Renaissance, the Enlightenment, the era of Romanticism, the early twentieth century, and the late twentieth century. Each of these periods has been marked by its own myths and metanarratives that have, in turn, conditioned the attitudes of the writers who endeavored to revive the runic tradition in their day. And occasionally some of these writers and thinkers—Johan Bure and Guido von List, for example—have been the source of insights that serve to shape events in their own and subsequent epochs.

Each chapter of this book will also take into account two different approaches, that of the scientific and that of the esoteric, which are often very independent but are sometimes related or overlap. The interests of *scientific* runology are properly limited to those things that are logically provable, or that belong to a comparative model capable of shedding light on the runic tradition. *Esoteric* runology, by contrast, assumes that the runes have some sort of mysterious meanings or powers *in and of themselves* and seeks to unravel the methods of discovering and/or utilizing these features. Academic or scientific runology can exist apart from esoteric runology, but the best of esoteric runology, in imitation of a sort of Platonic model, is founded on factual and academic runological findings. However, it must also be admitted that much of actual extant esoteric runology exists in a world quite separate from the academic realities.

Over the past few decades academic runology has become more and more narrow in its scope and now tends to be focused mainly on linguistic concerns. In part, this situation has come about as a reaction against the earlier and excessive use of "magical" interpretations among academic runologists of the early twentieth century. The more recent academic abhorrence of such interpretations may also be a response to the growing popularity of runic esotericism or "runic occultism" in our own time. The excesses of the New Age approach can rightly be seen as a disappointing turn of events for more levelheaded academics. However, as this study will show, the serious esoteric dimension of runic studies is something that has always been a part of runology. It is not likely to go away, so it is perhaps better to improve and refine the esoteric approach than to reject it entirely.

On the other hand, it is also the case that in recent years the study of the history of esotericism in general, and "Western Esotericism" in particular, has entered the world of academia as an interdisciplinary program. Unfortunately, some of the initial products of this nascent discipline have been shallow or have lacked a fundamental grounding in linguistic and general historical and cultural knowledge. There are, however, several shining examples of erudition. One of these is Antoine Faivre, who has provided a widely accepted general theoretical model of approaching the subject of esotericism (see Faivre 1994, 10–35).

Faivre identifies six major components that are present in esoteric thought and practice. The first four are considered primary, while the latter two are seen as secondary or "relative." The six major components are:

1. **Correspondences.** There exists a mysterious system of correspondences between a higher and lower world, and between and among the contents of these worlds.

2. **Living Nature.** The natural world of physical phenomena is seen as "essentially alive in all its parts, often inhabited and traversed by a light or hidden fire circulating through it" (Faivre 1994, 11).

3. **Imagination and Mediations.** These complementary concepts indicate the presence of a faculty of the soul for the discovery of the hidden reality (*imaginatio*) and the further possibility of employing this knowledge through mediations between the worlds; for example, by using symbols and rituals.

4. **Experience of Transmutation.** The overall effect of esoteric endeavors is nothing less than a practical and fundamental change in the nature of the subject (the esotericist himself or herself) and/or an object in the world itself. The esoteric is not merely content with idle intellectual speculation.

5. **The Praxis of the Concordance.** This is the tendency to try to establish common denominators between and among various (or all) cultural traditions and is the expectation of "obtaining an illumination, a gnosis, of superior quality" (Faivre 1994, 14). By

these methods a perennial philosophy is discovered that is alleged to be at the root of many traditions. There are generally two attitudes toward this process: the genetic and the transgenetic. The former seeks links only among linguistically, culturally, and historically related traditions; for example, within the Indo-European system. The latter believes in a common core shared by all traditions, be they Chinese, Hebrew, Egyptian, Celtic, or from some other source.

6. **Transmission.** Here we have the idea that esoteric knowledge must be passed from master to disciple, bound in a relationship that is more or less understood to exist within a certain school of thought.

Taken together, these components describe and define what is meant by the term *esoteric* in a scientific or academic understanding. In the course of this study when the word *esoteric* is used, it is to be conceived of in these terms.

The exoteric perspective, by contrast, is not categorically opposed to the esoteric, although many individuals in the exoteric field are philosophically opposed to the intrusion of esoteric concerns into their discipline. Rather, the exoteric is a necessary corollary to the esoteric. The exoteric should be intelligible to the logical mind and explicable in terms of logic alone. It is the literal meaning of a text, while the esoteric attempts to penetrate beyond this to the spirit of the text. Paradoxically, esoteric texts can be read from an exoteric perspective, and exoteric texts can be interpreted from an esoteric angle. As we will see, this "debate" has been an ongoing theme in the history of runology: the distinction between the so-called skeptical and imaginative runologists.

There are several other key concepts in Faivre's delineation of what constitutes esotericism (Faivre 1994, 19–35). These concepts help to clarify and focus the six components above.

The first such concept is gnosis, knowledge. This is an

extraordinary form of experiential knowledge that is turned inward and in which both intelligence and memory participate (Faivre 1994, 23). Second, there is theosophy—not to be confused with the teachings of Helena Blavatsky's Theosophy—which is a cosmosophic view of the universe that endows the cosmos with mythic meaning. The theosopher begins with a "revealed given"—one of his myths. This could be, for example, the Norse myth of Ragnarök. To this he applies active imagination and thus evokes symbolic resonances (Faivre 1994, 26). Then there is the concept of secrecy or mystery. This is not conventional secrecy; these mysteries are not consciously withheld from the public; rather, they can only be revealed individually and according to an initiatory process. These are "the mysteries of religion, the ultimate nature of reality, hidden forces in the cosmic order, hieroglyphs of the visible world—none of which lends itself to literal understanding" (Faivre 1994, 32). Finally, there is the concept or claim that occult practices constitute a valid tool for increasing human empowerment, wisdom, and other benefits. The secret knowledge of the cosmic order is both to be gained by, and demonstrated through, occultism; that is, through practices rooted in the theory of correspondences, such as magic and divination.

All of these factors have to be understood when we invoke the idea of the esoteric. Academic or exoteric runology is not always excluded by esoteric runology, but historically it most often has been. By the same token, academic or scientific runology does not have to exclude or reject the dimension of esoteric runology, although it most recently has tended to do so. In fact, in the history of ideas, these two schools are related models, yet they are distinct and separate in their aims and methods. I hope that the message of this book will help bring about a runological synthesis by which these two often antagonistic views of the runes can be brought together in a cooperative model. One of the first steps in this process is to gain a firm understanding of the history of this problem.

OVERVIEW OF THE PRESENT BOOK

To understand the revival of the runes that has occurred in more recent centuries, one must have a basic understanding of the runic tradition as it was during its period of establishment. Our book therefore begins with an outline of runic history from its emergence in antiquity to the time of its decline between 1300 and 1500. The history of the runic revival as such begins after about 1500. The first phase of the revival, which lasted to about 1700, is dealt with both in terms of exoteric study and usage, and esoteric or mystical work. Generally, this pattern will be followed in all subsequent chapters. The runes can be seen as a purely utilitarian, practical script used for various kinds of interhuman communication. This being said, their use was always tinged with ideas of secrecy and certainly with a marked expression of *identity*—as a feature of Anglo-Saxon, Scandinavian, or generally Germanic culture. The second phase of the revival, 1700 to 1900, will also follow the fascinating story of the rediscovery of the runes from an increasingly academic, scientific perspective. From the turn of the twentieth century to the fateful year of 1933, the runic revival enjoyed one of its most lively periods with esoteric interest on the rise and with academic attention also becoming quite intense. Between 1933 and 1945 in Germany the runes were incorporated to some extent into the program of the National Socialist German Workers' Party (NSDAP). After the war that ended the regime of that party, the runes began a new phase of renewal, but the shadow of the Nazis would continually be something with which runic revivalists would have to deal. The years between the end of the Second World War and the mid-1970s were fairly bleak in the world of the runic revival, although in the academic world, progress continued to be made. From the mid-1970s onward, the first stirrings of a more widespread, global revival of the runes started to be felt. This latest stage of the revival has been a phenomenon of mixed results.

The conclusion of our present volume is an essay wherein I present a way forward for the runic revival, in both its exoteric and esoteric dimensions. Here I reassess the distinction between these two approaches and discuss the most harrowing challenges we face in the future.

As I have mentioned in my preface, this volume also officially constitutes the second part of a larger trans-epochal project on the "History of the Rune-Gild" in the broadest sense. From the *esoteric* and internal standpoint of the modern-day Rune-Gild, the latter organization actually represents a continuation of the ancient Gild. The modern Rune-Gild makes no claim that there was a continuous "apostolic succession" from ancient times but rather that the spirit and "Odian mandate" present in the original Gild is likewise present in the current organization.* To explore this avenue of thought, the present project was conceived. It is therefore essential to trace the original Gild back to its origins, and that involves the centuries-long transition from the ancient and medieval network of rune-users to the present day.

In *Revival of the Runes,* we will concentrate on the various phases of the revival, or reawakening, of the spirit of the ancient Gild. This revival was not always accomplished with a consistent level of quality, as will be seen. But it has very often been done with great power and conviction, carried forth by passionate people moved by the Odian spirit—the spirit of *seeking the mysteries* that the runes represent. As we see it, integral runology is an expression of a mosaic of interests—art, accurate use of language, poetry, literature, craftsmanship, and magic—bound together under the inner exhortation of *Reyn til Rúna!* ("Seek the Mysteries!"). Keeping this unifying factor in mind, this is not merely a volume about mystics and magicians using runes but is just as much a history of the academic and intellectual pursuit of runology in the halls of academia. Since the beginning of the runic revival in the days of

---

*The term "Odian" refers to someone who strives to emulate the mythic actions—for example, the quest for runic knowledge—of the god Óðinn (Odin), as opposed to simply worshipping the deity in a religious sense. For a more detailed explanation of the implications of the term, see Thorsson, *The Nine Doors of Midgard,* ix–xi.

the grandfather of runology, Johannes Bureus (Johan Bure), the ideas of magic and science have been inexorably bound together in the pursuit of runic knowledge. So it was, and so it continues to be—often much to the chagrin of both wild-eyed mystics and narrow-minded academic pedants. Although this particular subtext is present in this book, it is not something I will continually harp on or emphasize.

My aim here is to present an objective, informed, and empathetic exploration of a movement that took place over several centuries to reawaken knowledge of an ancient writing system and an ancient ideology. This movement and its representatives constitute a fascinating historical phenomenon in the annals of European and American intellectual life. It is a heroic and often quixotic tale with the occasional touches of Till Eulenspiegel. But we can learn to expect the unexpected when we begin to engage with the mysteries that the runes were apparently originally designed to convey from person to person and from men to gods and ghosts. So now, let us leave this lofty peak of Hnitbjorg and descend into the world of human history once more.

CHAPTER ONE

THE RUNIC TRADITION— AN OVERVIEW

To study the revival of the runic tradition, we have to outline what that tradition was in ancient times before it died out. Most serious esoteric runologists today agree with the exoteric ones regarding the basic facts about what that tradition was in its external form. This was originally a system of twenty-four signs, each of which stood for a sound value in the contemporary Germanic language. Over time this system underwent a number of elaborations and modifications, which can be described and interpreted. It took scientific runology centuries to figure out this system and its history in all its details, as we will see.

Esoteric runologists, on the other hand, historically often create runic systems that are at odds with exoteric runological facts. This runs the gamut from Johan Bure's *Adulruna* to Guido von List's *Armanen Runen* (Armanic runes). It appears that some current would-be esoteric runologists also cannot help themselves from somehow altering the best-known facts about the tradition; for example, by changing the order or names of the runes to suit idiosyncratic interpretations. It is such whimsical alteration that often causes would-be esoteric runologists to lose any shred of respect they might have otherwise gained from the academic world.

THE OLDER FUTHARK

In this chapter I propose to discuss the nature of the futhark system and its historical manifestations. The word *futhark* (or *fuþark**) would appear to be the invention of nineteenth-century scholars, and it is an acronym formed from the phonetic values of the first six staves of the rune row, f–u–þ–a–r–k (see below). However, the principle of having the first few staves stand for the entire row was one used in ancient times as well. Part of the inscription on the sixth-century bow brooch of Aquincum reads:

Under no circumstances should it be forgotten that the term *rune* is a complex one. It has the primary definition of "*mysterium, arcanum,* secret lore" and is only secondarily defined as the sign or symbol representing an individual sound of the contemporary spoken Germanic language.

The runic system is a complex of factors, all of which interrelate to form an organic structure. The basic ingredients in this structure are:

1. Name (indicating a phonetic value and an idea)
2. Shape
3. Order (number)
4. Tripartite Division

---

*The letter known as "thorn," þ, which ultimately derives from the Germanic runestave Þ, corresponds to the phoneme now represented in English by the digraph *th*.

Thus, each runestave has a distinctive name that conveys a kernel concept in the runic ideology, while the first phoneme in the name indicates the phonetic value of the stave in writing practice. It must be borne in mind that the staves were also often used as ideograms; for example, ᛃ could stand for the concept "good harvest" as well as for the sound [j] (pronounced as in English /y/). The shape of the stave can also be considered ideographically and could suggest or denote mythic content to the poetic minds of the ancient runemasters. The ordering of the staves (and the resulting numerical values) constitutes the first element of the inter-runic network of meaning. Through number, connections between different runes are revealed and bonds can be made. The next level of the inter-runic connectivity is expressed by the division of the futhark system into three sets later called in Old Norse *ættir* (sg. *ætt*), meaning "families, kindreds." This, too, communicates a new set of connections and makes a new level of bond-shaping possible. These interconnective factors are features that should also be familiar to the poetic mind-set; they allow for connections to be made between and among things that would otherwise seem unrelated.

As can be seen from the various futhark systems outlined in the coming pages, there is a remarkable level of consistency in these factors. It can scarcely be doubted that a great tradition underlies the systematic consistency of these factors over at least a thousand years of runelore. There are essentially two great historical periods for the runic tradition: the "older" and the "younger." The period of the Older Futhark of twenty-four staves probably spans from the beginning of the Common Era to about 750 CE. The second period begins circa 750, when the system was transformed into the Younger Futhark of sixteen runes. This second system was in use throughout Scandinavia during the period generally referred to as the Viking Age (ca. 800–1100 CE). This younger system gradually fell into disuse after it was subsumed by an *alphabetic* runic system. Although alphabetic runestaves continued to be used in inscriptions well into the nineteenth century in certain specific areas (the Swedish province of Dalarna, on the island of Gotland,

and in Iceland), knowledge of the runic script had generally died out in Scandinavia by about 1500.

Tables 1.1, 1.2, and 1.3 in this chapter provide the various futharks with indications of their divisions into *ætt*-systems, numerical and phonetic values, along with their names and the English meanings of those names. It is unclear as to when these names were originally applied to the runic characters, but it is likely that they were part of the archaic system since these names could have given the continuity and context that allowed the system to thrive for centuries across many tribal boundaries.

How do we know about the existence of the runic tradition? Upon what evidence can we base a history of this kind? To begin with, and what we must constantly come back to, it is the corpus of runic inscriptions themselves that provides the most compelling evidence for the existence of an ancient network of runecarvers. In all there are more than five thousand of these artifacts. The greatest number of these runic artifacts were carved in Scandinavia (especially in Sweden) between about 980 and 1130.

During the earliest period, from the beginning of the tradition to about 750 CE, runic inscriptions were carved in the twenty-four runes of the Older Futhark. It has been remarked that the runic system of sounds formed a "perfect fit" for the Germanic language used by the carvers at the time of the invention of the script. For every sound in the language, there was a sign. In all there are only about five hundred inscriptions known to us from this early period, half of which are found on bracteates (stamped gold medallions) made between about 450 and 550 CE in Scandinavia, especially in Denmark.

The runic tradition may have begun as early as about 150 BCE or as late as about 50 CE. The runic system of writing was ultimately based on one or more Mediterranean scripts such as the Greek, the North Italic, but most especially the Latin alphabet used by the Romans. It was probably the invention of a single individual who was either well placed in an existing network of workers in language—poets, magicians, and storytellers—or who was indeed the creator of a new network that arose based on his invention of the writing system to be used by runemasters among all Germanic tribes.

Historians who study the development of writing systems have determined that the origin of a particular script usually lies somewhere between one and two hundred years prior to the first surviving attestation of that script. For many years it was thought that an ornamented spearhead found in Øvre-Stabu, Norway, and dated to approximately 150 CE featured the oldest extant runic inscription. In 1979 an inscription on a brooch from Meldorf in present-day Germany came to light, which has been conclusively dated to somewhere about 50 CE. The only question in this regard is whether the Meldorf inscription is actually *runic* or not. Using these dates and the general criteria for the origin of scripts, the time of the invention of the runes would again be somewhere between 150 BCE and 50 CE, with the median falling approximately circa 50 BCE. This would roughly correspond to the time of increased Roman-Germanic interaction that began in the era of Julius Caesar. By the advent of the Roman Empire under Augustus (reigned 27 BCE–14 CE), this cultural exchange had become more intense on economic, military, and perhaps other levels.

Various theories exist as to the manner in which the runic system came into being. These theories fall into two main camps: the autochthonous and the exotic. The autocthonous view contends that the runes were invented totally within the Germanic world and were formed from preexisting holy signs. Adherents of such a theory hold that the runes are of extreme antiquity; they may even claim them to be the origin of the other scripts of the world. Autocthonous theories were believed in by various runologists from Johan Bure to Herman Wirth. As it turns out, there is really no good evidence for an autocthonous origin of the runes. Most scholars recognize that the Mediterranean alphabets such as the Greek, North Italic, or Latin/Roman script are older than the runes and that the runes are based on one—or possibly a combination— of these Mediterranean scripts. A reasonable middle ground, perhaps, between these two theories would acknowledge that the majority of the runes were based on Mediterranean letters but that some of them are of indigenous origin and may have even been based on preexisting signs used by the Germanic peoples before they actually wrote in runes proper. A review of all of these theories is contained in my book *Runes and Runology* (Flowers 2020).

In any event, most runologists agree that by the early years of the Common Era the Older Futhark of twenty-four runes was established and in use among the many Germanic tribes that were spread over three million square miles of Europe. Runes were probably not found in every tribal group, but they were known to many of them in all parts of Europe and all along the pathways of tribal movements during the great Migration Age (300–550).

The original runic system appeared as it does in table 1.1 (see p. 16), which shows the Older Futhark and indicates the sequence of the rune-signs, their basic phonetic values or sounds, and their particular names along with a translation of each name. There are many problems in determining the exact qualities of these rune-names, as no direct record exists of them from the earliest time period. However, because the Old English runes and the Scandinavian Younger Futhark runes had well-established and copiously documented names that indicate a high level of agreement between these systems, most scholars agree that the earlier Proto-Germanic forms of the rune-names can be reconstructed with relative accuracy and that these names—or similar ones—were attached to the signs from the beginning.

The shapes of the individual runestaves were remarkably consistent. A few of them also showed a high degree of variation. This is especially true, for example, of the **u**-run (ᚢ ᚢ ᚢ), the **k**-rune (ᚲ ᚴ ᚲ), the **j**-rune (ᛃ ᛃ ᛃ ᛃ), the **s**-rune (ᛊ ᛋ ᛊ ᛊ), and the **ng**-rune (ᛜ ᛜ ᛝ). Some of the most important things to realize about the system are that there were twenty-four runes in it, no more and no less; that the runes were arranged in a certain order; and that each rune-shape was characterized by certain visual characteristics that distinguished it from the others. A summary of the system is presented in table 1.1.

TABLE 1.1. THE OLDER FUTHARK

No.	Sound	Shape	Name	Translation of Name
1	f	ᚠ	*fehu	livestock/money
2	u	ᚢ	*ūruz	aurochs (wild bison)
3	th	ᚦ	*þurisaz	thurs (a giant)
4	a	ᚨ	*ansuz	a god (*Wōðanaz)
5	r	ᚱ	*raidō	wagon/chariot
6	k	ᚲ	*kēnaz	torch
7	g	ᚷ	*gebō	gift (sacrifice)
8	w	ᚹ	*wunjō	joy/pleasure
...				
9	h	ᚺ	*hagalaz	hail(-stone)
10	n	ᚾ	*naudiz	need (distress)
11	i	ᛁ	*īsa	ice
12	j	ᛃ	*jēra	year (harvest)
13	ei	ᛇ	*eihwaz	yew tree
14	p	ᛈ	*perþrō	fruit tree
15	-z, -R	ᛉ	*elhaz	elk
16	s	ᛋ	*sowilō	sun
...				
17	t	ᛏ	*teiwaz	the god *Teiwaz
18	b	ᛒ	*berkanō	birch(-goddess)
19	e	ᛖ	*ehwaz	horse
20	m	ᛗ	*mannaz	man, human being
21	l	ᛚ	*laguz	water
22	ng	◊	*ingwaz	the god/hero Ing
23	d	ᛞ	*dagaz	day
24	o	ᛟ	*ōþila	ancestral inherited property

The data presented in this table can be considered the bedrock of runic tradition. This is a tradition often fraught with certain problems of detail that have been endlessly argued over by scholars, but most of it is fairly well established as far as most runologists are concerned. A review of the problems associated with the names of the runes is contained in my book *Runes and Runology*. The next level of solid tradition is formed by the texts of the medieval rune poems, which explain the various runestaves in mythic and cultural contexts. These poems are presented, translated, and discussed in my book *The Rune-Poems* (Flowers 2019).

THE ANGLO-FRISIAN FUTHORC

Sometime during the fifth century runemasters practicing along the shore of the North Sea in the tribal territories of the Ingvaeones—the Saxons, Angles, and Frisians—began to add supplemental runes to the existing futhark to account for linguistic changes that were occurring in their dialects of the language. To some extent this addition of new signs to the system seems also to have been motivated by how the dialectal-phonological changes were causing the sounds contained in the distinctive names of the runes to be altered. For example, the Proto-Germanic word for a "god," **ansuz,* became *ōs* in Old English, so the name of the fourth rune now began with an "o-" rather than an "a-." These changes did not cause a fundamental revolution in runic ideology—that is, in the way runes were thought to function and the purposes for which they were used— as would be the case with the transformation of the Older Futhark into the Younger one in Scandinavia. Rather, the Anglo-Frisian model was a highly conventional response to language change: new signs were added to the old system to extend it in a practical way. This spirit of innovation, the willingness to add and invent new runes, would be a continuing hallmark of the Anglo-Frisian runic tradition. The Anglo-Frisian system went through two major phases: a sort of pre–Old English phase in which the supplemental runes appear to have been just that, and not seen as a fundamental reform of the system; and then a later phase that was more formally understood as a tradition of its own. But the Anglo-Frisian system does not appear to have ever been understood in an entirely *fixed* form, such as the Older or Younger Futharks were. The Frisian runes were in use in Frisia (present-day Holland and adjacent regions in northern Germany) from about 425 to perhaps as late as 900 CE. While the Anglo-Saxon Futhorc is well attested, we have no independently recorded Frisian Futhorc either in epigraphical or manuscript form, but the evidence clearly shows that both of these futhorcs were part of a common North Sea runic tradition, having evolved from the same source or set of practices.

Despite the fact that the runic tradition began within a pagan, or pre-Christian, context, it survived the Christianization process and even thrived in a Christian context, cultivated by men in ecclesiastical roles in English culture for centuries. As a result, runelore was widely recorded in a lively manuscript tradition mainly produced by Anglo-Saxon monks, often working in Continental monasteries. However, the culture shock brought on by the Norman Conquest in 1066 proved to be the death knell for the runic tradition in England.

The best general survey of the Anglo-Saxon runic tradition remains *An Introduction to English Runes* by R. I. Page (1999), while my little book *Anglo-Frisian Runes: A Concise Edition of Old English and Frisian Runic Inscriptions* (Runestar, 2019) provides an overview of the whole corpus of epigraphical evidence. New English inscriptions are constantly being discovered by metal detectorists in Britain.

A summary of the Anglo-Frisian system appears in table 1.2.

TABLE 1.2. THE ANGLO-FRISIAN FUTHORC

No.	Sound	Shape	Name	Exoteric Meaning
I	f	ᚠ	*feoh*	cattle, wealth
2	u	ᚢ	*ūr*	wild ox
3	þ/ð	ᚦ	*þorn*	thorn

No.	Sound	Shape	Name	Exoteric Meaning
4	o	ᚩ	ōs	a god (or mouth)
5	r	ᚱ	rād	(a) ride, riding
6	c [k]	ᚳ	cēn	torch
7	g [y]	ᚷ	gyfu	gift
8	w	ᚹ	wynn	joy
9	h	ᚻ	hægl	hail
10	n	ᚾ	nȳd	need
11	i	ᛁ	īs	ice
12	y	ᛄ	gēr	year
13	ï	ᛇ	ēoh	yew
14	p	ᛈ	peorð	dice-box/"pear"
15	x	ᛉ	eolhx	elks/sedge reed
16	s	ᛋ	sigel	sun
17	t	ᛏ	tīr	Tīw/sign or glory
18	b	ᛒ	beorc	birch/poplar
19	e	ᛗ	eh	warhorse
20	m	ᛗ	mann	man (human being)
21	l	ᛚ	lagu	sea
22	ng	ᛝ	ing	the god Ing
23	d	ᛞ	dæg	day
24	œ [ay]	ᛟ	œthel	ancestral property
25	a	ᚪ	āc	oak
26	æ	ᚫ	æsc	ash
27	y	ᛦ	ȳr	bow
28	io/eo	ᛡ	īor	serpent
29	ea	ᛠ	ēar	earth-grave
30	q	ᛢ	cweorð	fire-twirl (?)
31	k	ᛣ	calic	cup, chalice
32	st	ᛥ	stān	stone
33	g	ᚸ	gār	spear

THE YOUNGER FUTHARK

The system of twenty-four runes, as seen in table 1.1, was used in ancient times from the dim beginnings of the runic tradition to about 750 CE in both Scandinavia and Germany. At that time, there was a smooth and regular transition to the sixteen-rune system of the Younger Futhark in Scandinavia. In this table, as in those for all the other systems, the numerical value, name, phonetic value, shape, the exoteric meaning (the literal translation of the name), and the esoteric meaning (the underlying significance of that name in the runic context) are given.

The sixteen-rune system of the Younger Futhark was historically in use throughout the Viking Age, which lasted from about 800 to 1100 CE. Some knowledge of this system was preserved in secret throughout the Christianized medieval period, even though cultural forces attempted to destroy the runic tradition in its true form. The Younger Futhark is an unusual and conscious reformation of the Older Futhark system. It is highly unusual that at a time when the Scandinavian dialects were becoming linguistically *more* complex and developing *more* sounds, the writing system used to represent this language was simplified by *reducing* the number of signs available to represent those sounds. This is almost unheard of in the history of alphabets. What made this possible was the fact that the runes were not being reformed by or for those who were interested in maintaining a utilitarian script. The rune-row was reformed by men who were more akin to priests (the runemasters) than to scribes or grammarians. The signs were reduced in number, according to an orderly method in which the symbolic and phonological values of the runes that were eliminated were absorbed by the remaining ones. Thus, a streamlined system was created.

The *ætt*-system of internal divisions in the futhark became even more vigorously represented in the Viking Age. For example, the use of rune-codes based on the *ættir* was widespread during this period. It should be noted, however, that each Younger Futhark *ætt* begins with the same stave as in the older period. This is evidence for the importance of the *system* to the runemasters. It was imperative to maintain the tripartite division of the futhark, and that each of the *ættir* began with the same rune as they had in the older period.

TABLE 1.3. THE YOUNGER FUTHARK

No.	Sound	Shape	Name	Meaning
1	f	ᚠ	*fé*	cattle, money, gold
2	u/o/v	ᚢ	*úr*	drizzling rain, aurochs
3	þ/ð	ᚦ	*þurs*	thurs (giant)
4	a	ᚬ	*áss*	the god (= Óðinn)
5	r	ᚱ	*reið*	a ride, thunderclap
6	k/g/ng	ᚴ	*kaun*	a sore
...				
7	h	ᚼ	*hagall*	hail
8	n	ᚾ	*nauð*	need, bondage, fetters
9	i/e/	ᛁ	*íss*	ice
10	a	ᛆ	*ár*	good year, harvest
11	s	ᛋ	*sól*	sun
...				
12	t/d/nt/nd	ᛏ	*týr*	the god Týr
13	b/p/mb	ᛒ	*bjarkan*	birch(-goddess)
14	m	ᛘ	*maðr*	man, human
15	l	ᛚ	*lögr*	sea, waterfall
16	-R	ᛦ	*ýr*	yew, bow of yew wood

The motives behind the systematic and sweeping reform of the runic system remain a matter of scholarly controversy. Some believe it was done to shield runic literacy from unqualified readers; that is, the inscriptions were becoming too legible to the uninitiated, so a new system was devised that would further obfuscate the inscriptions. This reformed futhark of runestaves would have then functioned as a kind of code unto itself, serving to preserve and promote the profession of runecarving. If this was the motive, it seems to have been effective in the sense that runic inscriptions became more prevalent in Scandinavia than they ever had been before—at least on large and permanent monuments. Any theory involving linguistic factors appears to be wishful thinking, since the reform runs entirely counter to linguistic utility. The Norse dialects were becoming more phonetically complex at the time, so the reduction of signs would have been counterproductive if there had been a goal to better represent these sounds.

ESOTERIC DIMENSIONS OF THE RUNIC TRADITION

Runes and Magic

Now we must consider the uses of runes in ancient and medieval times (pre-1500) that indicate they were employed in magical or divinatory practices. The chief distinction between the modern-day speculative (or imaginative) runologist and the skeptical runologist hinges on the question of whether the runes were ever considered by the ancient Germanic peoples to have been imbued with some sort of magical power, force, or special symbolic essence that made them something sacred and set apart for an extraordinary kind of communication or whether they were just a writing system like any other that was occasionally used in what might be called "magical" spells.

Perhaps the best answer to this question is provided by an anonymous runemaster who lived sometime in the late sixth century and who carved on a stone the words:

ᚱᚢᚾᛟᚹᚨᚺᛁᚱᚨᚷᛁᚾᚨᚲᚢᚾᛞᛟ [. . .]
runofahiraginakudo [. . .]
runō fahi raginakundo . . .
"(A) rune I color, one stemming from the gods, . . ."

I would say that this runemaster knew better than any modern-day runologist as to what the nature of the runic tradition was, at least in his day. This is clear and direct evidence that the runes were believed to be derived from a divine source. Later Old Norse literary evidence also continues to point us in this direction. Virtually every time runes are mentioned in saga literature, for example, they are ascribed to some magical or mystical meaning. Some skeptics have tried to suggest that this attitude was imported to the North by Christianity, which seems highly unlikely as Christianity was largely *opposed* to the sentiments expressed in this runic material. Also, the spiritual and magical power ascribed to the runes in pagan sources was actually a continuing challenge to the aspect of Christian prestige that was tied to the use of the Latin language and the Roman script.

It can be conceded that the runes may have had a profane origin and served as a practical script for the first few centuries of their use, and only somewhat later were they imbued with magical and mythical associations. This can be said only because there are no *overtly* magical runic inscriptions before the fifth century. The earliest inscriptions are often one-word formulas, and these are too brief to provide direct evidence that would prove beyond any doubt whether the motivation of the carver was operative or magical. However, it must also be said that few inscriptions dating from before the Middle Ages give any outward sign that they are, in fact, a purely profane and ordinary form of communication between two humans.

Runes may have been in use as early as 150 BCE, but whenever they were invented, they were most likely the work of a single individual. We may reasonably posit that the originator of the runic system was an aristocratic man at home in what is now Scandinavia, probably a warrior by profession (a member of a warband), and also a poet or storyteller. He may have served in some capacity in the Roman army for a time, as the runic system appears to have been loosely based on the Roman alphabet. He became familiar with Roman writing and then returned home to the North and innovated his own system. The rune-using culture

that developed over time was thus connected to a high prestige population; it was the instrument of an elite group of men with some significant ties to the Roman world (whether as a result of military service, or
through trade, and so forth). The spread of the runic system would have
occurred through some sort of intertribal network and may have been
closely attached to a central mythological patron, to be identified with
the high god *Wōðanaz (the Germanic deity whose name later evolves
into Óðinn in Old Norse, Wōden in Old English, etc.).

The ancient Germanic peoples at the dawn of the first millennium
lived in a prehistoric time. This means that there are no significant
written records produced by them other than the brief inscriptions
they made. Our knowledge about these early Germanic societies largely
derives from Greco-Roman descriptions of them. The rune-using culture within these Germanic groups must have formed a continuous
and dynamic lineage. We know it was continuous because the lack of
written records precludes the tradition being revived based on written
sources after a period of decay. The orality of their culture ensured the
necessity for a continuous oral chain of master-pupil relationships being
at the core of their society. Their situation can be contrasted to that of
the Hebrews and Egyptians, who had written records that allowed for
periods of decay in which teachings were "lost" and then later revived
based on preserved written texts. The old Germanic rune-using culture
was also dynamic in that the nature of the data seems to have changed
over time, reforms occurred, and so on.

The history of the runic tradition can be compared with that of
Greek writing. The Greek alphabet was adapted from the Semitic
Phoenician alphabet, with the significant innovation that all sounds of
the language, including the vowels, were assigned phonetic characters.
The Greek alphabet was first used by the merchant class, and only later
did the letters take on any philosophical or mystical meanings. This esoteric aspect is evident in the writings of philosophers such as Pythagoras
and Plato. The Greek system is characterized by borrowed letter names
(*alpha, beta, gamma,* etc., based on Semitic *alef, bet, gimel,* etc.) and the

fact that the earliest attestations of writing are in the milieu of merchants and government.

One of the stone-cold facts about all runic inscriptions that must be taken into account in each and every effort to interpret an individual inscription is that every inscription is an effort at an act of communication. The following sequence of three questions then arises: Who is the performer of the communicative act? Who or what is the object or intended recipient of the communication? And what, if anything, is expected as a response to that initial message?

Regardless of their origins and original purpose, after about 400 CE we see a proliferation of overtly magical uses of the runes. A few examples of this will show what an unquestionably magical (operative) inscription looks like.

Our first example is the fifth-century so-called amulet of Lindholm.

A: **ekerilaRsawilagaRhateka:**
B: **aaaaaaaaRRRnnnxbmuttt:alu:**

Line A is perhaps best read as *ek erilaR sa wīlagaR ha(i)teka*, "I, the Erulian, am called the crafty one" (Krause and Jankuhn 1966, 70). Line B consists of a series of twenty-one runes, which are not intended to be natural language, concluding with the familiar formulaic word *alu*.

In the Lindhom inscription the runemaster identifies himself by a title that empowers him to perform the operative act, characterizes the nature of his performative act (being "crafty" or "tricky," i.e., dangerous), and then unleashes a runic formula, the purpose of which we can fairly well guess at based upon the examples of later formulas that bear a close resemblance to this one, such as the curse formula known from a section of the seventeenth-century *Galdrabók* (see Flowers 2005, 55–56). The whole sequence, which really constitutes a self-contained ritual formula, concludes with the sanctifying word *alu*. This inscription is analyzed in some more detail by Flowers (2006, 72–79). It appears that the overall formula, probably a preexisting one that was used repeatedly, is here imperfectly executed, as it was obviously intended to consist of twenty-four runes on each side, but the runemaster left out one, an **i**-rune in line A. Therefore, it might be said that the formula in its entirety originally had some intended numerical symbolism. Both lines were probably supposed to have twenty-four runes. We can only speculate that the meaning of the number twenty-four would have been as a signature of completeness and totality, and hence the number itself is a sign of some intrinsic power.

One of the most well-known magical formulas in the older tradition is found on the Stentoften stone in southern Sweden. Another stone from the same region, the Björketorp stone, has some of the same formulas. The Stentoften inscription is dated to about 650 CE, and its runes can be seen here:

These can be read as follows:
I. **niuhAborumR**
II. **niuhagestumR**
III. **hAþuwolAfRgAfj**
IV. **hAriwolAfRmAgiusnuhle**
V. **hideRrunonofelAhekAhederAginoronoR**
VI. **herAmAlAsARArAgeuwelAdudsAþAtbAriutiþ**

The text is normalized to the following:

I. *niuha-būrumR* II. *niuha-gestumR* III. *HaþuwolfR gaf j(āra)*
IV. *HariwolfR magius nū hlē* V. *h(a)idR rūnō [ronu] felheka hedra*
gino-r(ū)noR VI. *hermala(u)sR argeu wēlad(a)ud sā þat briutiþ.*

This may be translated as something like: "To the new farmers, (and) to the new foreigners, Haþuwolf gave good harvest. Hariwolf is now protection for his (son retainer?). A row of bright runes I hide here, magically charged runes—restlessly because of 'perversity' a deceitful death (has) the one (who) breaks this (monument or stone arrangement)." One of the main functions of this inscription is clearly stated as a curse on anyone who would disturb the arrangement of rocks of which the stone was a part.

Bracteates were made from thin sheets of gold that were embossed with images stamped from a wooden dye. The round gold disk was then fitted with a beaded rim and a loop so that it could be worn as an amulet. They were apparently worn mainly by women, as they are typically found in gravesites belonging to women. But more commonly they are found as hoards—a collection of gold objects that were intentionally buried, perhaps in hopes of sending the gold to the otherworld where the one who buried it will be enriched. The Germanic gold bracteates were all manufactured between about 450 and 550 CE.

These bracteates, inscriptions on which account for half of the older runic record, are categorically *magical* objects. The vast majority of extant bracteates do not have runic content, but there are about 250 that have been found with runic texts. Their particular form of magic works on three levels: (1) the object as such—that is, a gold medallion obtained as a cult site; (2) the iconography on the object; and (3) the inscription, which often appears in conjunction with the image.

A typical example of a runic bracteate is offered by Tjurkö I-C (Ikonographischer Katalog 184), which is shown in the image on page 28.

The runic text on this bracteate reads:
wurterunoRanwalhakurne ·· **heldaRkunimudiu** ···
wurte rūnōR / an walha-kurne ·· *HeldaR Kunimu(n)diu* ···
"Held worked the runes on Welsh grain for Kunimund"

The phrase *an walha-kurnē*, "on the grain of the 'Welsh,'" is per-haps a kenning for "gold" (= the bracteate). "Welsh" is here a general Germanic term for "foreign" or "southern" as opposed to northern (cf. ON *valskr*, "foreign, esp. French"; OHG *wal(a)hisc*, OE *wealhisc*, "for-eign, esp. British or 'Welsh'"). This usage shows that Germanic speakers probably also referred to Romans with this word. The Tjurkö I-C brac-teate is clearly an amulet with a runic inscription that specifically dedi-cates its intended effect: to bring prosperity to Kunimund.

The iconography of this style of gold bracteate (called type C by the specialists) was inspired by Roman coins depicting the emperor on horseback. The Germanic person seeing the latter sort of depiction would have naturally reinterpreted it as representing the mounted god *Wōðanaz. The image was then radically restylized according to indig-enous aesthetics to create a new and uniquely Germanic form of sacred art with these objects.

The *Poetic* (or *Elder*) *Edda* provides many examples of the runes in a magico-mythic context. These references have been cataloged and studied by several scholars over the years, for example by Wolfgang Schöttler (1948) and Francois-Xavier Dillmann (1976). The most conspicuous and meaningful of these passages is the section concerning the mythic origin of the runes themselves. In stanzas 138–39 of the *Hávamál* poem, we read about how the god Óðinn (<*Wōðanaz) hung himself on a tree (i.e., the World Tree, Yggdrasil) in a ritual of self-sacrifice, and through this ordeal he discovered the runes (i.e., the cosmic secrets):

> *Veit ek, at ek hekk   vindgameiði á*
> *nætr allar níu,*
> *geiri undaðr   ok gefinn Óðni,*
> *sjálfr sjálfum mér,*
> *á þeim meiði   er mangi veit,*
> *hvers hann af rótum renn.*

> *Við hleifi mik sældu   né við hornigi,*
> *nýsta ek niðr;   nam ek upp rúnar,*
> *æpandi nam,*
> *fell ek aptr þaðan.*

Throughout Old Norse and Old English literature, references to runic use and the meaning of the etymon *rūn-* (which underlies ON *rún*, pl. *rúnar;* OE *rūn*, pl. *rūna~rūne;* with corresponding cognates in all the older Germanic languages) consistently point in an esoteric and magical direction, and we can only conclude that those living in the Middle Ages during the era when these documents were produced had a more complete idea of what this concept meant than most modern scholars can imagine. It is also interesting to note that while the original sense of a *rune* as mystery has its origins in the indigenous Germanic (and Celtic) tradition predating the coming of Christianity, this term was, for an initial period at least, gladly folded into Christian terminology. Insofar as it could be understood to correspond to a universal concept, the term seems to have transcended religious differences.

From the beginning, perhaps, the Proto-Germanic word *rūnō may have indicated *both* a mystery and the individual signs or symbols with the capacity to communicate mystery. In this we are reminded of the terminology surrounding the Greek letters, which are called στοιχεĩα (*stoikheîa*). The latter term not only denoted written signs used in representing language but also the *elements* of the cosmos. Terminology of this sort is a reflection of the sense of awe that some cultures showed toward the process of writing. This sense of awe may be lost to the modern mind-set, but that means little in our attempts to understand the ways those living two thousand years ago might have thought.

With regard to the corpus of early runic inscriptions, a chronological arrangement of the data appears to show various phases for the magical use of runes. For the first two hundred years or so of the tradition, only very short texts are known. These provide identity between the carver and the object, or with the act of writing itself. After about 100 CE the possibilities of practical influence on the already established tradition of runic writing may have been felt from the Greco-Roman world through the conduit of the Mithraic cult, practiced by Roman soldiers on the northern borders, or *limes,* of the empire, among whom were many Germanic recruits. Then, after about 300 CE, these and/or other influences from the south and east increasingly led to more complex and more overtly magical inscriptions. All of this speaks to the intrinsically dynamic nature of the runic tradition. It was not created and then perpetuated in a stagnant way; rather, its generally consistent core was a structure capable of absorbing and adapting influences on a continuous basis. At least this seems to be the best model of understanding the historical dimension of the runic data.

Questions concerning the early magical use of runes are dealt with in great detail in my book *Runes and Magic* (Flowers 2014). I would refer the reader to that book for a thorough discussion of the ideas of magic in connection with the runes in the earliest period of their history. *Runes and Magic* is not a book of esoteric runology; it is a scientific observation of early runic data using the lens of an interdisciplinary academic approach.

The whole runic tradition gradually decayed and became more and more geographically limited over the years. Learned men used Latin with its Roman letters, and even made some inscriptions in Latin using runes. At the same time, rudimentary use of runic writing became restricted to pockets of traditionalists living in the Dalarna and Gotland regions of Sweden and in Iceland.

Two obscure sources demonstrate that runic knowledge was partially kept alive in learned circles and even exported in some way from Scandinavia. The first of these sources is the fourteenth-century manuscript Sloane 3854, now housed in the British Library. The manuscript is a jumble of pages, poorly bound and with many parts missing. It is actually a Latin translation of the *Kitāb al-Istamātīs,* a hermetic treatise that is the source for the *Ghayat al-Hakīm,* generally known by its Latin title, *Picatrix.* Originally, this was an Arab-language manual of magic. The runic features in this translation appear to be innovations unknown in the original. Scandinavian runes are used to designate halves of the signs of the zodiac, and each rune is ascribed to one of the four classical "elements." All of this is presented as a preparation instructing the magician how to use these signs to communicate in a secret way with the universe, but unfortunately the practical section of the manuscript is missing! These cryptic signs are designated as *runae.* The runes in question are derived from the pointed, or "pricked," form of runes that were used in the "runic alphabet" in Scandinavia after about 1100. The second such source is found in the Prague manuscript XXIII F 129 from the second half of the fifteenth century (ca. 1475). It stems from the Alemannic linguistic territory (southwestern Germany and Switzerland). This is generally a manual of human medicine. Throughout the text, sections appear in which certain key words are written in runes. Again, these are the Scandinavian "pointed" runes. Both of these sources generally indicate that runes were still thought to be heavily tinged with a magical aura, even in areas far from where the runes would have been at all familiar.

When we look back on the earliest manifestations of the runic craft, it is very plausible to suggest the idea that these practitioners of an expert skill—the writing of specialized texts in a particular script, probably often in exchange for money or position—should have formed a whole cosmology based upon the particulars of their craft. Such a process is normal and expected. The most conspicuous and well-known example of this phenomenon is that of the medieval stone *masons* (whose work originally may have developed out of earlier institutions involved in the construction of wooden structures in the North). The masons, builders of buildings, developed a whole mythic worldview in which the technology of their craft was symbolically interpreted and revalorized. A similar course of development may have taken place in many other such guilds that cultivated specialized knowledge in areas ranging from warcraft to handicrafts, to the arts of language and poetry.

Systematic runic knowledge of all sorts had generally died out in all but a few areas by about 1500. It is only after such a demise that we can begin to speak of a rebirth or revival of such knowledge. Almost as soon as the traditions of runic usage were lost, men began to try to recover them. This is a clear indication of the original importance of runic knowledge to the cultures in various Germanic lands from England to Germany, and especially in Scandinavia. But whether exoteric or esoteric, this renewed knowledge would be hard-won and difficult to recover. Precisely because this knowledge was now disestablished and rejected, it was ripe for "occult" speculations and practices. And this would have been doubly true in light of the copious indications that the runes had been used for magical purposes in antiquity. The following chapters of this book contain the story of the endeavor—as often misguided as not—to revive runic knowledge in all its facets and functions.

As we will see over the course of our survey, the field of academic runology has undergone many phases of development, and it is still subject to varying influences and ideological positions today. The twentieth century, for example, was especially lively with its pendular swings between what R. I. Page called skeptical runologists and imaginative runologists. Because of profound changes in the world of Western academia—namely, its recent domination (especially at the administrative levels) by materialists, advocates of Marxist critical theories, and politically driven activists—the possibilities for the work of the "imaginative" runologists in academic establishments have become extremely limited.

As a necessary analytical tool in this book I will discuss the ideas of exoteric and esoteric runology in separate ways. However, when we look at the older, traditional period of runology—that belonging to the premodern use of runes—we should realize that these two parts were actually part of *one* phenomenon. My general theoretical stance is as follows: although a certain quality of understanding can be gained by observing runic data through these two separate lenses (exoteric and esoteric), ultimately it is only by viewing the tradition from a holistic, or integral, perspective that the data can be fully understood. The integral runologist of the future will be one who can enter into the mindset of the traditional runemasters in an experiential way. Much like the experimental archaeologists of today, who learn the *physical* crafts of the ancients and thereby achieve a greater understanding of the ancient objects they study, the integral runologist will learn to *think* like an ancient runemaster and thus be better able to understand the process by which the runic inscriptions were created and the messages they convey. However, this being said, I do see the value in both ends of the polar extremes, between the entirely esoteric and the purely rational approach. Each has something of value to convey to our process of understanding. No whole or complete history of runology can dispense with any aspect of the role that the runes have played in the story of our cultural lives.

CHAPTER TWO

THE DECLINE
OF THE TRADITION

(900–1500 CE)

To understand the life and characteristics of a cultural feature that later
undergoes a reawakening or revival, it is generally useful to know how
it declined and became moribund. As we have seen, the runic tradition
never fully died out everywhere. But in many of the cultures where it
had once thrived, it did completely disappear, only to be rediscovered
centuries later. Despite its spotty survival in certain areas of Sweden
and in Iceland, it must also be acknowledged that the runic tradition
had probably once been an important feature of the symbolic culture of
the social elite of Germania in the early centuries of its tradition (from
about 150 BCE to 400 CE).

The transition from the Older to the Younger Futhark should not
really be seen as a sign of the decline of the tradition as such. Instead
it was a reorganization of that tradition signifying a rebirth or reformation, which provided new vigor to the tradition. Although the use
of the Younger Futhark was more limited in terms of its geographical
coverage, the intensity of that use seems to have far exceeded what took
place in the older period.

As we noted in the previous chapter, the rune rows that evolved from the Older Futhark developed quite differently in Scandinavia as compared with what took place in the North Sea region with the Anglo-Frisian runes. In Scandinavia, the reduction of the inventory of available graphemes to represent a language that was actually producing more phonological variation runs counter to the natural and expected process found in the history of other writing systems. In the Anglo-Frisian system of runes, by contrast, we see the normal and expected progression with new runes being invented and added to the inventory to account for sound variations. Moreover, in the Anglo-Saxon sphere it is also evident that a number of these new runes were treated in the spirit of the ancient tradition—endowed with names, and four of them were even given runic stanzas (see the *Old English Rune Poem*).

The Scandinavian reformation of the runic tradition began as a piecemeal alteration of older runes in what is called the transition period between the older and younger systems. This transition period was historically brief, and then, rather suddenly and thoroughly, a new system was codified and established in a manner that strongly suggests there was some sort of organized effort behind it. The reformation brought with it a heightened level of activity among runecarvers, which seems to have culminated in a gildlike organization behind the industrious production of memorial stones in Sweden from the tenth to the twelfth centuries.

The newly reformed system also made runic texts more difficult to read, with single runes being made to stand for a variety of sounds. One might logically ask: Why was this obfuscation deemed necessary? Since the phenomenon did occur, and because it runs contrary to the normal and expected development of a writing system, we must assume that it was the result of a conscious plan. Here the simplest answer is probably the right one: The system was made more difficult so that it could not be casually learned by those outside the gild of runecarvers. Thus, the meaning of the runes was effectively hidden from those who might be attempting to learn to write outside the professional class of carvers.

The latter group was probably adjunct to the school of court poets of Viking Age Scandinavia, and this reform would have helped preserve their exclusive status.

This picture is a familiar one in the history of writing. Most of the great writing systems of antiquity, from the cuneiform of the Sumerians to the hieroglyphics of the Egyptians, were invented by and for a professional organization of scribes. The scribes had nearly exclusive control over those systems, which outsiders could not learn without years of study. (Today we see the same trend among the "IT guys" who keep things complex and ever-changing to ensure future employment.) It was the Greeks who departed from this model for the first time, creating a writing system that could be easily learned by any clever fellow. Now certainly, we cannot believe that the ancient scribes of Mesopotamia or Egypt were too stupid to invent a simple system; rather, they developed the complexity of their systems as a safeguard on their institutional power. All that is being suggested here is that the reform from the Older Futhark to the Younger, and the reduction of signs to make the system more difficult to read, was most likely motivated by needs akin to those we see elsewhere in the history of writing.

We might now ask: What had been the characteristics of the rune-using culture in the times when it was flourishing? The answer to this question is multileveled.

1. It was a male-only profession or activity. We know this because self-references to the runecarvers in early times are exclusively in the masculine gender. This was probably because runes were used in conjunction with other male-only activities such as trading, poetic performance, and membership in war bands. We can also see that when women do begin to be referred to as runecarvers—for example, in a German inscription from Neudingen/Baar circa 600 CE—this occurs in a place that was being Christianized and thus in a time when the old traditional institutions must have been in flux and/or demise.

2. The culture seems to have been one patronized or "sponsored" by the god *Wōðanaz (whose name becomes Óðinn in Old Norse). This god was seen as the discoverer of the runes, the originator of the runic system, and the agent by which the runes and their usage were transmitted to human practitioners.

3. The runes and runic inscriptions served the interests of what we would today call practical religious functions: they memorialized the dead (thus perpetuating their spiritual existences in the memory of men), manipulated the essences of named persons or things as to their location or activity, and acted as signs for communication between the realm of the living and dead, between gods and men, and between men and their environment.

4. The runes maintained their traditional order (f, u, þ, a, r, k, etc.), which is indicative of an indigenous organizational principle inherent within, and particular to, a special cultural group.

Each of these factors broke down as the tradition began to go into decline. Women began to carve in runes, which only indicates that the knowledge had lost its special "trade-secret" status. Certainly, as the Germanic world was slowly Christianized, the sponsorship of the high god of the Germans had to be called seriously into question. In the transition from the traditional indigenous religion of the ancient Germanic peoples to that of Christianity, there is no direct and incontrovertible evidence for the idea that Christ became a new sponsor for runic knowledge, but there is some circumstantial evidence for this syncretic process. Runes and runic use appear at first to have been not only undiminished by the coming of Christianity but also actually increased in its intensity. The runes appear to have lost some of their special status as signs for practical religious communication as the Latin alphabet was being introduced and literacy spread in a more general way in Germanic-speaking areas. Finally, the special indigenous organizing principles of the runic tradition gave way to that of the Latin alphabet, which is indicative of the loss of some of the special identity of the system.

The traditional transmission of runic knowledge fell into decline in different regions of the Germanic world at different times. In Germany, this occurred about 700 CE, after which time no more inscriptions were being made in the region we now know as Germany itself. However, runic knowledge was kept alive there in clerical settings; that is, in learned works being produced in monasteries, often due to Anglo-Saxon influence. This influence from England was the result of monks coming to monasteries in Germany in the eighth century. In England itself the demise of runic usage came in the wake of the Norman Conquest (1066), such that after 1100 runic inscriptions were no longer being made there. The greatest early native German exponent of runic knowledge is thought to have been the Frankish monk Hrabanus Maurus (780–856), to whom the treatise *De inventione litterarum* (On the Invention of Letters) has been traditionally ascribed.

Runic use in Scandinavia persisted for a very long time. In more remote areas, such as the island of Iceland, the province of Dalarna in Sweden, and the Swedish island of Gotland in the Baltic Sea, runes continued to be used in a fairly lively way into modern times. Runes were found in agricultural contexts among farmers, and so on, as well as among the learned and literate writers of manuscripts. In Iceland, these manuscripts were often concerned with magic.

During the Middle Ages a system was developed whereby the Younger Futhark runes were expanded into an alphabetic system. Here a runic character was assigned to each of the Latin letters as they were used to write the Scandinavian languages (and Latin) at the time. This was accomplished in part by adding points or dots to the existing runes or by inventing new characters. At first this was done in an unsystematic way during the eleventh century, as certain runes were "pointed" to indicate more precise phonetic information; for example, ᚴ, ᛁ, ᛏ, and ᛒ were pointed as ᚷ, ᛂ, ᛐ, and ᛔ, respectively, to indicate the sounds *g, e, d,* and *p*. By time of the reign of Valdemar the Conqueror (1202–1241) the system was finally codified as a fully developed runic alphabet, which generally replaced the Younger Futhark for most actual runic inscriptions. The runic alphabet was altogether easier to read, but nevertheless the lore surrounding the sixteen runes of the Younger Futhark also continued to be cultivated and preserved for another two centuries. Eventually this knowledge, too, fell into disuse. (See table 2.1, p. 40.)

As the culture that supported and promoted the runic craft underwent profound changes, the use of runes changed and then fell into decline. The aristocratic warrior class was transformed by religious and political developments. These changes were especially profound during the fifteenth century in Scandinavia, the last bastion of runic culture. As evidenced by inscriptions as early as the sixth century in Germany and in Old Norse literature written in the thirteenth century and after, women began to carve runes. This practice had previously been reserved to an all-male domain. With the official conversion of the populace to Christianity, the longtime patronage of the runic craft by the god Óðinn was largely lost, although awareness of his role in the runic endeavor was retained in poetic circles. It must be recognized that in Germania, as elsewhere in the world, religions did not change suddenly. Instead, there was a syncretic period of "mixed faith," if you will, that lasted for several centuries. Knowledge of the old gods and their power died only slowly and at different rates in various regions throughout the Middle Ages. But by 1500 the old gods and goddesses were in a deep slumber.

The Christianization process did not at first interfere with the use of runes, nor did the medieval introduction of Latin as a "sacred language." There are even medieval Latin inscriptions written in runes, mostly of a religious or magical nature. This body of evidence bears witness to the fact that the runes continued to be considered somehow powerful as a medium for the conveyance of messages of a magical character, despite the fact that the culture in which they originated had been overcome by the Latinate world of the church. The fact that Roman letters never seemed to be considered as anything but a practical tool, in contrast to the reputation of the runes, can also be taken as evidence for the attitude of the Scandinavians in particular toward the original nature of the runic script.

TABLE 2.1. THE MEDIEVAL NORSE RUNIC ALPHABET

Rune	Letter	Commentary on Form
ᛆ	a	Younger Futhark **a**
ᛒ	b	Younger Futhark **b**
ᛍ	c	Variant of ᛎ
ᛑ	d	Dotted Younger Futhark **t**
ᛂ	e	Dotted Younger Futhark **i**
ᚠ	f	Younger Futhark **f**
ᚵ	g	Dotted Younger Futhark **k**
ᚼ	h	Younger Futhark **h**
ᛁ	i/j	Younger Futhark **i**
ᚴ	k	Younger Futhark **k**
ᛚ	l	Younger Futhark **l**
ᛘ	m	Younger Futhark **m**
ᚿ	n	Younger Futhark **n**
ᚮ	o	Based on Younger Futhark **a**
ᛔ	p	Dotted Younger Futhark **b**
ᚴ	q	Younger Futhark **k**
ᚱ	r	Younger Futhark **r**
ᛌ	s	Younger Futhark **s**
ᛐ	t	Younger Futhark **t**
ᚦ	þ	Younger Futhark **x**
ᚢ	u	Younger Futhark **u**
ᛦ	R/y	Younger Futhark **-R** (*ýr*)
ᚤ	y	Dotted Younger Futhark **u**
ᛎ	z	Variant of ᛍ
ᛅ	æ	Younger Futhark **a** (variant of ᛆ)
ᚯ	ø	Based on Younger Futhark ᚬ

The general loss of the order of the runic system in the indigenous futhark sequence and its rearrangement in the alphabetic order was one of the most significant aspects of the runic decline. Nevertheless, it is clear that awareness of the old order remained in some circles, as evidenced by the survival of the rune poems into the fourteenth century. These retained the order and number of runes inherited from the Younger Futhark.

The runes themselves can be seen as a sign of authentic, integral, traditional culture. As factors developed—or were introduced—that compromised the traditional culture in general, the runes naturally fell into decline as they increasingly lost their mythic support. It is interesting to note that although the runes were replaced by the Latin alphabet as a consequence of a new religion being introduced, the new *letters* themselves do not seem to have been interpreted as having any special or awesome powers. Yet—as the use of runes to write Latin prayers or Mediterranean magical formulas indicates—the runes retained their status as a sacred script even into the Christian period.

We can see how all sorts of archaic Germanic cultural features, including the runes, were reconfigured to conform to new outer forms, which then entered into the historical record as "folklore." Symbolic motifs were reduced to mere decorative or ornamental features, with their original significance becoming lost. The German Romantics would later refer to this type of material as *versunkenes Kulturgut,* "submerged cultural features." In the first half of the twentieth century especially, much folkloric research would be pursued regarding allegedly ancient motifs that had found their way into common objects through various expressions of folk art including pastry shapes, architectural features, house marks, and masons' signs. It must be remembered, however, that any possible "runic" connection to such features could have only come about if the specific crafts and customs themselves were rooted in times so archaic that they were shaped when the runes were in more widespread use. Runic speculations regarding folk arts and customs may therefore be entirely modern interpretations or projections onto forms that only coincidentally resemble runes. In these cases, then, what we are dealing with is a fanciful or wishful reinterpretation, whereby the unconscious mind has projected runic significance onto shapes that were never consciously intended to be related to runes. We will have more to say about this phenomenon in chapters 7 and 8.

Another dimension of runic demise lies in their displacement from the most elite ranks of society and the centers of cultural and economic power to fringe areas—both socially and geographically. But evidence shows that this transition was in no way sudden, nor was it violent or extreme.

Finally, it can be said that by the year 1500 runic knowledge had become almost entirely isolated and repressed by the unrelenting effects of the transformation of society and culture from a traditional basis to one shaped and reshaped according to the values and cultural norms of the Roman Catholic Church and its ideas about politics and religion. For all intents and purposes, the runes were now a moribund cultural feature. It is only after this point that we can begin to speak of a true runic *revival*.

CHAPTER THREE

FROM THE RENAISSANCE TO THE BAROQUE

The Revival Phase I: 1500–1700

The Western world underwent tremendous cultural changes about the year 1500. Historians identify this approximate date as the beginning of the Modern Age. The Middle Ages, which were marked by popular faith and the prevailing influence of the church over many areas of life, thought, and politics, were passing away and a new world, more rooted in reason and science, was rising up. The Western Hemisphere was "discovered" by Europeans (1492), Copernicus demonstrated the heliocentric model of the immediate cosmic order (1543), and Martin Luther successfully challenged the authority of the Roman Catholic Church (1521). These and other developments sent the world into a flurry of changes and brought many centuries-old assumptions into question.

In northern Europe these changes were most profoundly felt because it was there that the existing church authority was first broken and a new spiritual model established in the form of Protestantism. There was a new emphasis on nations, as each Protestant country was to have its own church organization with the monarch as its highest officer. Protestantism also promoted widespread education and literacy: the

Bible was being translated into the vernacular languages and the people were expected to be able to read it. Furthermore, because of the earlier invention of the printing press by the German Johannes Gutenberg (1436), literature of various kinds also began to flourish.

In the northern Italian city-states such as Florence, a Renaissance had already begun a few decades earlier. This was a rebirth and a renewal of interest in classical antiquities as a source for new human values. A handful of elite Italian thinkers, such as Marsilio Ficino (1433–1499) and Giovanni Pico della Mirandola (1463–1494), and artists, such as Sandro Botticelli (1445–1510), turned to ancient Greece and Rome for a renewed identity and direction that set them apart from the orthodox Christian mores traditionally promulgated by the Roman Catholic Church. This movement was fueled by the rediscovery and study of ancient texts, such as the dialogues of Plato and the recently acquired *Corpus Hermeticum.* The latter is a body of texts in the Greek language that reflects Neoplatonic, Gnostic, and Hermetic ideas from pagan late antiquity. This zeal for the past was imported into northern Europe, where it was expressed as humanism; that is, an interest in perennial human values, scientific knowledge, and the cultivation of classical studies.

The perfect storm of influences in northern Europe led to the Protestant Reformation, interest in national traditions, and a new dedication to intellectual pursuits. In the North, Renaissance ideas were more widely disseminated throughout society and tied to a more liberal and practical application of emerging science and technology. There was a pronounced sense of turning inward—to individuality and hence to nationalism—as interest grew in one's own natural culture and to the values of the more "common man."

In Italy the old gods of Rome could be revived quickly and easily, a process that has been studied in works such as Jean Seznec's *The Survival of the Pagan Gods* (1961). The source material for this revival was readily available in the form of pagan Latin literature, and all educated men could read the texts. In the North the situation would be very different. First of all, the source material that would be needed had mostly been destroyed by the church, or was never recorded. The treasure trove of Icelandic texts that did exist had not yet been discovered in any comprehensive way by European humanists. That development would have to wait until the seventeenth century. Secondly, the languages in which the old material was recorded would have to be learned and decoded by a new generation of scholars. Methods of understanding them would require significant philological work that would take centuries to develop. Finally, there had developed a certain prejudice against all things Northern, which even the Northerners themselves had often adopted in favor of Greco-Roman learning. This latter bias is generally a by-product of Christianization.

One of the greatest intellectual heroes of the Northern Renaissance was Theophrastus Bombastus von Hohenheim, better known as Paracelsus (1493–1541). He pioneered methods of scientific inquiry as applied to medicine and pharmacology, two disciplines of which he is considered the modern "father." He was also a magician, alchemist, and astrologer. Paracelsus would greatly influence the general thought of men such as Johannes Bureus a few years later. This topic was the subject of Sten Lindroth's 1943 book, *Paraceslismen i Sverige, till 1600-talets mitt* (Paracelsism in Sweden to the Mid-Seventeenth Century).

The rediscovery of the runes by the learned elite of northern Europe, and the subsequent publication and teaching of these discoveries to a wider public, begins at this time, but it would be a long and winding pathway over several centuries. Once forgotten by the cultural elite that first dealt with them, the deeper secrets of the runes would not reveal themselves again without a significant and prolonged intellectual and cultural ordeal.

THE BROTHERS MAGNUS

A pair of brothers, Johannes and Olaus Magnus, who were two of the last Catholic archbishops of Sweden, found themselves in exile in Rome due to the growing Protestant Reformation in their homeland. Their work was essential in the process of the runic revival. Although they were largely driven by a desire to save the prestige and reputation of their country in the eyes of Catholic Europe, their historical volumes were among the first to bring the ancient runes to the attention of a learned public. As a result, they were among the earliest writers to publish in *printed form* a reference tool for the renewal of runic writing beyond the limited areas where it had survived in Iceland—Dalarna, and Gotland. In 1554, Johannes Magnus (Johan Store, 1458–1544) published a compendium of Gothic and Swedish royal biographies from biblical times to his present day titled *Historia de Omnibus Gothorum Sueonumque Regibus* (History of All Kings of the Goths and Swedes). A Swedish translation did not appear in print until 1620. Olaus Magnus (Olof Store, 1490–1557) published another history of the Nordic peoples entitled *Historia de Gentibus Septentrionalibus* (A Description of the Northern Peoples) in 1555. There he presented his "Gothic Alphabet" along with its corresponding sound values. The brothers Magnus considered the many runestones that dotted the Swedish countryside as proof of the extreme antiquity of Swedish civilization, maintaining that the Swedes were literate before the Romans knew how to read or write. They also claimed that the ancient Northmen used birch bark as paper. The runestones, they thought, must have been erected by giants in some antediluvian age. Olaus Magnus had the *Carta Marina,* one of the earliest accurate illustrations of the Scandinavian peninsula, printed in 1539. On this map was the image of the saga-age hero Starkaðr holding two runic tablets. The runes depicted are of the same style as would appear in the later woodcut of the "Gothic alphabet" from 1555. This is a runic alphabet (in ABC-order) with Latin transcriptions over each of the runes. According to the brothers Magnus, runes were used as a cryptic mode of communication in times of war, but no special mention is made concerning their esoteric value or connection to the pre-Christian religion (although such is implied by the fact that they were considered to have existed before the time of Noah).

The brothers Magnus were among the earliest contributors to a new Gothic mythology that would come to be known to historians as *Storgöticism* (Meglo-Gothicism). Although these brothers laid some of the foundation for Storgöticism, this would historically become a movement connected to the Protestant wave of thought interested in demonstrating the cultural and intellectual achievements of the North and separating it from the Roman and Latinate world. For the brothers Magnus, however, these general concepts were conceived of as a way of showing that the North had a venerable culture worthy of respect in the family of nations. I will return to the topic of Storgöticism later in this chapter.

Fig. 3.1. The "Gothic alphabet" published by Olaus Magnus in 1555

THE BROTHERS PETRI

Like their predecessors the brothers Magnus, two other brothers, Laurentius Petri (1499–1573) and Olaus Petri (1493–1552), who succeeded the Magnuses in their ecclesiastical offices, also wrote on runes. The brothers Petri were both essential contributors to the process of turning Sweden into a Protestant, and then specifically Lutheran, realm. Their real (non-Latinized) names were Lars and Olof Petersson, and their interests included the promotion of Swedish national identity and the use of the Swedish language in all areas of life. They were instrumental in producing a Swedish translation of the Bible. One important aspect in the task of shaping a national church, with the king as its head, involved rehabilitating the view of the national—and hence *pagan*—past. Olaus began to study the pre-Christian monuments in the Swedish countryside and wrote about the pagan names of the weekdays. Both brothers wrote manuscripts that remained unpublished but were archived and used by subsequent generations of Swedish scholars. They noted that runes had continued to be used in a fashion parallel to the Latin script, and Laurentius wrote a manuscript later referred to as *Mäster Larses Runekänsla* (Master Lars's Runology). All in all, however, rudimentary studies and texts such as those produced by the brothers Magnus and Petri mainly served to point out how the general runic tradition had fallen into relative obscurity and disuse, even in the areas of the North where they had best survived.

THE BIRTH OF MODERN RUNOLOGY

Since the runes had largely fallen into obscurity over almost all of the Germanic world, and remained only a limited part of life in certain more remote areas of Scandinavia, the stage was now set for a true *revival* of runic knowledge as we will see in the work of the Swedish Storgöticist and Rosicrucian Johannes Bureus. But the mystical aspect of Bureus's efforts was only one part of his contribution. His role as what can rightfully be called the first modern runologist is perhaps more important, as he planted the seeds for the growing interest in the runes that would take hold in the halls of academia throughout Europe. The story of the scholarly runic revival is every bit as fascinating as the revival connected with magic and mysticism—and eventually, as we shall see, these two worlds will begin to reconnect with one another.

In the two centuries between 1500 and 1700, the initial groundwork for the scientific study of runes was laid. During this period, academic study was still significantly clouded by superstition and medieval prejudices. These hindrances would be able to be overcome only with the development of better scientific tools and the moderate loosening of the grip of the church and the state over freedom of thought.

As Klaus Düwel (2008, 217–18) points out, the study of runes during the earliest part of this time was dominated by certain ideas that would only be disproved over time. One was that the signs were of extreme antiquity, going back to biblical times and even antedating the Great Flood described in the Old Testament Book of Genesis. Most thinkers at this time still accepted the medieval idea that Hebrew was the oldest language, or the original language of mankind, and therefore the runes and all other forms of writing must have somehow derived from the Hebrew letters. Because the most commonly found runes— and the ones with the most magnificent monumental presence, appearing as they did on the great memorial stones of Sweden—were written with the signs of the sixteen-rune futhark, it was believed that this was the *older* system, whereas the few inscriptions that had been found and identified with various additional signs (many of which bore a greater resemblance to the Latin alphabet) were assumed to represent a younger and more recent system.

As we have already noted, the whole study of runes in Scandinavia was also made part and parcel of that great political and cultural movement known as Storgöticism. In connection with these ideas, the study of runes gained a symbolic value in the political and economic struggles taking place between the two great Scandinavian powers of the time: Denmark and Sweden. This seems to have been much more important to the Swedes than the Danes, which was mainly because the Swedes became the power rising in the North after their victory in the Second Northern War (1655–1660), whereas the Danes had historically held the upper hand. From the Swedish perspective, they identified the ancient Goths with the inhabitants of their country known as Götar (in Väster- and Östergotland, for example) and on the island of

Gotland. The ancient tribes known as the Ostrogoths and Visigoths, together with the kindred Vandals and Burgundians, had all gained great historical prestige in the Migration Age (300–550). Their histories became the stuff of legend, and their leaders and kings, such as Alaric and Theodoric, achieved mythic status. Although the Goths had disappeared from history after about the eighth century in Spain, their legendary prestige could be harnessed as a source of political power. The history and legends surrounding the Goths thus became intertwined with the runic symbols in a new and powerful modern mythology.

The deep roots of Storgöticism go back into the Norse Viking Age when the Goths entered the world of myth and legend. In the *Poetic Edda* the plural designation *gotar* is used honorifically to mean men of great power and the word *goti* is used for a valuable horse, as Gothic horses were highly esteemed. So by the time Nicolaus Ragvaldi, the archbishop of Uppsala in the mid-1400s, made his famous speech at the Council of Basel in 1434 extoling the virtues of the Goths, the traditions of giving a high place of honor to the Goths, and of the Swedes identifying with this people, was already well established (see Svennung 1967). Gothicism spans over several centuries of Swedish and Scandinavian history, and some might say that glimmers of it still exist today. Generally summarized, Gothicism is a combination of the belief in the special antiquity and prestige of the Goths, their identity with various local populations (Swedes, English, Spaniards, and others), and the attempt to harness this identity and ideology in the service of greater military and political power for the nation. As we will see in the case of Bureus, Gothicism could also go in a quite mystical direction. The apex of Swedish Gothicism was probably reached in the works of the Swede Olof Rudbeck (1630–1702).

The chief effect of Storgöticism on the history of runology is that the belief arose that the Swedish runestones, which number in the thousands, were somehow the most splendid and ancient examples of runic activity and so the sixteen-rune futhark that they bear must, for this reason, be the oldest and most original form of the runic tradition.

This false assumption prevailed for a number of years in the sixteenth and seventeenth centuries. How do we know it is false? Simply because the language represented by the Older Futhark, Proto-Germanic or Primitive Norse, is *closer* to the Indo-European root language than is the language of the Viking Age, which is represented in the Younger Futhark inscriptions. Archaeological contexts also clearly show that the Older Futhark of twenty-four runes occurs in environments older than that of the sixteen-rune system. Moreover, the runic alphabet developed in the Middle Ages is directly based on the Younger Futhark.

JOHANNES BUREUS AND THE *ADULRUNA*

Since I first wrote about Johan Bure in *Runelore* (Flowers 1986), considerable interest has arisen in the work and personality of this remarkable scholar-mystic. Unfortunately, information about Bure has been

Fig. 3.2. The symbol of Bure's *Adulruna*

rather difficult to acquire. His own written works—which fill many volumes in Swedish archives—have gone for the most part unpublished. Works about Bure are also relatively rare. The first extensive treatment of his life and work in Swedish was perhaps the 1908 study by Hans Hildebrand, "Minne af riksantikvarien Johannes Bureus" (A Remembrance of Johan Bure, National Antiquary), published in volume 23 of the *Svenska Akademiens Handlingar* from 1910 (pp. 55–435). Subsequently, a good deal of work has been done in Sweden by scholars such as Susana Åkerman, Håkan Håkansson, and especially Thomas Karlsson. The most extensive work about Bure in English can be found in Thomas Karlsson's "The Adulruna and the Gothic Cabbala," which comprises the second part of his book titled *Nightside of the Runes* (Karlsson 2019).

It is as an early practitioner of what can be called radical runology that we wish to approach the figure of Johannes Thomæ Agrivillensis Bureus (= I.T.A.B.), as his full name appears in the Latinized version that was fashionable in his day. As we briefly move through his life and work, remember that here we have a man living and thriving within the circles of power close to the royal Swedish government a scant four centuries after the destruction of the "heathen" temple at Uppsala. Interest in a nationalistic Swedish (Gothic) Renaissance had already been ignited by his predecessor, Johannes Magnus, but it was Bure who would synthesize the intellectual precision of scholarship with the inspired passions of magical enthusiasm. From our "postmodern" perspective we must forgive Bure his spiritual intransigence in the paradigms (myths) and terminology of Christianity. As one comes to understand who and what Bure was, one comes to see that his words encode deeper meanings than perhaps even he was fully able to grasp or articulate at the time.

THE LIFE OF JOHAN BURE

Johan Bure was born on March 25, 1568, at Åkerby, about one mile northwest of Uppsala, Sweden. The child was christened Johannes

Fig. 3.3. A portrait of Johan Bure from 1627

Thomæ Agrivillensis Bureus. His father was the Lutheran parish priest of Åkerby, and his maternal grandfather had also been a priest.

In 1570, Johan's father died and his mother remarried another parish priest that same year. But she, too, would die just ten years later. Johan's stepfather was kind to the boy and supported him in his early schooling.

By the time young Johan was nine years old, he was in school under Magister Olaus Andreæ in Uppsala. At the age of fifteen he went to Stockholm to study at King Johan's Collegium under Ericus Schepperus. In 1590 he received a position in the chancellery of the collegium.

Throughout the years he continued to learn various languages: besides the Latin that was basic to all education at the time, he learned Hebrew (beginning as early as 1584) and Greek. He even began teaching himself Arabic at the age of sixty.

At the time when he received his position in the chancellery, his interest was piqued in all sorts of antiquities. By the next year, 1591, these interests had developed a mystical tendency. In the summer of that year he read the Latin grimoire known as the *Arbatel* or *De Magia Veterum* (On the Magic of the Ancients), and he developed an enthusiasm for the Kabbalah. Perhaps it was contact with the family of his first wife, Margareta, whom he married in January of 1591, which set Bure's mind in this direction. Margareta's father, Mårten Bång, was involved with certain occult pursuits. These ended badly for him as he was beheaded for heresy in 1601. Bång had instructed a certain woman on occult teachings, who then began to report publicly on her "heavenly journeys." The contents of these reports were judged to be heretical so she was burned and Bång, who was charged with being her instructor, was beheaded. This story demonstrates the mortal danger from established authorities that such interests could incur at this time.

In 1593, Bure received a new position as *corrector* (editor) of religious publications. This necessitated a move from Stockholm to Uppsala. But just before he left Stockholm, he visited the Franciscan cloister on Riddarholm (a small island that lies within Gamla stan, the city's old town area) to assess material in the library there. While on this visit, he caught sight of an ancient runestone that had been set in the threshold of a door. The practice of removing stones from their original places to be used as building materials (especially for churches) had been fairly common in medieval Sweden. Of course, Bure had been familiar with the sight of runestones in the countryside from his childhood, as the region around Uppsala is scattered with hundreds of such stones. But when he saw *this* stone it is said that "his curiosity was awakened" (Hildebrand 1910, 75).

From that time forward Bure focused much attention on learning the language reflected in the stones and on the mystical significance of the runic characters themselves. It is said that he went into the "backward"—or culturally conservative—province of Dalarna to the northwest of Uppsala and there learned to read runic characters from the farmers in the region. This is quite credible because farmers in that region were still known to be using runes into the nineteenth century, three hundred years after Bure's time.

Throughout the period of his government service, which was not a well-paid position, Bure earned extra income with handicrafts—he made copperplate engravings, inscriptions in stone, and repaired clocks.

By 1595, at the age of twenty-seven, Bure formally entered the university at Uppsala, where he began to study theology. He was promised the parish of Börstil in northern Uppland, but he never took the final step of becoming a priest. During the time of his studies, he traveled to the south, visiting both Germany and Italy. Bure also began an extensive expedition to record runestones in the Swedish countryside. He set out on August 8, 1599, and concluded the trip on April 5, 1600. In 1602 he was named professor in the *artes liberales* by Duke Karl. His teaching fields were to be *runska* (Runic Studies) and Hebrew.

The following year Duke Karl ascended to the throne of Sweden and became King Karl IX. The king then named Bure as his "antiquarian," although no formal government post had previously existed for this function. Karl was intensely interested in Swedish prehistory, both for its own spiritual sake and for the political advantages that could be derived from the results of such studies.

An example of this latter use of prehistory can be seen in connection with the Mora stones from a parish southeast of Uppsala (fig. 3.4). Karl sent Bure to investigate this group of carved stones that bore not only runes but also a representation of the triple crown insignia of the Swedish monarch. The legitimacy of such a find would demonstrate the great antiquity of the Swedish royal house (since it was believed that the runes were, or could be, antediluvian) as well as the ancient hegemony of Sweden over the other two Scandinavian countries (Denmark and

Fig. 3.4. The Mora stones

Norway). Such a stone monument indeed exists, but the crowns were obviously carved at a much later date than the runic inscription.

In 1604, Bure began taking part in the instruction of the young crown prince, Gustav Adolf, and thus a friendship was inaugurated that would last for three decades.

Throughout the first few years of the 1600s, Bure's work on the exoteric interpretation and esoteric significance of the runes was intense. By 1599 he had completed a copper engraving titled *Runakänslones lärospån* (Runology Chart), which was meant to instruct on how to read runic inscriptions (fig. 3.5). This was followed with several other manuscripts, culminating in 1603 with the *Runaräfst* (Rune Investigation), a scientific study of runelore. By 1605 the first version of his masterpiece of runic esotericism, *Adulruna Rediviva* (Noble-rune Resurrected), was complete. However, it must be noted that this, like so many of Bure's other works, was never published in the conventional sense. Over the decades that followed he would revise this text many times until 1642, when he himself deemed it ready to go to a printer.

To appreciate fully the pioneering character of Bure's work, one must realize that relatively little was known about the runes or Norse

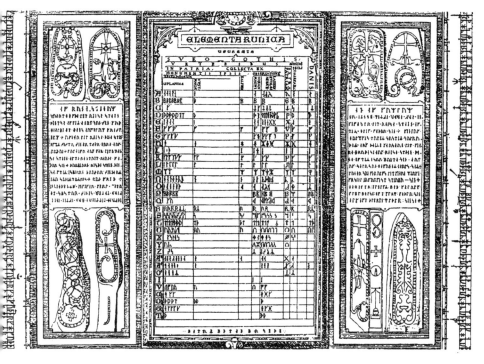

Fig. 3.5. Detail of Bure's runology chart, *Runakänslones lärospån* (1599), with illustrations of runestones and runestaves together with interpretations of rune rows

mythology at the beginning of the 1600s. Bure and his contemporary rival, the Dane Ole Worm (Olaus Wormius), had virtually initiated the academic study of runes, and, as far as mythology was concerned, the *Codex Regius,* a manuscript containing the corpus of poems that would come to be called the *Poetic* or *Elder Edda,* would only be discovered in 1643. For these reasons, as well as the general cultural and religious climate in which Bure found himself, we can perhaps forgive him what now might seem to be wild eccentricities. It was simply a matter of not having quality primary sources readily at hand.

One conclusion reached by Bure in his studies during the first decade of the 1600s was that the runes had been suppressed by the Christians and that a return of the use of the runes was tantamount to a return of the Swedes to a place of honor. In this idea there is an implicit neo-heathenry. Bure went on to write and have published *Runa ABC-boken* (The Rune ABC Book; 1611), which served as a handbook to teach contemporary Swedes how to write their language in runes.

It is at the time of the publication of *Runa ABC-boken* that Bure becomes a regular companion of Gustav Adolf (Gustavus Adolfus). He continued to instruct his royal patron on matters of both Swedish prehistory and esoteric matters until the latter's departure for battle in Germany in the midst of the Thirty Years' War in 1630. This book may have aided Swedish forces in using runes as a military code in Europe during this war (Enoksen 1998, 184).

The second decade of the 1600s saw a deepening of Bure's work in the esoteric. He mysteriously refers to the year 1613 as the time when he says that he "received knowledge concerning the hidden truth, and when I found it, I knew it to be my duty to become its apostle" (quoted in Hildebrand 1910, 75). Evidence seems to point to the *Rosicrucian* nature of his enlightenment.

Historians of the Rosicrucian movement will not be disturbed by the dates here, for although the first Rosicrucian manifesto, the *Fama Fraternitatis* (The Story of the Brotherhood), was not published as a printed document until 1614, it had circulated in manuscript form at least as early as 1612 (see Yates 1978, 41). It is not necessary to assume that the contents of the *Fama* alone exercised this influence on Bure. It is more likely that since Bure was intimately connected to the international Protestant esoteric intelligentsia through his personal relationships with Kings Karl IX and Gustavus Adolfus, he was exposed not only to potent manuscripts but also to oral teachings of what might best be described as proto-Rosicrucianism.

Let me hasten to add that we are not left to speculate as to Bure's Rosicrucian connections. In 1616 there appeared a Latin poem under the title *Ara foederis theraphici F.X.R. assertioni Fraternitatis R.C. quam Roseæ Crucis vocant, consecrata* (Altar of the Theraphic [= Physicians'] Brotherhood F[raternitatis] C[rucis] R[oseae], dedicated to the Assertion of the Fraternity R. C., which they call the Rosy Cross).

On the last page of the eighteen-page document there appeared a text actually *signed* by Johannes Bureus.

It would, I think, also be a mistake to assume that Bure and his royal companion were passive participants in the Rosicrucian adventure. However, Bure's version of these teachings seemed, at their deepest levels, to be related to the symbolism of the runes.

According to Bure there was something exalted and hidden about the runes—there were ordinary runes (as used to carve on stones), but there were also *adulrunor* (or *adelrunor*), "noble-runes," which behaved in ways he compares to Egyptian hieroglyphics or Hebrew letters. A good idea of how this system worked can be gained from the synopsis of the contents of *Adulruna Rediviva* in the next section of the present work. The essential idea of the *adulrunor* was in place by 1605, but the esoteric realizations of 1613 in a certain way completed the picture for him. Many of Bure's ideas appear related to those of the English philosopher John Dee (1527–1593) on a multiplicity of levels.

In 1616 he delved deeper into the mysteries with the production of a short text titled *Buccina veteris iubilei* (The Old Jubilee Trumpet). This is an esoteric text that Bure used as a focus for his teachings. He began to gather group after group of students to whom he transmitted the mysteries of the text. Students even came from Germany, which brought him in direct contact with Prince August of Anhalt in Saxony, who is known to have had interest in the secret sciences.

The 1620s were a period of intense scholarly activity for Bure. In 1624 he published the first edition of *Monumenta Sveogothica hactentus exculpta* (The Hitherto Carved Suedo-Gothic Monuments), which was the first attempt to create a scientific collection and edition of the vast corpus of runic monuments in Sweden.

This period was, of course, also rich with esoteric discoveries and explorations. Bure came under increasing attacks for his heretical ideas, but he was solidly supported by the royal house against any and all critics, the majority of whom were members of the Lutheran clergy.

A fair amount of Bure's new esoteric work at this time centered on dreams and their interpretation. One interesting anecdote reported in Bure's diaries, which are fairly extensive and detailed for this period of his life, relates how Gustav Adolf told Bure of a dream he had in which one of his boyhood tutors by the name of Henrik Horn appeared and the king took him to be Satan himself. In the dream the king asked "Horn" if he believed in Jesus Christ, and the figure answered "No" and said he had received a new revelation. What is most interesting is that Bure interprets the dream figure of "Horn" as a stand-in for himself. This darkly reveals Bure's own self-conception.

In 1626, Bure's first wife, Margareta, died. Together they had conceived eight children—almost all of whom died in childhood. The sad circumstances of his children's mortality grieved him greatly. Bure was a man of emotion and sentiment. His diaries reveal his grief over his dog, Sultan, who was killed by wolves.

On May 20, 1630, King Gustav Adolf officially created the *Riksantikvariet,* the National Office of Antiquities, and named his friend and mentor, Johan Bure, as its first head, the *riksantikvarie* (National Antiquary).* Just a few weeks later the king departed for the battlefields of Germany, where he and his Swedish troops would turn the tide of fighting in the Thirty Years' War. The antiquarian-mystic was with his friend and student up until just a few hours before the warrior-king departed. Sadly, Bure would never see his friend again, as the king was killed at the Battle of Lützen in 1632.

In 1636, when Bure was sixty-eight years old, he remarried. He and his new wife had one child, whom he named Margareta. But she, too, was to die in childhood.

Bure remained active as *riksantikvarie* until 1648, when he had to leave his post due to failing health. He spent the last years of his life as an invalid, though he continued to dictate works to the last. He died at his longtime home at Vårdsätra on October 22, 1652.

---

*This office, now officially referred to as *Riksantikvarieämbetet,* the National Heritage Board, remains an active part of the Swedish government to this day.

BURE'S CONCEPT OF *ADULRUNA*

Bure begins his *Adulruna Rediviva* by laying out the function of the runic system as a *mediator* between the divine and human levels of existence. He says that the *creative word* of God is a mediator between God and his creations and that in the human realm this is mirrored in *languages,* which act as mediators between speakers and listeners. This notion is extended then to *writing,* which is also God-given, as a mediator between writers and readers. Bure notes that Jesus uses a metaphor by which he refers to himself as a writing system: "I am the Alpha (A) and the Omega (Ω)" (Revelation 1:8). Bure also refers to a *stone* as the most noble and lasting of all things. Clearly, then, a *runestone* is more than just an archaeological artifact for Bure—it is a *mediator* between the divine and human minds.

According to Bure, everything that exists is either creative or created, but between them there is another level, which is creation. This is the creative process itself. For this reason, Bure states that the originators of the runic system made the rune row in three groups of five staves. The first group of five is designated as the progenitor (Sw. *födare*), the second as that of generation (Sw. *födelse*), and the third as that of the generated (Sw. *foster*). Here we find the reason why Bure did not want to recognize ᛆ as an independent rune. Only with its identification with **r** can the number of runes be reduced to fifteen.

Although Bure was somewhat familiar with the newly reemerging data on the runes—such as their traditional shapes, names, and the poetic stanzas attached to each—he dismissed this information as exoteric and relied on his subjective vision to unlock the secrets of the *adulrunor.* This accounts for the non-traditional elements in the system of *Adulruna Rediviva.* It must be kept in mind that what little was known and had been published about the runes from ancient manuscripts appeared after Bure had already codified the essentials of his esoteric system. This codification took place between 1605 and 1613.

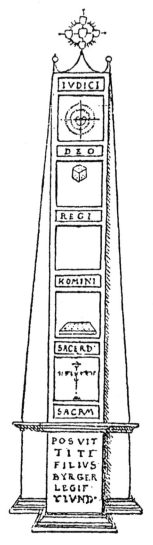

Fig. 3.6. Bure's illustrative runic monument

BURE'S RUNOLOGY

Bure's runology is represented in table 3.1, the left side of which was printed in his 1611 text *Runa ABC-boken* (p. 11). It shows both the *adulrunor* and the common runes used in writing, which Bure is interested in formulating for use in writing modern Swedish. (The section at right presents another more readable version of Bure's table.)

TABLE 3.1. BURE'S RUNOLOGY

Runa ABC according to the Swedish ordering

Alphabetum Scanzianum ordine proprio.'

Ᵽ	Frey.	F. Ᵽ/v confona.	1
↑	V r.	ᛏ/u.ᚾ/v.ᚾ/y.ᚾ/ů.	3
◁	Tors.	Ⲧ / th. ᚦ/dh.	5
ᚻ	Odhes.	ᚼ/ð.ᚼ/ð. ᚼ/ᚼ/ᚼ/ð.	7
ᚱ	Rydhur.	ᚱ/r. ᛉ/r/ er fin.	9
ᛉ	Kyn.	Ᵽ/ᚠ/c. Ᵽ/Ⲩ/g.ᛋ/q.	10
ᛉ	Haghall.	H/ Gh / Ch.	30
↓	Nadh,	N. ᛁ/nfin. ᛁ/dn.	50
ᛁ	Idher.	I voc. J/ᛁᚾᛁ/ᛁ/e.	70
ᛏ	Æru.	Æ.. ᛁ/a. ᛏ/an.	90
ᛏ	Sun.	S pr.ᛋ/s. ᛋ/ᚠ/ss.	100
↑	Tidhr.	T. ᛏ/tt. ᛏ/d.	300
◁	Byrghal.	ᛒ/b. ᚠ/ B/ p.	1500
ᚱ	Lagher.	L. ᚠ/ ll.	700
Ψ	Man.	M. Ψ/mm.	900

Ᵽ	Fräy	F. Ᵽ v consonant.
↑	Ur	ᚾ u. v cons. ᚾ y. ᚾ å
◁	Thors	Th. ᚦ dh. ᚦ dhdh
ᚻ	Odhes	ᛁ o. ᛁ å. ᚼ ᚼᚼ ö
ᚱ	Rydhur	ᚱ r. ᛉ r final
Ⲩ	Kön	Ᵽ k c.Ᵽ g ᛋ q.
ᛉ	Haghall	H Gh Ch
↓	Nådh	Nᛁn final ᚾnn. ᛏ ån
ᛁ	Idher	I vowel j cons. ᛁ e.
ᛏ	Åru	Å. ᛏ a.
ᛏ	Sun	S pr.ᛋ s ᛋ med. ss
↑	Tydhr	T. ↑ tt in fi. ᛏ d.
◁	Byrghal	B.ᛒ p in pr. alias ᛒ ᚠ
↑	Lagher	L. ᚠ ll
Ψ	Man	M.Ψ mm

BURE'S INTERPRETATION OF THE RUNESTAVES

Ᵽ is Freyja's (*Fröja*) stave. *Fröja* meant *fru* (lady) in the older language. This comes from *frö* (seed), having to do with fertility, and from this the word *fröken* (young lady) is derived. In the rune-rhymes it is called *fä* (beast; cattle; fool), having to do with abundance. This can be compared to Hebrew א (*aleph*) meaning "ox."

↑ (*ur*) signifies the force of origin and expansion. It corresponds to: (1) Latin *ab* or *ex*; (2) the *ur-* in *urväder* (bad weather; hard wind with snow or rain); and (3) the *ur-* in *urverk* (clockwork), which signifies motion.

ᚦ is linked with the name of Thursday and is the most important sign of *freedom*, because *töras* (to dare) means to venture out, which is also connected to *törna* (to turn back to shore). Bure links this rune with many geographical features in and around Sweden showing where borders between peoples change or meet.

ᚼ is connected with the name of Oden's day (Sw. *onsdag*) and is called the Odin-stave (*Mercurii litera*) or the Öden-stave (stave of fate = *fati litera*). Otherwise it is also connected to *öde* (fate), and *öud*, which indicates "possession." Bure claims that those who say "Wednesday" or "woensdag," and so forth, have forfeited their rights to use the rune script.

ᚱ stands for *råda* (to advise, rede), ride, rudder (by which a ship is controlled). It is a sign of dominion and justice (*rätt* = right). Bure identifies the **ᛣ** as the *original* form of ᚱ used in final position. The **ᛣ** shows a straight line descending right down between the two arches. *Råda* was exiled to the end of the row, outside the fifteen-rune system, and designated with the ordinary name *stupmadher* (inverted man).

Y is the sign of sex (*kön*) or kin. It is the *generosæ naturæ litera* (stave of noble nature). A shack **ᛣ** is inverted to **Y**, which shows the stave's original kingly character, linked also to the concept of ability (*kunna*).

ᚼ is called *hagel* (hail), that which encloses (Sw. *hagar*) everything and/or makes everything that is most favorable (Sw. *haglek* = art and craft) and protected (Sw. *hagelig*).

ᚾ bears either the name *nöd* (need) or *nåd* (grace). Bure sees the shape of the stave as an illustration of the relationship between the two alternate names and concepts of *nöd* (need/distress) and *nåd* (grace; gift), in that grace is shown by the raised stroke on the right side (note the *subjective* perspective here) and distress by the downward stroke as one moves to the right.

ᛁ is defined as *poententiæ litera* (stave of repentance) due to its simplicity, or as the *studii litera* (stave of pursuits). Bure notes offhandedly that the poems refer to it as "ice."

ᚤ Bure notes, has a variety of sound values and hence must have a variety of names. Among these he counts *ära* (honor/glory), *år* (year), and *ari* (eagle). He provides a list of Latin glosses: *gloria* (glory), *perpetua requies* (eternal rest), *littus* (shore), *aquila* (eagle), *annus* (year), *annona* (yearly produce, harvest), and *sufficientia* (plenty). The shape of the stave illustrates its meaning as glory ending in tranquillity, because the stroke is raised forward moving to the right, the reversal of *nöd* (need).

T is the sun-stave, and the son-stave. The sun is named after the light created on Sunday—the sun is linked with the Son of Light. To this stave belong the words *sona* (to make amends), *suna* (to be forgiven by the Son), and *ransuna* (to redeem that which has been stolen). The poems speak of the sun as the highest in heaven. T is called "hanging sun" because the rune hangs from the back of the serpent ᛍ. This latter form, says Bure, was adapted from the Greek Σ and is called "kneeling sun."

↑ is the tide-stave (cf. Tuesday). It signifies time and holidays or ceremonial divine services. In ancient times priests were called *tidmän* ("time men") and *tijar* ("godly ones"). The name *tak* (roof) is used because of the shape of the stave. This is also connected to the tar torch and whip (swingle).

B *byrkal* = *byr-karl* is the one who is lord over the farmsteads; or *byrgall* (*byrg-all*), which contains everything and is contained in everything. It corresponds to the beginning (*börja*). As a compound of *byr* + *ger,* the name indicates the patron of the home, fatherland, or city. Some translate the name as "son of war," as we know the *ger-man* is a "man of war."

ᚱ = lays, law. The name of Saturday, which Bure calls the seventh day of the week, is *lördag* (wash day) in Swedish. This comes from *lög* (bath). Also, law (*lex*) comes from *laga* (to arrange), so law is connected to laying. Also note the connection with *sam-lag* (sexual intercourse) and *hjone-lag* (connubial union).

Ψ is the last rune of the row in Bure's system. Because it is the runesound [m], made with the lips closed, that "closes the mouth." It is linked with Monday, and so to the Moon, and to man. The form of the stave indicates a man with two uplifted arms or, as on some stones, a man scratching his head ⵉ.

✦

These interpretations of the meanings of individual runestaves are a mixture of philological evidence, folk etymology, and Bure's own spiritual insights. It is unknown how many of Bure's ideas are derived from the lore of the farmers and learned men of Dalarna, from whom he is known to have learned something of the runes. It is also curious to note that some of the more speculative innovations found in the Armanen system of Guido von List seem to have some parallels in the ideas of Bure. These parallels are not likely to have resulted from List and others having *read* Bure's works, because the latter were never widely published or translated.

THE ESOTERIC RUNOLOGY OF BUREUS'S *ADULRUNOR*

Exoteric runology is concerned with the inner meanings of the runestaves used for writing ordinary language, but it is seen that this is a reflection of the esoteric runology of the *adulrunor*. So, the *adulrunor,* as delineated by Bure, are not identical in form to the *uppenbara runor* (evident or ordinary runes).

The fifteen *adulrunor* are said to be inscribed on a cubical stone that fell from heaven as a sign of the powerful divinity of the mediator between God and Man (fig. 3.7 shows Bure's own illustration of this stone). On three of the sides of the cube there are groups of five staves organized in the form of a cross.

Again we see the typical Burean system of 3 × 5. The forms of the staves of the *adulrunor* are often quite different from ordinary

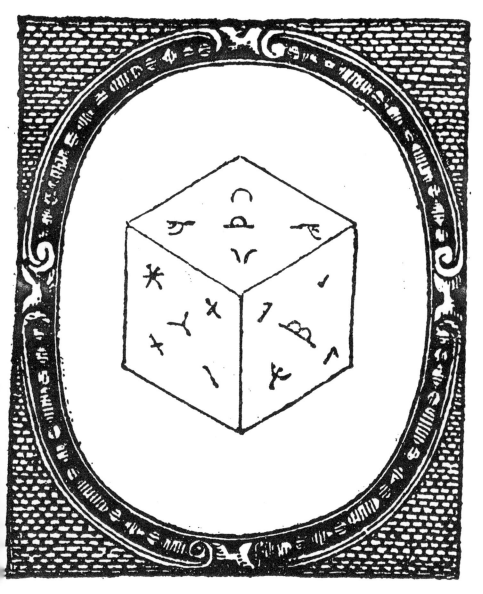

Fig. 3.7. The cubical runic stone

versions of the staves. The difference is often a matter of rotating the stave ninety degrees, or the use of the rare Hälsinga rune-forms for Π and R, which are ⟩ and ⟨, respectively. In the first quintet the five signs appear:

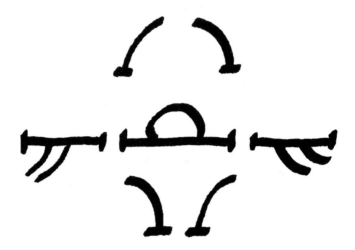

The three central runes ᚦᚨᚠ (*t, o, f*) refer to the triune divinities of Thor–Odin–Frey. According to sixteenth-century "tradition," these gods were inherited in Sweden from Noah and his son Japheth. Bure insists that only later did Asiatic masters of magic (Sw. *sejd*) and wizards (Sw. *tollare*) arrive, pretending to be incarnations of the true Gods. But the true religion of the ancients held sway for a much longer time in the North than in southern Europe. Bure, like many other mythologists of his time and earlier, used the Old Testament as a text for basic data, which in Bure's case was then coupled with a primitive understanding of Saxo Grammaticus and perhaps of Snorri's *Edda,* copies of which had surfaced in the mid-1500s.

One of the innovations of the religion instituted by the wizards was that instead of a triune godhead, the people should worship Thor in life, Frigg at birth, and Odin in death. Here Bure wishes to maintain the primal monotheism of the ancestors and ascribe pantheism to a later, decadent, phase of history. This decadence represents the beginning of the dimming of the knowledge inherent in the *adulruna.*

Bure then proceeds to interpret the individual *adulruna*-staves of the first quintet, which as a whole signify *birth,* or the beginning of things.

⟟⟊⟊ is the freest and functions everywhere and in everything. This is the highest and most powerful force, and it is equated with the Norse god Thor. This force is actually androgynous. Bure points to an image of Thor found in Uppsala that is masculine in the upper body, feminine below. (Later commentators have identified this image as a badly damaged early depiction of Christ.) Thor is linked with Jove, and hence to Jehovah. The icon 𝛺 shows the door of a lodge at the horizon. It is flanked by ⟊ and ⟊, Odin and Frigg, who with outstretched arms show the way to the door.

⟊⟊ is the *adulruna* of Odin, the son of Thor, according to Bure. This interpretation of Odin as Thor's son was common in the early studies of Norse myths, which were heavily influenced by comparisons with classical mythology. To Odin belongs all property and estate and all offices of state. The name Odin is equated with Latin *fatum,* "divine foresight," due to the similarity between the god's name and the Swedish word *öde,* "fate."* This *fatum* is seen as the origin of all created things. The originators of the runes concealed Odem, or the "blood-red one," Ådam, behind the image of Odin—or Mars, the destroyer. Of this Ådam it is said that in his wrath all the power of the enemy shall be destroyed by his blood.

⟊⟊ is on the left side of Thor, and hence on the day *after* his day. This signifies Frigg (or Fröja), the daughter of Thor and wife of Odin. Bure identifies Freyja (Fröja) with Frigg and says that the Swedish ancestors worshipped the true breath of holiness under the name of Fröja. This is further identified with the spirit that "moved upon the face of the waters" (Genesis 1:2). This is the one who distributes all good gifts.

Below the horizon and *outside* the door are the twins (*u, r*), which appear as ram's horns ⟊⟊. They indicate the password to the whole divine work, which emanates from above and is in perpetual motion and

*This is an example of folk-etymologizing on Bureus's part; there is, in fact, no historical relation between these words.

expansion. Bure indicates that everything emerges from the *one,* and returns to the *one,* and cites a comparison of three biblical passages— Daniel 7:10 and Matthew 13:41 and 22:30—as a key.

But above the horizon the twins (*r, u*) are paired *inside* the door thusly: ⌒⌒. This is a password to eternal rest and union with the highest God. Bure cites the "Egyptian Trismegistus":

> *Those chosen by God are of two kinds,*
> *the one are those who migrate,*
> *the other those who are still,*
> *and these are the highest holiness of souls.*

The second quintet of *adulrunor* appears:

This is the quintet of birth or generation, as the first had been that of the progenitor (the progenitor = father, birth—the process that the father initiates, but not identical with the father). The central triad of this group of five is NotAriKon—those who bear the governments of the three realms signified by the three crowns in the Swedish national symbol. The ✝ on the right side signifies grace/mercy, while the ✝ on the left side means glory in the Promised Land. Ψ is the ruling governance of the *kyn* (kin) of the realm, which is invisible. *Kyn* is split in two at the top like two branches of a tree. This indicates that the tree of life stands on both banks of the river that emanates from God's throne.

The *adulrunor* of this quintet create a progressive sequence that demonstrates the interrelationship of the three kingdoms:

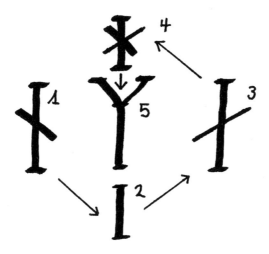

One emerges from the valley of grace/mercy (✝) over the narrow passage of repentance (*ider*) into the plain of honor (*ärevidden*). From there one must pass through a torrent of hail (*hagelfors*) to ascend to the summit of character (*kynnahöjder*). Bure compares this progress to the migration of Israel from Egypt over the Red Sea and through the wilderness into the "redemptive land of peace." Further, he equates this process to the movement of the High Priest at the Israelite Temple from the outer court (1), before the brazen altar (2), into the holy temple (3), before the holy golden altar (4), and from there into the Holy of Holies (5). Only the one who understands these progressions can understand this quintet of *adulrunor*. He will understand the office of the mediator priest (✝), the lying stone (I), the royal government (✝), the falling stone (✳), and the office of judges (Y).

The third quintet is that of the offspring:

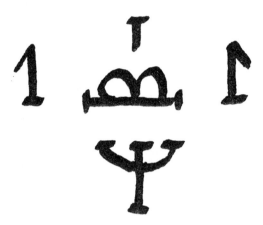

This quintet can be observed from two distinct angles: either (1) horizontally (1ᴀℓ) or (2) vertically (ᴛᴀᴪ).

In the first arrangement, a password is formed by the three-forked office of mediation here in this world—of mediating between sun (ᴛ) and man (ᴪ) through the central lord (*drotten*) and king (ᴀ), flanked by the priests (*tidemän*) on the right and judges (*lägmän*) on the left. All three—king, priest, and magistrate—act as mediators between the sun (*sol*) of righteousness and his servants.

In the second vertical view a column is created between *sol*—the most excellent of all visible things, which here has the high seat (seat of honor)—and the moon (ᴪ, *månen*), which illuminates the night. The former is likened by Moses to Eden (Genesis 2:8) and by Solomon to the "heaven of heavens" (II Chronicles 2:6), while John likens it to the New Jerusalem (Revelation 21:2), which requires no sun because it has itself become a sun, and no moonlight because it is its own reflected light. This new world is called Paradise by the Lord and an enclosure in Eden by Moses. However, in the midst of this is the present dungeon (*fjätterhyddan:* the "fetter-hut"). For this reason, we must await salvation. The twins 1 and ℓ remind us that everything has its *time* and *place* (*tid och lag*).

These two interpretations of this quintet point to the strongly ambiguous and even apparently paradoxical meaning of the *adulruna*: in the one instance it is the mediator (king and lord); in the other, the mortal clay of the body. The reconciliation of these two meanings reveals a profound understanding of the role of the material universe in the cosmology of the ancient Goths as well as in the modern world newly emerging in Bure's time.

ADULRUNA: THE PRIESTLY OFFICE

The third section of *Adulruna Rediviva* deals with the office of the pastor or priest. This section is an extensive commentary on a cruciform arrangement of *adulrunor* widely used by Bure, yet seldom fully explained. The symbol appears as depicted in figure 3.8. Note the three

Fig. 3.8. The cruciform symbol of the priestly office

crowns arrayed at the top of the cross and above each side of its horizontal beam.

The mythical priest-figure Byrger, who is said by Bure to have been an originator of the runic system, is used as an archetype of the ancient priesthood. Byrger illustrates the seven eternal *adulrunor* in a cruciform arrangement according to the seven days of the week.

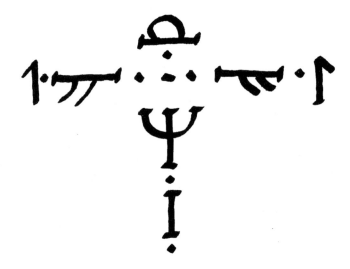

Each of these is shown to correspond to the image of the crucifix—the image of Jesus Christ (= Byrger) hanging on the cross—as shown in table 3.2.

TABLE 3.2. THE *ADULRUNOR* OF THE CROSS

on	stands		marked here			
1 head	♎		▷		♃	Jovis
2 left arm		}		}	♀	Veneris
3 left hand					♄	Saturni
4 feet		stave		day	☉	Solis
5 chest	ψ		ψ		☽	Lunae
6 right hand					♂	Martis
7 right arm					☿	Mercurii

This esoteric runic information is combined with the words of Jesus: "Whosoever will come after me, let him deny himself, and take up his cross, and follow me" (Matthew 16:24). The practice of "taking up the cross" is equated with the daily meditations known as the Stations of the Cross. This, like other Christian forms of practice and belief, was seen as something that actually belonged to the original faith predating the time of the historical Jesus.

Although Bure's melding of mystical Christian and runic iconography may seem at first to be indicative of his subjectivist approach, one should not be so quick to judge his ideas harshly. Studies have more recently shown the degree to which early medieval Christianity was in fact "Germanized" centuries before the first Christians ever came to Sweden (see Russell 1994).

Bure maintains that Thursday is considered by Swedes to be the holiest of days. He takes this as an indication that the secret spiritual heritage of the Swedes (embodied in the *adulrunor*) antedates that of the Jews (whose holy day is Saturday) or the Christians (whose holy day is Sunday). Bure traces the Swedish tradition back to King Ninus of Babel, who established the holiness of Thursday in memory of his father, Bel, who is identified with Jupiter (Jove = Jehovah). From this primeval time until the coming of Roman Christianity, the Swedes had kept their holiest day as Thursday.

There are two groups of four runes each, which form the actual cross under the body of Byrger/Christ—one group of four runes horizontally across the arms, the other vertically along the length of the body. The runes positioned across are ᚱᚢᚾ (*RUNA*) = *literatura, experientia* (because *runa* is, according to Bure, derived from *rön*, "experience").* These *adulrunor* can also be combined as follows:

---

*Bure's etymology is insightful here: as with Old Norse *rún*, "rune," and *raun*, "experience" (the latter word being formed through ablaut from the same stem, *rūn-*, that underlies the former), the modern Swedish words *runa* and *rön* are etymologically related.

to form an image of grace and honor opening a gate to eternal peace and rest. These same four runes are also significantly combined as ⊁ᚴᚩ (*AURN*) = *örn, aquila*—the eagle. These are equated with the eagle standards of Caesar Tiberius, which represented Gothic soldiers from the Pontus under Pilatus. The runes that form the vertical beam are ᐋ|⁎Y—which Bure says can be read as *PIGKind* = *virginis filius* ("son of the virgin"). He comments that the sequence shows the "son of the virgin," the righteous guide, leading his followers out of bondage (the "fetter-hut") by means of *ider* (repentance) through the embrace of the all-containing ⁎ (a combination of ᚠ grace and ᛏ honor) and throughout into the highest level of freedom in ♎.

So the vertical column describes the initiation of an individual from a state of bondage to one of liberation, while the crossbeam is the experience (*rön*) of the mystery (*runa*) of the world.

Four *adulrunor* are identified as the shepherd runes as depicted here

and that guard an inner seven, which is identified as the flock. The shepherd runes consist of the divine trinity Thor–Odin–Frigg (ᚦᚭᚠ) along with ΔΔ, which is the valor of the shepherd. The image of the ΔΔ is likened to the breasts of the maiden, which feed the shepherd, as well as to the double doors of a sheep pen for the entrance and exit of a flock. The runes signifying the "flock" are shown in figures 3.9 and 3.10.

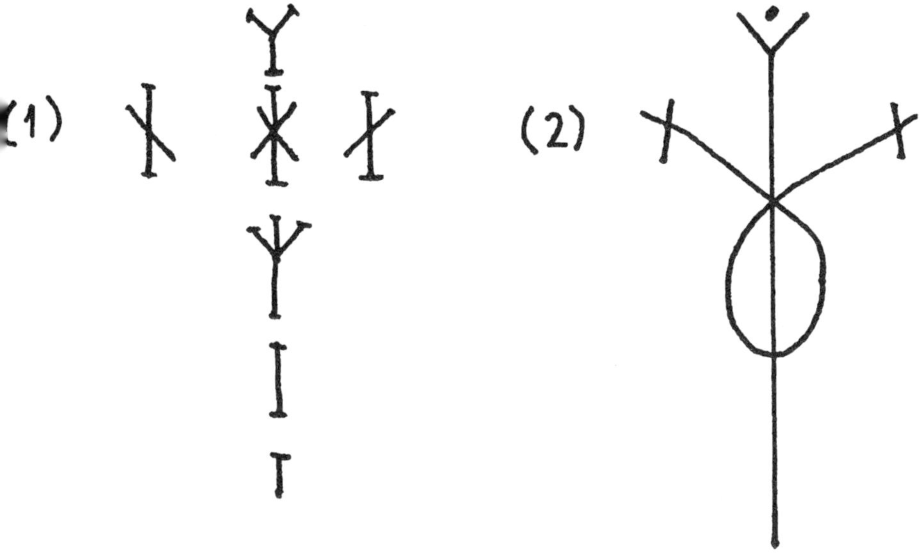

Fig. 3.9 and Fig. 3.10. The seven cruciform runes and the sevenfold Holy Spirit

From these seven cruciform runes (fig. 3.9) is formed a glyph (fig. 3.10) that signifies the sevenfold Holy Spirit united with the Word of God. These runes can be arranged from above to below to form the phrase ᛉᚭᛯᚼᛘ' = *gæghn mis* = *ocurre mihi* (run to meet me). This is the voice of the one who calls from above, and those who answer from below call out 'ᛁᛉᚼᛯᚭᛉ *sim äghn k(ynd)* = *simus possessionis filij, quasi unus* (we are of the property of the Son, as if one). Note that ᛉ is here read by Bure as an ideographic rune and that the formula is created by reading the seven runes from the bottom upward, reversing the order of the original "call."

The remaining four runes at the outermost arms of the cross are ᛏᚱᛁᛚ = *trol(l)* (trolls), the "evil spirits," daemons—indicating the spiritual wolves that seek to scatter and gobble up the flock. At first these wolves seem to entice the flock with both ᛏ and ᛚ (time and space, *tid och lag*)—and then they drive members of the flock down into the infernal regions with a three-pronged fork ᛉ (trident). The reversal of this formula is ᛚᚱᛏ (*lort*) [Sw. *lort*, "dirt, filth, muck"] *defraudatorum symbolum* (sign of the deceived)—those who have been lured by the trap and snares.

Bure has the mystical Byrger lay out the *adulrunor* in two groups: a horizontal one of nine staves and a vertical one consisting of seven staves. The horizontal row defines the two outstretched arms of him who calls (*kallare*), and on the "caller's" heart stands the ᛉ, which radiates sacrality. On the right arm stand the signs ᚾᚢᚱᛞ (= NORD). At first glance this reads *nord* (north), but Bure interprets the initial rune as an ideograph: N(*ådens*)ORD/N(*ödens*)ORD = Word of Grace/Word of Need. Read in reverse, this yields ᛞᚱᚢᚾ *tron*, meaning *fides* (faith). On the left arm we find the runes ᛡᚠᚢᛚ, which can be read *åful*, "permanent fullness." But this, too, can be interpreted with an initial ideograph ᚠ (*äro*, "glory"), thus *Ä(ro)FUL* = "glorious." Bure reasons that since the "caller's" right arm is God's Word, then it follows that the left arm must be the Holy Spirit: because without these two, he says, no one could be called or follow.

The runes ᛚᚢᚠ (*lof*) can also be read as meaning "praise," but, according to Bure's esoteric reading, these signs should be understood as ᛚᛁᚠ (*lyf*) = "love." From *lyf* Bure alternatively reads *l(i)uf–ful* ᛁᚠᚢ ᚢ·)·ᛚ, which refers to faithfulness—with all its legal hooks and bitter barbs ᛚ, and also to the gospels and the grace-full horn of oil ᛋ).

The group of seven staves depicts the "collector's" vertical body, the head of which is ᛤ, while the feet are ᛉ. Between these extremes, however, are the five-runged ladder (see next page).

On the downward climb the "caller" began in Thor's stave and completed the journey in *byrgall*—and there the ones who have been called are to turn around and begin their ascent up the ladder. In Thor (**ⵔ**) the return journey is complete. The descent begins by passing through doors from which all good gifts come. The first rung is Y— the highest realm of the Father. The second is ✴ (*hagal*)—the one that completes the Father's will. The third is Y (*man, manna*), which is the heavenly bread. The fourth is I (*ider*), which is repentance as the result of sin (guilt). The fifth is ᛏ, which shows the rays of the sun—take note of temptation (Rev. 16:8), the sun does the same (Luke 22:31). The one who is in ⵠⵠ is sitting in fetters or bonds, being threatened with death. The savior wishes that all those who doubt will come to know that life is the great reward.

The shepherd himself made the ascent into heaven along the ladder of staves described here.

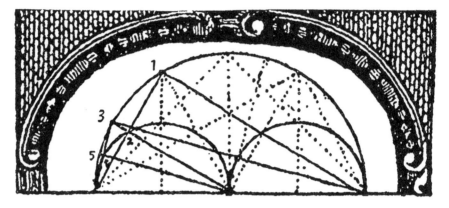

Fig. 3.11. The ascent to heaven

Figure 3.11 shows the immeasurable power received by those who have been united with God.

ADULRUNOR AND THE SECRET CALCULATION OF TIME

Bure uses the cruciform figure of the *adulrunor* to measure time in mysterious ways. The right arm of the cross renders 1 (300), ↑ (5), 𝖂 (1), and ✝ (60) = 366—the number of days in a complete circuit of the Sun. The fifth stave ✶ = 30: the number of days in a lunar cycle from new moon to new moon. This is the heart of the bride being embraced by the bridegroom, which is the Sun. This cosmic embrace of the primeval masculine and feminine first took place in Paradise. The staves to the right: ⫫⟩⫪ = 90 + 1 + 3+ 700 = 794. According to Bure's calculations, this is the number of years between the conjunctions of Jupiter and Saturn—the two highest planets of (medieval) astronomy. These numbers were used by Bure to arrive at cosmological dates—such as 1648, which was to be the date of the next "embrace" of the Sun and Moon (794 x 2 + 2 x 30 = 1648 AD).* Thus, the Incarnation of

---

*The year 1648 marks the end of the Thirty Years' War with the signing of the Peace of Westphalia. Many scholars of the history of ideas consider this to be a turning point in which the Enlightenment period begins.

Christ occurred at one of the conjunctions of Saturn and Jupiter. The importance of such a conjunction to Bure is linked with the esoteric interpretation of the planet/god Saturn with the "Gothic" god *Oden* (fate) = Odin.*

Another of Bure's calculations concerns the sum of the vertical runes of the cross ᐃᐃ.ᛌ.ᛁ.ᛉ.ᛡᘯ (500 + 100 + 70 + 900 + 30 + 5 = 1605). The year 1605 is the one in which Bure received the idea of the *adulrunor*—the idea descended upon him, and with and from this concept, or Word, he spent the rest of his life ascending the ladder of the runes.

The numerological and eschatological speculations embedded in Bure's work are often extremely obscure to the outsider. Some of Bure's contemporary detractors accused him of trying to speculate endlessly, and irrationally, about the date of the "end of the world," and they tried to make it seem that he had become mentally incompetent. The facts do not bear out this interpretation, which now seems to be politically motivated rhetoric at the court of the king. However, his speculations in this direction are obscure and leave themselves open to such attacks. For anyone who can penetrate his code of thought, illumination might accompany their insights.

THE THREE CROWNS

Bure traces the origin of the national symbol of Sweden, the three crowns, back to the mythical figure of Byrger Tidesson, who advised

*The ongoing attempt to link Christ with Odin is further illuminated in studies such as G. Ronald Murphy's *The Saxon Savior* (1989).

that the administration of the land be divided into three functions: that of the king, the high priest, and the judge. Accordingly, the power to govern was divided into three and so was the land they governed. Each of the three parts of the land received a crown as its symbol— and thus the coat of arms of all three crowns is a symbol of the whole of Sweden.

THE SCIENCE OF *ADULRUNA*

Since the time when I first wrote the text of this section about Johan Bure in 1998, great strides have been made in the studies surrounding this Swedish runologist and mage. We can especially point to the work of Thomas Karlsson, who was actually inspired by the magical words I originally wrote at the end of this section, *"Någon har mycket att göra."* This call was heard and now I can say, *Någon har mycket gört!*

At one point Bure created a table with which he wished to show the place of the *adulrunor* in the great scheme of philosophy and the sciences of his day. In his own Renaissance spirit, he was already laying the foundations for an integral runology of the future.

TABLE 3.3. BURE'S TABLE OF THE RUNIC SCIENCES

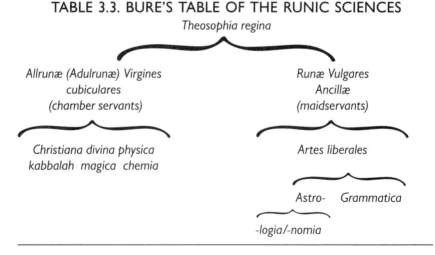

Theosophia regina

Allrunæ (Adulrunæ) Virgines
cubiculares
(chamber servants)

Runæ Vulgares
Ancillæ
(maidservants)

Christiana divina physica
kabbalah magica chemia

Artes liberales

Astro-   *Grammatica*

-logia/-nomia

Table 3.3 not only gives us a map of Bure's esoteric universe of ideas, but it also articulates these ideas into a meaningful series of relationships. Royal theosophy is divided into an inner and outer aspect. The inner aspect is identified with the pristine *adulrunor*, which are articulated into the three sciences of "kabbalah," "magic," and "alchemy." The "common runes" are the "maidservants" known as the liberal arts. These support and promote the esoteric pursuits, and from them the liberal arts branch out further into astronomy/astrology and grammar. From Bure's life and work it is clear that he realized the magical significance of *grammar*—the meaningful arrangement of sounds/letters. He saw this as being intimately bound up with the concept of a *rune*. Bure recognized (correctly) the etymological link between the Swedish words *runa* (mystery; letter) and *rön* (experience, observation, understanding). The definition Bure gives of *"adulruna"* at this point is *nobilis experientia quæ potissimum constat in naturæ cognitione,* the "experience of nobility, which it is agreed (is) in the knowledge of nature." *Adulrunor* are those things by which we may investigate the noble or exalted aspects of objects—natural or supernatural.

The study of the ideas of Johan Bure is fraught with difficulties. His esoteric works largely remain unpublished today. They are stored away in archives in Stockholm, Uppsala, and Lund. This circumstance makes a difficult study twice as hard as it would be otherwise. Bure's ideas are, I suspect, extraordinarily sophisticated and complex. Yet their meaning is shrouded behind an obscure language of symbols that would be difficult to understand completely even if all his works were readily available in convenient editions and/or translations. It is almost certainly the case that Bure only revealed the *key* to his thought and language to those students who took the time and effort to come and learn with him in person. So, when we are left to speculate on his meanings or evaluate his thought based on the fragments of printed material and commentaries on the latter, we are confronted with the magnitude of the task of unlocking the mysteries of Bure's system.

OLAUS WORMIUS

Olaus Wormius (Ole Worm, 1588–1654) was a Danish physician, natural historian, and antiquary who was a true Renaissance man. His father, Willum, was wealthy and at one time the mayor of the city of Aarhus. Wormius studied widely—first theology in Marburg, Germany, and then medicine in Basel, Switzerland, where he was promoted to doctor of medicine in 1611. In 1617 he received a Master of Arts degree in Copenhagen, where he taught Latin, Greek, physics, and medicine for the rest of his life. He eventually became the personal physician to King Christian IV of Denmark.

Although both Bureus and Wormius can be considered the contemporary grandfathers of modern runology, they were men of very different temperaments: Bureus was a mystic at heart; Wormius was more purely scientific in his approach. Another practical contrast between the two is that Bureus produced much of his work in manuscript form only, whereas Wormius published a good deal more of his work in printed books.

In general, Wormius made many important contributions not only to the field of antiquities, such as runic studies and medieval literature, but also to medicine and natural history. The small bones that fill the gaps in the human cranial sutures—the Wormian bones—are named after him. He collected fossils and specimens of animals from around the world. He had a pet great auk bird from the Faroe Islands, his illustration of which is the only known depiction of this now extinct animal drawn from a living model. He also famously disproved the existence of the unicorn and showed that the horns widely attributed to them were actually from a sea creature, the narwhal.

The contributions of Wormius to runology were significant. He traveled widely in Denmark and Norway in search of runic monuments. In 1626, Wormius published the *Fasti Danici* (Danish Chronology) containing the results of his researches into runic lore; ten years later he came out with the ᚱᚢᚾᛁᛦ *seu Danica literatura antiquissima* (*Runer,* or the Most Ancient Danish Literature; 1636, with a later edition appearing in 1651). In this work he tried to explain the origin and development of runic writing. Generally, he maintained that all scripts originated from the Hebrew alphabet as it was the oldest of all scripts. The similarities between Greek, Latin, and runic signs were taken as evidence that all of them were descended from a common archetype, identified with the Hebrew alphabet. He did note that he believed that the runes were older than either the Greek or Latin systems. His *Danicorum Monumentorum* (Danish Monuments) appeared in 1643 and was the first printed collection of transcribed runic texts taken from runestones and presented in any sort of systematic way. Some of the work of Wormius, like that of Bureus, contains depictions of monuments that have since been "lost." In such instances, these illustrations and descriptions may be our only evidence for their existence. He wrote his works exclusively in Latin.

Wormius himself succumbed to the plague in Copenhagen while treating the sick during the epidemic.*

RUNIC ANTIQUITIES IN SWEDEN AFTER BUREUS

Johannes Bureus was succeeded as the head of *Riksantikvariet* by Georg Stiernhielm (1648–1651), Johan Axehielm (1652–1657), and even by his own kinsman Laurentius Bureus (1657–1665). An important figure who emerged at this time in Uppsala was the antiquarian Olaus Verelius (1618–1682). Verelius served as National Antiquary between 1666 and 1675 and was also the founder of what became known as the Hyperborean School of Swedish antiquities and history. This held that the Swedes were the people referred to in Greek literature

---

*As a *weird* footnote, we may mention that in the stories of the early twentieth-century American horror writer H. P. Lovecraft, Wormius is cited as the translator of a Latin version of the fictional grimoire of magic known as the *Kitab al-Azif* or *Necronomicon*. Perhaps Lovecraft got Wormius and Bure confused?

as the "Hyperboreans." This school is the successor to Gothicism and enjoys some adherents in esoteric circles to this day. Verelius was in fact the teacher of Olof Rudbeck. In 1675 he wrote a handbook of runic studies called the *Manuductio compendiosa ad runographiam Scandicam antiqvam recte intelligendam* (A Short Guide to Correctly Understanding Old Swedo-Gothic Rune-Writing), compiled the first Old Norse dictionary by a non-Icelander, and showed that the pagan temple of Uppsala was actually located where the present-day church is at Gamla Uppsala.

Johan Hadorph (1630–1693) became the National Antiquary in 1679 and served in that office until 1693. Hadorph began the work of collecting runic inscriptions for publication, as most of the work of Bureus remained in manuscript form. The work was to be called *Monumenta Runica Sueo-Gotica* (Swedo-Gothic Runic Monuments). Hadorph actually enlisted the aid of the entire Swedish population in the quest to hunt down runic monuments in the countryside. This mainly consisted of writing to church and governmental officials in all of the parishes to be on the lookout for runic artifacts. In 1666 he formalized the office of antiquities, for which the noble and influential university chancellor Magnus Gabriel de la Gardie was officially responsible. De la Gardie is also well known for his contribution of buying the *Codex Argenteus,* the sixth-century manuscript of Ulfila's Gothic Bible, which had been taken as booty from Prague by the Swedish army during the Thirty Years' War.

A persistent puzzle in the early study of the runes was the meaning of certain inscriptions found in the Hälsingaland region of Sweden. To most people they appeared to be nonsensical scribbles. A prize was offered to anyone who could read them. In 1675 the mathematician Magnus Celsius (1621–1679) gave a speech at Uppsala in which he demonstrated his decipherment of these runes. However, because Celsius died shortly after the speech, his solution was not published until 1707. As it turned out, the Hälsinga runes were actually those of the Younger Futhark with the "head-staves" (the vertical line) removed. This left only the branches.

In 1699, Johan Perinskiöld came out with an annotated edition of the *Vita Theodorici regis Ostrogothorum et Italiae* (Life of Theodoric, King of the Ostrogoths and of Italy), by the sixteenth-century German humanist Johann Cochlaeus. In this volume, Perinskiöld claimed that the runes had been brought to the North out of Asia by Magog, son of Japheth. To support the idea further, he claimed to be able to read the name "Magog" on the runestone of Bällsta in Uppland, which was a misreading of the runes.

During the Renaissance period in England, in which the English Reformation also took place, runes appear to have been studied by only a few antiquaries. In the earliest period these men were clerics, but by the seventeenth century, secular scholars also explored some runic knowledge as well.

OLOF RUDBECK

A visionary and latter-day Renaissance man named Olof Rudbeck (1630–1702) became one of the most radical Storgöticists in history. Rudbeck's father was Bishop Johan Rudbeck, personal chaplain to King Gustav Adolph, and his son, Olof Rudbeck the Younger, was a botanist and teacher of Carl Linnaeus. Olof Rudbeck was a physician, scientist, and linguistic historian, who was accomplished in many fields. He was a professor of medicine at Uppsala University but is perhaps best known today as a visionary historian.

Between the years 1679 and 1702, Rudbeck worked on the production of works of linguistics, history, and national mythology, which resulted in the publication of the four volumes of his magnum opus *Atlantica* (Swedish version: *Atland eller Manheim*). In this work he endeavored to show that the fabled land of Atlantis mentioned by Plato was actually located in Sweden and that Sweden was the land of the original Paradise and the origin of all civilizations and languages. The runes and runic inscriptions were a pivotal aspect of his theories.

Fig. 3.12. An illustration from *Atlantica* (1689), in which Rudbeck depicts himself in the company of Hesiod, Plato, Aristotle, Apollodorus, Tacitus, Odysseus, Ptolemy, Plutarch, and Orpheus

Rudbeck, following in the footsteps of Bure before him, went into the countryside around Uppsala and learned how to read runic perpetual calendars carved on long staves by often illiterate peasants who had preserved ancient knowledge.

Rudbeck also plumbed the depths of classical works to discover that the Roman historian Pliny had determined that the original Greek alphabet consisted not of twenty-four, but of only *fifteen* letters: A, B, Γ, Δ, E, I, K, Λ, M, N, O, Π, Σ, T, and Υ.

The other eight letters were added later over time. This led Rudbeck to conclude that the ancient Greek alphabet and the runic futhark were one and the same. He also began to note the similarities between

Greek and Old Swedish words, taking into account certain systematic changes (for example, Swedish /h/ corresponds to Greek /k/, as can be seen with Sw. *hiarta* and Gk. *kardía,* both meaning "heart"). Rudbeck was recognizing what would become established linguistic science some years later with the discovery of the Indo-European family of languages. For Rudbeck, however, these relationships were taken as proof of the *Swedish* origin of all alphabets and languages.

Like every other scholar of his day, Rudbeck thought that the sixteen-rune futhark was the original runic system, but in his own visionary way he saw them as being derived from the shape of the caduceus of Hermes/Mercury.

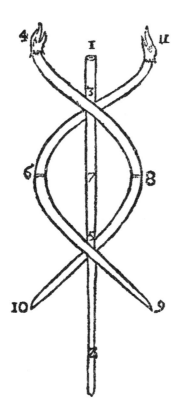

All the runes can be derived from this shape using the numbers as guideposts. For example, the ᛏ-rune can be made by connecting 2 to 5

and 10 to 9. This schema was the instrument by which the Swedish god Heimdall (= *hem-taler:* "secret speaker") taught writing to the Greeks. The fact that Hermes was considered the originator of writing among the Greeks served to further substantiate the theory in Rudbeck's vision.

Rudbeck's theories gained little respect outside of Sweden, but in his native land they made him immortal. In May of 1702, a fire broke out in Uppsala that destroyed two-thirds of the city, including Rudbeck's home and library. While the fire raged, Rudbeck attempted to direct firefighters from his rooftop. Rudbeck's biographer, David King, describes the aftermath of the fire in this way:

> As his life's work turned to embers and ash, Rudbeck showed all the strength for which his long journey had prepared him. In some ways this was his finest moment. Far from complaining, losing hope, or succumbing to bitterness, Rudbeck showed the inner strength and wisdom that he always believed had existed long ago in a golden age under the North Star. (King 2005, 250)

True to form, two weeks after the great fire had ravaged three-fourths of Uppsala, Rudbeck entered the council chamber with drawings of plans to rebuild his beloved town.

Just four months later Rudbeck would die peacefully in bed. He would be entombed in Uppsala Cathedral at the transept. Subsequent Swedish monarchs were often crowned atop his grave.

Rudbeck's descendants would carry on some of his more fantastic work, as his son Olof the Younger theorized about the reasons for Sweden's great political and military power, and also sought to show a relationship between the Sámi language and Hebrew. A nephew, Petter Rudbeck, also wrote books trying to show that the events of the Trojan War actually took place in southern Sweden.

An objective yet sympathetic picture of Rudbeck is provided in David King's book *Finding Atlantis,* where he points out that although Rudbeck's specific theories about history and language (and the runes) were inaccurate, many of his operating assumptions—for example, that ancient artifacts could be dated according to how deep they were buried in the ground, or how distant languages might be related to one another despite how different they might seem to be—anticipated new scientific breakthroughs in the fields of archaeology and linguistics. It does appear that Rudbeck was a true visionary and that his mythic vision acted as a sort of potent national magic in Sweden.

CHAPTER FOUR

THE ENLIGHTENMENT

(1700–1800)

The historical period most commonly referred to as the Enlightenment is also sometimes known as the Age of Reason. This period roughly encompasses the years 1650 to 1800. The Enlightenment was a radical critique of the Renaissance, in that the Renaissance tended to look for new and alternative sources and authorities for knowledge, whereas the Enlightenment ideal was the questioning of all sources and the rejection of authority on principle. This led to a relative disinterest in the past and a striving for more universal truth as based entirely on rational models.

The cultural roots of this period stem from three main sources. First, there was increased religious or sectarian tolerance. This followed the fiasco of the Thirty Years' War (1618–1648), which had essentially been a civil war within Christendom between Catholic southern Europe and Protestant northern Europe. Secondly, there was a continued growth in strong nation-states, which led to political nationalism. Finally, there was a general acceptance of the idea of rationalism as a way forward for humanity. Both orthodox Christianity and Greco-Roman philosophy were increasingly doubted as being dogmatic authorities based on tradition. The Enlightenment looked to subject all such "received knowledge" to an empirical test.

The Enlightenment was marked by a desire to attain new kinds of intellectual and artistic achievement, free from traditions and cultures of the past. With the passage of time, however, there was a return to the more open admiration and imitation of classical (Greco-Roman) forms in art and literature. In its latter phase of development, the Enlightenment became what is known as Classicism or Neoclassicism. This is distinguished by the use of the aesthetics of the Greeks and Romans with an emphasis on clarity, precision, and simplicity.

Generally, this phase in the history of ideas meant that interest in the spirit and aesthetics of the "barbarian" past of the nations of northern Europe became greatly reduced. This was the time of hyperrationalism and the past was only admired insofar as it corresponded to a (largely fictionalized) version of Greco-Roman culture and aesthetics. However, tools of science were developed, and methods of observation were pursued that would be of great use later as interest in the indigenous pasts of the various nation-states of northern Europe redeveloped in the Romantic period.

JOHAN GÖRANSSON

Considered to be the last of the great Storgöticists, Johan Göransson (1712–1769) is also often called the last Rudbeckian. Born into a farming family, he became a Lutheran priest, runologist, antiquarian, and archaeologist. He entered the University of Lund in 1740 and graduated in 1744 with a dissertation on the topic of *Skadinaviens urgamla inbyggare* (The Ancient Inhabitants of Scandinavia). The next year he enrolled in Uppsala University, and it was there that he became especially enamored with the teachings and theories of Olof Rudbeck. In 1745 he began to teach at Lund University, and in 1747 he became a priest in Karlstad. He later continued his career within the church, earning more academic and ecclesiastical offices (in this early modern period, church offices and duties within the Lutheran Church were alternatives to university life for scholars). Göransson developed a great reputation for his intelligence and mental powers—so much so that he came to be referred to as *Sveriges ljus,* the "Light of Sweden." He wrote an unpublished academic study of the Hebrew language, but mainly he devoted himself to the history and ancient traditions of Sweden and Scandinavia in general.

The influence of Rudbeck's ideas are evident in his works such as *De genealogia regnum Suioniæ* (On the Genealogy of the Royalty of Sweden; 1746), in which he claims that Sweden's earliest kings are descended from Saturn and Jupiter, while in the introduction to his edition of the *Edda* titled *De yfverborna Atlingars eller Sviogöters ok Nordmänners Edda* (Edda of the Hyperborean Descendants, or Swedo-Goths and Northmen; 1746) he maintains that this text was written at a time contemporaneous with Moses and discovered in Sweden during the reign of Queen Disa, three hundred years prior to the siege of Troy, and that they were originally written on brass tablets.

Göransson was also an important editor and translator of Icelandic sources in Sweden. He published parts of Snorri's *Edda,* translating the passages into both Latin and Swedish. Similarly, he edited the first poem of the *Poetic Edda,* the "Völuspá," also attempting a Swedish translation.

As far as runology is concerned, Göransson made two important contributions: one scholarly and exoteric (for the most part!), and one thoroughly esoteric and in the Rudbeckian tradition.

Göransson not only continued in the spiritual track of Rudbeck but also that of Bureus, Peringskiöld, Hadorph, and others whose unpublished manuscripts became sources for his scholarly work with runic inscriptions. In the realm of more scientific runology, Göransson produced his volume *Bautil, det är Svea ok Götha rikens runstenar* ("Memorial Stone," that is, Runestones of the Kingdom of the Swedes and Goths) in 1750. This was the largest collection of runic inscriptions made up to that time and encompassed 1,173 artifacts. In the introduction to this work, Göransson put forward the idea that Swedish was older than Latin and that the northern tongue was actually the mother of the language of the Romans. In the production of the volume he made use of material found in storage at the archives of the University of Uppsala that had been created and collected by previous generations going back to Bureus. When Göransson published this material under his name it caused considerable controversy, which soured him on the academic life. Although this work is filled with ideas stemming from Stogöticism and the Rudbeckian school of thought, the work remains valuable for its publication of many Swedish runestones now lost.

His most striking esoteric work is a book from 1747 titled *Is Atlinga; Det är De Forna Göters, här uti Svea Rike, Bokstafver ok Salighets Lära, Tvåtusend Tvåhundrad år före Christum, utspridd i all Land; Igenfunden af Johan Göransson* (Descendants of Is [i.e., the runes]; That is, the Letters and Doctrine of Salvation of the Ancient Goths, Hereafter the Kingdom of Sweden, Two-thousand and Two-hundred Years Before Christ, Distributed to Every Land; Rediscovered by Johan Göransson). For the most part he identified the sixteen-rune futhark as the original system and tied each of the runes to an epoch in biblical "history." The runes were used as tools for a biblical exegesis: as Göransson is well known for saying, "Every rune is a sermon." This book posited the runic order of signs as an outline of history, with different epochs being ruled by different runes. With this method Göransson could discover the secrets of the past and predict the future. In this he was again following in the footsteps of Johan Bure.

Göransson continued the ideas of the Storgöticists that Swedish civilization was the most ancient known to man and that all the gods of all people are really derived from the original gods of Sweden (Odin, Thor, and "Bore"). These were originally men who were so powerful and perfect that they came to be worshipped as gods, although they themselves were said not to be "heathens" but rather pious proto-Christians who foresaw the coming of Christ millennia before he even lived on earth. Göransson shaped an elaborate secret and mythical prehistory for

Sweden, which posited the grandson of Noah, Gomer, as the first ruler of the country. It was this Gomer, brother of Magog, who invented the runes. Göransson saw these sixteen signs as the origin of the Greek, Roman, and Etruscan alphabets.

A number of fantastic legends grew up around the personality of Göransson. He was thought to be a magician and a man of great wisdom (as we noted earlier, he was even referred to as "the light of Sweden"). Some believed he had power over the winds, the harvest, and sickness. His legend only grew after his death. A hundred and fifty years after his passing, people would still draw attention to a cypress tree in front of the church at Gillberga that had allegedly served as the site of a magical ritual done by him to bind the plague.

In discussing this last representative of the Storgöticists, it is a fitting place to point to a general feature in the esoteric thinking of individuals in European culture. Once Christianity had been firmly accepted for a few hundred years, and especially in the wake of the Reformation, it became almost impossible for individuals to entirely reject that religion and its theology and traditions. Broadly speaking, a bold religious revolution of that sort would only be possible for those coming of age in the twentieth century in the wake of figures like Darwin, Marx, and Nietzsche. But in earlier times there were two apparent options in men's minds: to Christianize the pagans (like the Storgöticists did, for example, by insisting that the national traditions of the North were older than those of Christianity and that the ancient Northmen actually prefigured or established at an earlier date what would become Christianity) or, as Guido von List would do later, to show that the ancient Northern or Germanic way was not destroyed by the coming of Christianity but rather that Christianity had to absorb and accommodate the secret teachings of the ancient Northmen and Germanic initiates (the Armanen, in List's terminology). In this latter case, we could say that Christianity, as it was practiced in the Germanic world, was a new form of the religion that blended the "Armanic" and Christian traditions. Both of these modes of understanding, which at first appear insane, have gains of truth to them. Indo-European myth and ritual had a decisive effect on Judeo-Christian religion from the beginning, and certainly the Roman Church did indeed have to accommodate the Germanic peoples of the early Middle Ages in a way similar to how, more than a millenium later, it would locally absorb indigenous religious features in the course of its missionary work in the Afro-Caribbean region (which simultaneously caused syncretized religions such as Vudoun, Macumba, Santería, and so on to form). This being said, the neo-mythologies created by men such as Rudbeck and Göransson can only be fully understood in their cultural and historical contexts.

What was noteworthy about the runic studies carried out in the Renaissance period and during the age of Storgöticism is the degree to which the esoteric dimension was somehow unified with the scientific study. This is what some critics have called the "heroic modern" approach. As the modern age progresses, however, an increasing rift will develop between these aspects of human thought—the esoteric and the scientific—and eventually an absolute division will be established between the signifier and the signified. When this occurs, the intellect has become dis-integrated, at least in the world of conventional thought.

In the half century that followed the publication of Göransson's *Bautil,* runic studies declined to a nadir of interest in Sweden. This was largely because the whole field of study was seen as the province of dilettantes and fantasists by the more sober-minded and anti-Rudbeckian antiquarians of the Enlightenment era such as Nils Brocman (1731–1770) and Olof von Dalin (1708–1763). The former held that runes and runic inscriptions were largely a Christian phenomenon, while the latter was an outspoken critic of the unreason displayed by the Rudbeckian school of thought.

As we will see, this period of skepticism was one more prelude to a rebirth of deeper interest in the runes and the ancient Germanic culture that would bloom in the time of European Romanticism.

CHAPTER FIVE

ROMANTICISM

(1800–1880)

The Age of Reason, with its promises of a rapidly perfected world based on the application of logic and rational problem-solving in a progressive manner, demonstrated its historical weaknesses and vulnerabilities in the throes of the excesses of the French Revolution. Long before that, however, many members of a younger generation had questioned the theoretical basis of Enlightenment thinking. It had ignored the particular in favor of the universal, the national in favor of the international. The revolution in the history of ideas that challenged the Enlightenment came to be called Romanticism.

Even before the broader Romantic movement had begun, in many parts of the Germanic world there were signs of disaffection with the Enlightenment approach to intellectual and artistic life. This was evident, for example, in German literary movements such as the Sentimentalist school influenced by Pietism and mysticism from 1740 to 1780, and *Sturm und Drang* (Storm and Stress) during the years 1767 to 1785.

The Romantic movement as such is thought to have run its course in mainstream culture by 1848, a year when there were general uprisings all over Europe in favor of national revolutions. These uprisings were generally suppressed by the monarchal powers, and the Romantic spirit became more of a matter of individual sensibility and of subcultural artistic expressions. Certainly, the basic ideas of Romanticism did not go away and remain as vibrant today as ever.

The importance of the Romantic impulse to runic study was this: scholars began to be more and more interested in national traditions, local phenomena, and organic and biological realities. This led attention increasingly away from things that made all peoples the same, and more and more toward those things that distinguished them one from the other. It was the unique, the individual, the national, and the natural that would become ever more compelling. The particular and peculiar art, literature, and even writing exemplified by the ancestors of the Germans, English, and Scandinavians at least became a topic of fascination and curiosity. But it would not be until the end of this period that enough data had been gathered, and the requisite methods made available, that would enable seekers to discover the real truth about the runes, their origins, and their true nature.

The late 1700s had been a period of especially widespread disinterest in Germanic antiquities, even in Sweden. There we find an overreaction to the excesses of Gothicism as expressed by men such as Rudbeck and Göransson. But the Romantic Age ushered in a new interest in the Germanic past, and one that was more a part of the artistic world as well as being relatively better informed with regard to history and linguistics. In Sweden this found expression in the organizations called the Götiska Förbund (Gothic Society), formed in 1811, and the Manhemsförbund (Manheim's Society), formed in 1815. *Manhem* is a term that harkened back to Rudbeck's work and signified the "world of men," the original golden age of humanity. The leaders of these Swedish societies were shaped by the ideals of Romanticism stemming from Germany at the time and by their own interests in renewing a patriotic sensibility. One of the leading lights of this movement was the poet, musician, and investigator Erik Gustaf Geijer (1783–1847), who wrote an influential chapter concerning runes in his work *Svea rikes häfder* (The Traditions of the Swedish Kingdom) in 1825. The historian Nils Henrik Sjöberg (1767–1838) of the University of Lund also reawakened general interest in the runes with his three-volume study *Samlingar för nordens fornälskare* (Collections for Aficionados of the North) published between 1822 and 1830.

The neo-Gothic movement in Sweden during the Romantic period was not principally focused on runic material, so I will have little more to say about it here. (However, it is a major focus of volume two of *The Northern Dawn,* my study of the greater Germanic revival from the Early Modern period to the present.)

A more exacting and scientific approach to the study of language emerged in the early part of the nineteenth century in conjunction with the spirit of Romanticism. Because of increased interest in indigenous culture, and due to the fact that so little had been preserved—and even less cultivated—with regard to the ancient Germanic past, ever more precise theories and intellectual tools had to be developed to uncover the long-buried truth of these matters. The process would not be quick, nor would it be easy. It would be fraught with many missteps and often beset by false assumptions. Nevertheless, it is in this period when the methods that would lead to a more perfect runic revival would begin to be developed.

Linguistic science made great leaps over the course of the nineteenth century. This was mainly due to the work of historical linguists of Germany and Denmark—for example, Rasmus Rask (1787–1832), Franz Bopp (1791–1867), Jacob Grimm (1785–1863), August Schleicher (1821–1868), and Johannes Schmidt (1843–1901). These scholars were able to show the relationship of the Germanic languages to one another and to contextualize them in the historical development of the greater family of Indo-European languages to which they belong. It was not until the middle of the nineteenth century that this linguistic science was sufficiently developed and established to begin to have a significant influence on the course of runic studies.

The rapid progress that took place in the field of linguistics found its way into runology much more slowly and with various degrees of success. In part this situation was exacerbated by the paucity of research material relating to runes and the lack of suitable scientific collections of runic texts that would enable linguistic scholars to pursue their work. Written sources, such as those in Old Norse literature, the Gothic Bible (written in the Gothic language of the fourth century), Old English literature, Old Saxon literature (such as the *Heliand*), and Old High German literature formed a large corpus of information, upon which serious scholars could toil away in their efforts to unlock the essence of ancient Germanic culture. By contrast, the runes were more difficult to gain similar access to at the time. The resolution of this enormous problem would not even be under way until the beginning of the twentieth century, when the great editions of the various bodies of runic inscriptions began to be edited and published.

A persistent misunderstanding was that the runes of the Younger Futhark were *older* than those of the twenty-four-rune system. This was undoubtedly due to the overwhelming number of inscriptions in the simpler system, which made the few inscriptions in the other system appear to be a decadent variant. However, the application of the growing knowledge concerning the languages in which these inscriptions appear would eventually make the picture clear. The even more comprehensive body of knowledge that was being amassed concerning the discovery and growing awareness of the truth about the Indo-European context of indigenous European culture and language would also aid greatly in this process.

The most important figure in the scientific field of runology since the days of Bureus and Wormius is that of Wilhelm Carl Grimm (1786–1859), who published a landmark study, *Ueber deutsche Runen* (On German Runes), in 1821. Wilhelm and his brother Jacob were, of course, pioneering figures in many fields, ranging from linguistics to mythology, folklore, and the history of the law and legal concepts. A year after Grimm's work appeared, the Dane Jakob Hornemann Bredsdorff would be the first to establish that the twenty-four-rune futhark was, in fact, the older of the two systems. During the middle part of the nineteenth century, several linguists worked on specific problems surrounding the runic systems and the correct reading of them in a basic way. Because the Older Futhark was more ancient, rarer in the record, and contained many puzzles relevant to the development of Germanic language at an archaic level, the study of them became increasingly interesting to all concerned.

Johan Gustaf Liljegren (1791–1837) published works under the title *Run-Lära* (Runology) (1832), which was a landmark work in the scientific study of the runes, and in 1833 his companion volume, *Run-Urkunder* (Rune-Records), appeared. The latter work contained illustrations and transliterations of only three thousand of the inscriptions.

A work that seems to represent a potential link between pre-Romantic and modern esoteric runology is the two-volume study published in 1856 and 1859 titled *Die Urreligion, oder das endeckte Uralphabet* (The Primordial Religion, or the Primordial Ancient Alphabet) by the Catholic bishop to Sweden, Jakob Laurents Studach (1796–1873). He was also a translator of the *Poetic Edda* (1829). In his *Urreligion* volumes, Studach forms all sorts of connections between Germanic and other mythic and magical symbolic and alphabetic systems, including the Egyptian and the Greek, as well as astrological lore. In the second volume of his *Urreligion* study, which is titled "Das Pentalpha des Runenalphabets" (The Pentalpha of the Rune Alphabet), an outline of his basic runology is given on pages viii–ix. I will provide a translation of this here, and the reader can make the connections between Bure and List, as well as others. Studach's Catholicism may have affected some of his peculiar associations in the text.

TABLE 5.1. THE STUDACH RUNE ALPHABET

No.	Shape	Sound	Name/Meaning
1	ᛈ	F	*fra, fre, frei, fro* (fraujo), *fé, fich, vrat, fir* (*vir–virgo* = Freyr–Freyja), *fyr, ax:* Free man, lord, god, riches (cattle, gold, hoard), child, boy, youth (fire), spruce tree [Ger. *Fichte*], ear of grain
2	ᚠ	U	*ur, vr, vraz, (dyr):* bull, storm weather, archer's bow, child, (*atrium,* "hall")
3	ᚦ	Th	*thor, thorn, thurs:* bull (hammer), thorn, triangle, giant, (blister [Ger. *Beule*])
4	ᛅ	O	(*henc*), *os, ors, hors* (*odil*): (*patibulum* [= crossbar for cross used in crucifixion]), estuary, horse, cross, (nobility)
5	ᚱ	R	(r-initial), *rat, rad, red, ræd, reid* (RT), *tir* (TR): wheel, rede, horse, god
6	ᚴ	K	(*diuot*), *kaun, kön, ken, chen, cen, chæn-thanne:* (Diut, Thiod, Teut, Tot), *genus,* type, (blister [Ger. *Beule*]), acorn tree
7	✳	H	*hagalc, hagilc:* H-chalice, holy vessel, (the seven chalices)
8	ᛐ	N	*naut, nöt, not:* ring, cattle, night, need (nemesis, eight, misery)
9	ᛁ	I	*is, iz, isc, Isch (isa):* ice, iron, man, Irmin column (isa) or the *jarn-, jar-, jær* = *war-, wær- wér-* sign (world-sign)
10	ᛏ	A	(r-medial) *ar:* river (Acheron), purifying fire-water, holy water
11	ᛋ	S	*sol (endi-sol):* sun (*Gin-sonne*, elf-light [*ignis fatuus*])
12	↑	T	*tyr, tir* (TR): god
13	ᛒ	B	*birc, birich, beorc:* birch, tree (*Leichenstossholz* [funeral pyre])
14	ᚱ	L	*laugr, lögr, lag:* lye, water (bathwater), law
15	ᛉ	M	*madr, man:* MN = *vir* and *virgo* (*mancipium* = freeman subject to the power of a Roman head of a family)
16	ᛉ	R	(r-final), *aur, ur, or, ör, yr, ir:* money, guild (debt), archer's bow

Appearing virtually at the same time as Studach's work was one by Franz Joseph Lauth (1822–1895) titled *Das germanische Runen-Fudark, aus den Quellen kritisch erschlossen und nebst einigen Denkmälern zum ersten Male erklärt* (The Germanic Rune-Fudark, Critically Revealed from the Sources and Explained alongside Some [Related] Monuments; 1857). Lauth was also an early practitioner of Egyptology when that discipline was fairly new. His particular obsession appears to have been the calculation of time using the runes as a guide.

Despite the advances in linguistic science—or, it appears, in some cases because of those advances—the idea that the runes actually had their genesis in the North and among the Germanic peoples, or that they sprang from a root common to all alphabets independently, persisted up to the middle of the nineteenth century. Scholars such as Gisli Brynjulfsen, W. Weingärtner, and F. Dietrich supported this idea, and Brynjulfsen stated that they had their origin among the "Gotho-Caucasian tribe." Apparently, the logic went, if the languages of the Germanic peoples have an ancient link to the Indo-Germanic heritage, so too must their ancient writing system. The fallacy of this should be obvious, but it stems from the lack of understanding of the essentially oral character not only of early Germanic culture but also that of the Indo-Europeans of the East.

When we look out over the whole sweep of the Romantic movement of the early nineteenth century in the Germanic countries (and at this time the United States could still be counted among these), we see a variegated picture with regard to the place of runes in this phenomenon. In general, it must be said that their role had become minimal. We see that runic symbolism had remained strong in Sweden for a very long time, especially under the sponsorship of the Gothicism of Rudbeck and Göransson, but elsewhere in Scandinavia they had slipped from the public's attention; in England (and America) runes had become the purview of dilettantes and eccentrics; while in Germany runes had remained largely unknown until the work of Wilhelm Grimm.

By the 1870s, however, the German world had been introduced to the runes at the level of "popular culture" in the form of Richard

Wagner's *Gesamtkunstwerke* (total works of art) otherwise known as "operas." In the *Ring of the Nibelungen* cycle of four such works, we see how Wagner used the concept of the runes as important symbols in his own personal and philosophical recasting of Germanic heroic mythology. The ring itself is said to be worked with runes, and the shaft of Wotan's spear is described as having runes inscribed on it. Runes, and the concept of runes as a method of conveying magical power, are deeply imbedded in Wagner's artistic worldview. It is from this time forward that the runes begin to gain a new attention in the German-speaking world and beyond. This is largely because Wagner's work was influential in many parts of Europe and the world.

In a forthcoming study titled *Wagner's Ring and the Germanic Tradition,* the philosopher Collin Cleary has recently reviewed the idea of the runes in Wagner's *Ring*.

> [W]e may note that there are numerous references to the runes in *Der Ring des Nibelungen,* where the term has the same variety of meanings it does in the Scandinavian sources. At times, it simply seems to mean letters or signs. For example, in Scene Two of *Das Rheingold* Fasolt reminds Wotan of the "runes (*Runen*) (*Runenzauber*) makes a ring from the gold." In the Prologue of *Götterdämmerung,* Brünnhilde says to Siegfried "I gave to you a bountiful store of hallowed runes (*heiliger Runen*)." And Siegfried says to her "in return for all your runes I hand this ring to you."

Clearly, Wagner had some ideas of his own concerning the symbolic and conceptual significance of the runes in Germanic lore. Wagner was a visionary in his own right, and the vision of art as a transformative agent in cultural revolution was the motivating factor in his work. The runes were brought into the consciousness of the Western world on a new level by Wagner's subtle inclusion of them on key symbols in his narrative. The golden ring of the Nibelungen appears to have been fashioned under the magical influence of the runes. The ring is a symbol of love and the cosmic power it wields—not only through the renunciation of love but also through giving love, receiving it, and withholding it from others. The other symbol upon which Wagner inscribes runes is Wotan's spear, a record of the god's binding contractual oaths involving the cosmos and other beings within it. The spear is a legal scepter of sovereign power. Wagner's use of these symbols prefigures both Freud and Jung.

Toward the last quarter of the nineteenth century, the world, and especially Europe and the United States, was beginning to engage in what would be called the Second Industrial Revolution. The technological, economic, and concomitant cultural changes this brought about would have wide-ranging repercussions on society at large and would be felt in the intellectual world in which the runic revival was taking place. On the one hand, scientific clarity was increasing, but on the other hand, there was a significant nostalgic reaction to the rapid and often ugly changes being wrought in society. Especially in Germany this would give rise to what came to be called the *Reformbewegungen*—the Reform Movements.

CHAPTER SIX

THE BEGINNINGS OF SCIENTIFIC RUNOLOGY AND NEO-ROMANTICISM

(1880–1900)

This brief chapter acts as a prelude and bridge to the great outburst of runic revivalism that will occur in the early twentieth century. But that revival did not spring out of thin air. The cultural preparations for it really took place in the twenty years leading up to the turn of the century.

The end of the nineteenth century was a time of great development in the world of ideas. Following the demise of the broader European Romantic movement in the wake of the failed revolutionary activity of 1848, alternative ideas began to go more "underground," into what we today recognize as subcultures. These subcultures continuously fight to make themselves more broadly influential in the mainstream of human culture. It remains so to this day.

More rigorous methodologies for the study of antiquity and the Middle Ages had become established in the academic world, and a considerable amount of sound, scholarly groundwork was laid in the early nineteenth century using the new tools of philology, linguistics, comparative mythology, archaeology, and other disciplines. Interest in the

Germanic past was growing and had matured by the late nineteenth century, to a certain extent due to the influence upon popular culture exerted by figures such as Richard Wagner, which we discussed at the conclusion of the previous chapter.

By the latter part of the nineteenth century, a number of aspects of life were being questioned, and alternative views were becoming ever more popular and acceptable. The ideas of major thinkers such as Karl Marx and Charles Darwin were being put into action on various cultural levels, and new ideas entered the mainstream through popular literature and other art forms.

In the realm of esotericism, the late nineteenth century was the period when the ideas that would bloom forth as the so-called magical revival were being developed. Popular interest in matters of the unseen and occult was on the rise as spiritual matters were increasingly taken out of the hands of churches and academics and progressively put into the hands of the masses. Several sometimes related, but often independent, spiritual groupings came into being. The Theosophical Society had been founded in America in 1875 and by the 1880s had put down roots in German-speaking Central Europe. Besides the Theosophists, there were offshoots such as the Anthroposophists and the Ariosophists as well as countless other groups like the German-Christians, the Germanic-Faith Movement, and all manner of mystically oriented organizations.

A number of broad alternative cultural movements were also on the rise during this period. In Germany especially, the philosophy of *Lebensreform* (life reform), as expressed through a loosely knit array of *Reformbewegungen* (Reform Movements) associated with it, had the goal of holistically reshaping various aspects of life—the environment, politics, economics, social and sexual relations, education, art, fashion— as well as the spiritual worlds of ethics, philosophy, and religion. This spirit of "Reform" has had a continuous effect on German culture since those days and was even exported to other countries to various degrees as well. For example, it has been convincingly shown that the American

"Hippie Movement" had its original roots in the German Reform ideas (see Kennedy's *Children of the Sun,* 1998).

The reformist spirit was largely motivated as a reaction to the sometimes grim and repressive aspects surrounding the Second Industrial Revolution, which began as early as 1870. But there were also positive effects that came about from the growth of new technologies. One of the most significant developments for the future of runic studies, both scientific and esoteric, is the great expansion in education and economic advancement of a burgeoning middle class. More people were being educated, and more people were earning the money with which to buy books and so on. It is from this time forward that we can trace the present state of socioeconomic life in the West.

In the world of academic runology, the most important development during the late nineteenth century was the work of the Dane Ludvig F. A. Wimmer (1839–1920), specifically his landmark study *Runeskriftens Oprindelse og Udvikling i Norden* (The Origin and Development of the Runic Script in the North), which appeared in Danish in 1874. But when this work was translated into German in 1887 as *Die Runenschrift* (Runic Writing) it gained a much wider readership and thus set off more general scholarly interest in runes in the years immediately following.

In the history of ideas, Wimmer's work came at the time when the two fields of historical (diachronic) linguistics and runology finally came together in a cooperatively productive way. The field of historical or diachronic linguistics had developed to such an extent that many of the difficult runological problems of the past could now be solved. In many respects this time period can be called a "golden age" of runology, with pioneering scholars undertaking the great task of producing comprehensive editions of the known runic inscriptions in their respective nations, as well as delving into bold systematic interpretations of the runic tradition, its origins, and its greater meaning.

Although collections of inscriptions had been made as early as the

Renaissance period, it was only after the stage had been set by Wimmer that this task could be undertaken in a systematic and coherent manner. The time was ripe for philologists working in the various lands where runes were to be found to think about creating definitive and comprehensive editions of these runic inscriptions. Toward the end of this incubation period, the first results of this collective project began to be published. This process is, however, so enormous and split up into various national spheres of interest that it would not even be completed in the twentieth century. (The work of producing a uniform edition of all the known runic inscriptions still remains unfinished today, but modern technological advances in the age of the Internet have, for the first time, made the realization of this enormous task foreseeable in the near future.)

In 1889, Rudolf Henning came out with a study titled *Die deutschen Runendenkmäler* (The German Runic Monuments), which discussed thirteen runic inscriptions from the territory of modern Germany, in which he included bracteates and Gothic inscriptions.

It was also during this period in the late nineteenth century that George Stephens (1813–1895) published his massive collections of runic monuments in English. His works were the four volumes of *The Old-Northern Runic Monuments of Scandinavia and England,* which came out between 1866 and 1901, as well as his *Handbook of the Old-Northern Runic Monuments of Scandinavia and England* in 1884. His works were elaborately illustrated with drawings of the runic monuments that remain interesting and useful to the present day. However, his treatment of the actual inscriptions was rather uninformed and uncritical. A balanced assessment of Stephens can be found in Andrew Wawn's scholarly history of the nineteenth-century "invention" and popularization of the Viking Age, *The Vikings and the Victorians* (Wawn 2002, 215–44).

As a continuing characteristic of the runic revival after the periods of the Renaissance and Storgöticism in Sweden, the scholarly world and the esoteric world generally seem to have kept their distance from one another. During the late nineteenth century, there was a general "occult revival" in various parts of the world, especially in Britain and France, while at the same time runic studies were certainly beginning to become more fixed and complete. It appears that it was during this time period especially that the present-day rift between those interested in the esoteric dimensions of the runes and those devoted entirely to the linguistic aspects of their study became established.

Perhaps a key catalyst in bringing about this rift was the Austrian mystic and poet Guido von List. We will examine List in more detail in the next chapter, but here it is relevant to briefly consider this pivotal figure in the light of the late nineteenth century so that we may appreciate the soil from which his esoteric vision would grow during the first few years of the following century.

Between 1877 and 1900, List wrote a wide variety of plays, novels, poems, and journalistic articles. None of them were overtly esoteric in the strict sense. However, it appears that in List's own mind his ideas were being synthesized into a more coherent esoteric vision before 1900. The key to his vision lies in the systematic treatment of the sounds of the German language, which are, in turn, eventually keyed to the runes. List's biographer, Eckehard Lenthe, notes that List began to use a pentagram in his signature from 1898 onward. Lenthe takes this as a sign of List's declaration that his intentions were magical and that he was dedicating himself to working to alter or influence the world in some way. During the decade of the 1890s in Vienna, List certainly would have been directly exposed to the personalities of men such as the Theosophist Franz Hartmann, the Anthroposophist Rudolf Steiner, and Dr. Carl Kellner, the alleged founder of the Ordo Templi Orientis. In 1900, List's poem "Wuotans Erwachen" (Wuotan's Awakening) was published in the Austrian journal *Der Scherer*.

The earliest epicenter of the neo-Germanic revival would be the city of Vienna, a city that was a great cauldron of social, political, and cultural upheaval, turmoil, and with all that a vibrant creativity that has rarely been matched in human history.

CHAPTER SEVEN

THE TURBULENT DAWN OF A NEW GERMANIC REBIRTH

(1900–1933)

The turn of the nineteenth century or, as it is also known, the period of the fin de siècle, was a time of extreme and dramatic development in human history. There were technological revolutions such as the invention of the lightbulb (1879), the motion picture camera (1891), powered flight (1903), radar (1904), radio (1906), and the affordable motor car (1908), all of which would transform society. These technical inventions also fired the imaginations of people on a popular level, and this was mixed with dramatic new ideas in social organization, such as Marxism (from the 1850s onward) and Social Darwinism (from the 1880s onward), and Freud published *On the Interpretation of Dreams* in 1900, ushering in a new era of psychology.

These events and developments affected every aspect of life in the Western world, and runology, both scientific and esoteric, was not exempted from these trends. Especially in Germany, where the ideas of the Reform Movement had established deep roots, the new wave of cultural development had significant effects. Radical solutions to age-old problems and questions were embraced with a special enthusiasm.

Following the year 1900 the number of editions cataloging the corpus of runic inscriptions began to proliferate. The scholars of each nation dedicated themselves to the production of comprehensive editions. The project in Sweden, due to its enormous size, has even to this day not been completed, but with the advent of the Internet and electronic databases, the project is now nearing completion. The most unfortunate chapter in this story is the lack of a comprehensive edition of the Anglo-Saxon runic inscriptions. (My concise edition of these inscriptions, *Anglo-Frisian Runes* [Flowers 2019] at least provides an organized checklist and basic readings for the corpus.)

The early twentieth century also produced a collection of brilliant runic scholars from each of the countries involved. In Germany, the names of Helmut Arntz and Wolfgang Krause are among the best known. In Norway, Carl Marstrander is someone we will meet again later. He was a student of Sophus Bugge and not only participated in the advancement of runology with his editorial work on the Norwegian runic inscriptions but was also a Celticist who jointly edited the journal *Ériu* with Kuno Meyer. Magnus Olsen was also a major participant in the Norwegian project. In Denmark, the names of Lis Jacobsen, Erik Moltke, and Anders Bæksted can be considered stellar. Sweden had a number of excellent scholars undertaking the great task of editing the huge corpus of Swedish inscriptions, among them were Otto von Friesen, Erik Brate, and Sven Jansson. Ludwig Wilser was one of the last writers with any scholarly credentials who upheld the theory of an indigenous origin for the runes, an idea that he defended as late as 1905.

In the world of scientific runology, the first half of the twentieth century was also a time in which a number of competing theories about the origin of the runic system were developed among scientific or academic runologists. Among a certain group of scholars at this time there was also a significant school of runology that focused on speculation concerning a numerological aspect to the runic tradition. This concept found its first proponent in Magnus Olsen, as exemplified in his 1916 landmark study "Om Troldruner" (On Magical Runes), and probably its last great champion in Heinz Klingenberg with his 1973 tour de force titled *Runenschrift—Schriftdenken—Runeninschriften* (Runic Writing—The Ideology of Writing and Runic Inscriptions). Not all of these numerical analyses were the same. Olsen simply proposed that the runemasters, such as Egill Skallagrímsson, used a system of rune-counting to compose and formulate inscriptions, especially if they were intended to have a magical effect.

Following the lead of Olsen and others, Hans Brix wrote a series of studies in the late 1920s and early 1930s on what he called *runemagi* (rune magic). He saw the numerical magic in what to others might appear to be ordinary memorial inscriptions. Brix took three numeric aspects of any given inscription into account: (1) words, (2) characters, and (3) dividing markers. An example of his method will demonstrate how his system worked. The Ulunda stone from Uppland, Sweden, reads:

halha x raisti x stin þina x aftir x hrulf x buanta x
sin x kuþ hialbi x at hans

"Helga raised this stone after Hrolf her husband.
God help his spirit."

The word-count of this stone is 12 (4 + 4 + 4).

The rune-count is 53, which, by reducing this number by the rune-count of the name in the sponsor, renders 48 (= 24 + 24).

The number of dividing signs is 9.

The three key-numbers for this runestone are therefore 53 (rune-count) + 12 (word-count) + 9 (sign-count). This makes 74 in all. Brix wants to subtract the numbers of the names of both the sponsor and the deceased (5 + 5 = 10) to render the "magical number" of the stone as 64. Furthermore, if the number of the sign-count and the word-count (21) is reduced by the number of the runes in the sponsor's name (5), we get 16. So here we see in the overall numeric symbolism references to the key-number of both the Older Futhark (24) and the Younger Futhark system (16). This sort of numeric symbolism forms a sort of meta-poetry, whereby meaning is conveyed by language and writing in ways that transcend the natural or normal modalities of communication.

During this phase of scientific runology, it was a Swedish professor from Lund, Sigurd Agrell (1881–1937), who most thoroughly developed theories of numeric symbolism with regard to runic inscriptions. He did not merely see the numeric patterns and claim there must be something "magical" about them; rather, he developed a whole historical and theoretical underpinning for the phenomena. He posited that the runes owed much to a connection with the Mithraic cult, into which many Germanic tribesmen were initiated, and that this cult was deeply involved with numeric symbolism—most particularly a method known to the Hebrews as gematria and to the Greeks as isopsephy. This entails the assignment of a numeric value to each letter of an alphabet and then adding together the numeric values of words or phrases to unlock hidden meanings and reveal formulas of magical power by means of the numeric symbolism. Such symbolism was widely known in late antiquity, as is well attested by the famous New Testament passage (Revelation 13:18) that refers to the "name of the beast" as either 666 or 616, depending on the manuscript one reads. Into this mix Agrell also threw a revolutionary new theory about the structure of the well-established futhark. He claimed that the system did not originally begin with the **f**-rune but with the **u**-rune. This made the **u**-rune the equivalent of the number one, the **th**-rune the number two, and so forth; and it thus meant that the **f**-rune was now the twenty-fourth rune. Agrell's assertion became known as the "Uthark-Theory." Unfortunately, there is no substantial evidence for this theory, other than the circumstantial evidence that some words when analyzed in this way seemed to him to correspond to numeric formulas found in the Mediterranean world. An example of this would be the famous runic formula ᚠᛚᚢ **alu**, which according to Agrell's Uthark-Theory would render the numeric formula 3.20.1 = 24 and thus the formulaic word *alu* could be seen as the symbolic equivalent of the entire runic futhark. By the same token, however, the gematria for the word using the supposed conventional numeric values would render 4.21.2 = 27 (2 + 7 = 9). Interestingly, the conventional system also causes the Old Norse word derived from *alu, öl,* rendered in runes as ᛏᛚᛁ, to result in the same sum: 10.2.15 = 27.

The most significant defense of Agrell's ideas can perhaps be found in the fact that there is actually a Kabbalistic technique, known by the technical Hebrew term *avgad,* that consists of replacing each letter by the next one, so that the first letter has the value of the last. Such a practice is also briefly mentioned by the runologist Klaus Düwel (2008, 182) as one of the later practices used with runic codes.

With regard to the use of runes as numbers and the gematria theory, it must be said that there is no solid basis for this in the runic record before the Middle Ages. As Prof. Dr. Klaus Düwel showed in his 1979 review of Klingenberg's work on runic gematria from 1973, there is no instance of runes being used as numerals, and when numbers are mentioned in inscriptions they are spelled out in words.

This objection does not, however, entirely dismiss the idea of numeric symbolism in the repertoire of the runemaster. The more modest and conservative theories put forth by Olsen and Brix, which hinge on the counting of runes in an inscription or meaningful (or otherwise "marked") segment of an inscription, appear to fit in well with the general ideology of the poet. In traditional Germanic poetry the syllables in a line are counted, stressed syllables are arranged in certain patterns (meter), and so on. The introduction of written characters among poets in an otherwise illiterate culture seems a plausible opportunity to take their poetic art to a new level. Poetic patterns in general (meter, alliteration, rhyme, and end-rhyme) are all measured in their artistry by the degree of meaningfulness and intentionality that is put into the text.

Rhyme for its own sake is referred to as doggerel. The patterns of poetry should indicate an extra dimension of meaningfulness in the message. As we saw in the discussion of the magical theory in chapter 1, the element of communication between realms of reality (between men and higher beings, or between men and nature directly) is essential. Poetry separates profane or mundane speech from sacred or magical utterances. The use of numeric patterns in visible speech (writing) would be just another level of this kind of thinking. We may therefore expect to find rules analogous to those that govern "registers" in the theory of sociolinguistics to be at play in the theory of magical communication, or what is called an operative speech act. Runic inscriptions themselves represent language performed in a higher register than ordinary, everyday speech.

Many of these numerological theories have been rightly and rationally criticized by skeptics who note that the rules for this practice posited by scholars such as Olsen, Brix, Agrell, and others are often highly flexible and arbitrary. All sorts of patterns can be made to fit the theory. Two responses suggest themselves: (1) The same thing is often true of other poetic rules; what pupil has not heard of "poetic license" at almost the same moment as the idea of *poetry* itself is introduced? (2) The idea of *intentionality* is key—if the writer intends to create various subtle patterns in his art, then they part of the overall effect of his work. That being said, discovering the specific intentionality that underlies an ancient literary text is admittedly somewhat of a speculative endeavor.

Due to a new, more scientific level of study and understanding of the ideas of religion and magic, it was also during the early twentieth century that many scientific runologists came to assume the intrinsically magical character of the runes and runic writing. These included Magnus Olsen, Carl Marstrander, Helmut Arntz, and Wolfgang Krause. This was a logical assumption to make considering that most runic inscriptions were not easily intelligible as any sort of purely secular communication, coupled with the fact that almost all early references to runes in Icelandic literature (including the Eddic poems) refer to runes and their use in a magico-mythic light.

Although scientific runology appears to have developed in accordance with its own intellectual traditions, those outside that stream of thought, perhaps caught up in the turn-of-the-century frenzy of innovation, also soon pulled the age-old runes into the picture. As opposed to the Renaissance tradition of a Johan Bure, who brought together the best scientific and the best esoteric methods of his day, the new esoteric runic revival, true to its modernistic roots, developed its own specialized systems apart from the world of academia. In the spirit of new and revolutionary applications of knowledge, the Austrian poet, journalist, and mystic Guido von List cast a vision of esoteric runology that is still felt today. Evidence shows that List was certainly well versed in the doctrines of Theosophy, an esoteric movement founded in 1875 in the United States and largely based on the writings of the Russian writer Helena Petrovna Blavatsky, which is a synthesis of Neoplatonism, spiritualism, Hinduism, Buddhism, and Egyptian lore. It holds that there is a secret organization of Mahatmas (great souls) who guide the organization. Theosophy teaches that there is a single divine Absolute and that the universe is a series of emanations from this source. In this respect it follows many religions and philosophies of the past. It also especially emphasizes the doctrine of reincarnation and the laws of *karma;* in other words, the belief that all action (Skt. *karma*) results in a reaction, positive or negative.

The century began with the publication in 1900 of a visually influential book by Friedrich Fischbach (1839–1908) called *Ursprung der Buchstaben Gutenbergs: Beitrag zur Runenkunde* (Origin of Gutenberg's Letters: A Contribution to Runology). Fischbach, who was a professional decorator and textile designer, brings the temperament of the visual artist to the questions of runology and speculates wildly about the iconic meaning of the rune-shapes. That is, he interprets the meaning of the runes in a pictographic way and links their significance to the practice of an ancient Aryan firecult. These ideas would inspire even more fertile imaginations in the early part of the twentieth century to come.

THE ARMANEN MOVEMENT
(Phase I: 1904–1919)

What can best be described as the Armanen Movement is a German-based neo-runic phenomenon founded and inspired by the Austrian writer, poet, and mystic Guido von List (born October 5, 1848, in Vienna; died May 17, 1919, in Berlin), whom we met in the previous chapter. His influence was considerable but has often been mischaracterized in later interpretations. In the German-speaking world, most rune-occultists in one way or another were inspired by his ideas, if not the system that he championed. List came from a fairly well-to-do family. It is noteworthy that List never published anything of a "practical" magical nature; his approach, at least as it was expressed publicly, was more philosophical and historical in character. His theories were, however, employed by more practically minded writers, such as Friedrich Bernard Marby, Siegfried Adolf Kummer, and E. Tristan Kurtzahn. The first phase of this movement took place during List's own lifetime and was shaped by his voluminous writings from this period. Most important for our purposes are *Das Geheimnis der Runen* (The Secret of the Runes; English edition: Destiny, 1988) and *Die Bilderschrift der Ario-Germanen* (The Hieroglyphs of the Aryo-Germanic Folk), published in 1910.

A more in-depth discussion and presentation of the practical or experiential aspects of early twentieth-century German rune occultism can be found the book *Rune Might* by Edred Thorsson (2018). There the reader will find a summary of the various techniques used by these occultists. Here we will instead concentrate primarily on the historical and runological aspects of their work.

Runologically, List's great contribution to the esoteric side of the runic revival was his development of the concept of an eighteen-rune futhork. Living as he did in a highly literate world, and emerging from an orthodox Christian cultural context, the power of *scripture* was undeniable in his world. List's eighteen-rune futhork is based on the *literary* evidence provided by a section of the Old Norse Eddic poem known as the *Hávamál*. This section, which composes the concluding twenty-eight stanzas of the poem, is known as the "Rúnatals þáttr Óðins": Óðinn's Story of the Listing of Runes.

List was a well-known and successful writer before he published his first groundbreaking esoteric work, *The Secret of the Runes* (1908). He was a poet, writer of fiction, playwright, and journalist. His most famous and successful work up to that time had been his *Deutsch-mythologische Landschaftsbilder* (1891), which was a two-volume collection of his travels to, and observations of, various unusual and historical landscapes, mainly in Lower Austria. The chronology of List's development, suggested by the contents of Eckehard Lenthe's biography of him, *Wotan's Awakening* (2018), indicates that List became ever more drawn into the world of the occult and magic during the course of the 1890s. Lenthe notes that List included a pentagram in his signature after the year 1898 and alluded to the idea that this marked him as a magus, a practicing magician, from that time forward (Lenthe 2018, 93). It was during the time Guido von List was temporarily blinded by arduous treatments for cataracts between April of 1902 and March of 1903 that his "inner eyes" are said to have been opened to a vast system of esoteric connections involving the development and structure of language. The runes would be basic and fundamental to the building blocks of this vast theory, which was ultimately given its final expression in his 1915 book *Die Ursprache der Ario-Germanen und ihre Mysteriensprache* (The Original Language of the Aryo-Germanic Folk and Their Mystery Language).

List was obviously heavily influenced by the literature and methods of Theosophy, and it is upon these mystico-magical methods that he based some of his insights regarding runic symbolism. It might be said that the eighteen runes of the Armanic Futhork have an *esoteric* heritage.

List claimed to have secret knowledge that the eighteen-rune futhork was indeed the *primeval* system out of which all others originated. No contemporary historian or philologist could ever agree with such a claim, as no epigraphical evidence exists for it. List struggled his whole life to try to get his theories of runes and language accepted by the academic world, a world that was almost entirely uninterested in his mystical approach. As we have seen elsewhere in this book, for centuries runologists thought that the sixteen-rune futhark was the most ancient form of the runic tradition, so List probably felt justified in his interpretation, since the Armanic Futhork is clearly an extension of the younger system.

This is not the place to enter into a lengthy or detailed discussion of the person or the numerous theories of Guido von List. Interested readers can consult the works of List himself, along with the aforementioned book about the practices of the early twentieth-century rune mystics, *Rune Might* (Thorsson 2018). The most important recent contribution to Listian studies is the aforementioned book *Wotan's Awakening* by Eckehard Lenthe, translated by Annabel Lee and published by Dominion Press in 2018.

For us it is here only important to outline List's basic *runological* theories. Clearly his ideas on the runes were fundamental to his whole approach, as he began his series of esoteric writings with the book *The Secret of the Runes* (1908), which in many ways encapsulates and exemplifies his larger philosophy.

List had not only a revolutionary approach to the runes but also to language itself. These linguistic theories are found in all of List's works, but a summary compendium remains *Die Ursprache der Ario-Germanen und ihre Mysteriensprache*. List's ideas about the German language, which must be characterized as entirely esoteric, have their origin in linguistic ideologies stemming from ancient India. This attraction to Indian thought only becomes intelligible with knowledge of the culture of the Theosophical Society and the popular interest of Germans in the concept of Indo-Germanic unity. Several of the "technical" terms used by List come from Sanskrit—for example, *kala, rita,* and *Garma* (= *karma*).

The learned linguistic structure of Sanskrit, reflected in its writing system using the Devanagari script, is *syllabic* in character. It is made up of syllabic "seed-words" consisting of combinations of consonants linked to vowels. Using this same principle, List devised a Germanic version of this system whereby he could analyze, on an *esoteric* level, the hidden meaning of any word in any language, ancient or modern.

While List can rightly be criticized for the inaccuracies of his theories from a purely linguistic standpoint, it is interesting to note that there is evidence that Icelandic scholars of language in the Middle Ages, and specifically the author of a work known as the *First Grammatical Treatise,* expressed similar ideas to those of List as regards the arrangement of sound in a syllabic system. It would seem that these theories or practices probably have their roots in runelore and are as much symbolic or mythic representations of language as they are practical linguistic exercises. (For a brief study of these Norse ideas, see my article "The Medieval Icelandic 'Grammatical Treatises,'" published in the volume *Mainstays* [Thorsson 2006].)

TABLE 7.1. THE ARMANEN FUTHORK

No.	Shape	Name	Meaning
1	ᚠ	Fa	*Fa, feh, feo* = fire generation, fire-borer, livestock, property, to grow, to wander, to destroy, to shred. "Generate your own luck and you will have it."
2	ᚢ	Ur	*ur* = *Ur* [i.e., "the primordial"], eternity, primal fire, primal light, primal bull (= primal generation), aurochs, resurrection (life after death). "Know yourself, then you will know all!"
3	ᚦ	Thorn	*thorr, thurs, thorn* = Thorr (thunder, thunderbolt, lightning flash), thorn. Thorn of life and death. "Preserve your ego."
4	ᚩ	Os	*os, as, ask* = Ase [i.e., one of the Æsir], mouth, arising, ash, ashes. "Your spiritual force makes you free."
5	ᚱ	Rit	*rit, reith, rath, ruoh, rita, rat* [English "rede"]. *Roth* [red]. *Rad* [wheel], *rod, rott, Recht* [right], etc. "I am my *rod* [right], this *rod* is indestructible, therefore I am myself indestructible, because I am my *rod.*"

No.	Shape	Name	Meaning
6	ʏ	Ka	*ka, kaun kuna, kien, kiel, kon, kühn* [bold], *kein* [none], etc. "Your blood, your highest possession."
7	✳	Hagal	*hagal* = the All-hedge, to enclose, hail, to destroy. "Harbor the All in yourself, and you will control All!"
8	✝	Not	*nauth, noth* [need], Norn, compulsion of fate. "Use your fate, do not strive against it!"
9	|	Is	*is, ire, iron* [Ger. *Eisen*]. "Win power over yourself and you will have power over everything in the spiritual and physical worlds that strives against you."
10	⟋	Ar	*ar,* sun, primal fire, *ar*-yans, nobles, etc. "Respect the primal fire!"
11	∫	Sig	*sol, sal, sul, sig, sigi,* sun, *sal*-vation, victory [Ger. *Sieg*], column [Ger. *Säule*], school, etc. "The creative spirit must conquer."
12	↑	Tyr	*tyr, tar, tur,* animal [Ger. *Tier*], etc. Týr, the sun- and sword-god; Tiu, Zio, Ziu, Zeus; *tar-* = "to generate, to turn, to conceal"; thus *Tarnkappe* [cap or cape of concealment], etc. "Fear not death—it cannot kill you!"
13	ß	Bar	*bar, beork, biork, birt,* song, *bier,* etc. Birth, life, death, rebirth. "Thy life stands in the hands of God, trust it in you."
14	ſ	Laf	*laf, lagu, lögr,* primal law, sea, life, downfall (defeat). "First learn to steer, then dare the sea-journey!"
15	ʏ	Man	man, *mon,* moon (*ma* = to mother, to increase; empty or dead). The exoteric and esoteric concept of man. "Be a man."
16	⅄	Yr	*yr, eur,* iris, rain-bow, yew-wood bow, error, anger, etc. Mutability of the feminine essence. "Think about the end!"
17	✚	Eh	*eh,* marriage [Ger. *Ehe*], law, horse, court, etc. "Marriage is the raw-root of the Aryans!"
18	⚡	Gibor	*ge, gi, gifa, gibor,* gift, giver, god, *gea, geo,* earth, *gigur,* death, etc. "Man, be One with God!"

Table 7.1 shows a general schematic outline of List's symbolic runic system as it appears in *The Secret of the Runes*. At least some of the appeal of List's system comes from the claim that it is based on a more archaic model than any other ever recorded. It is believed that the Master—as

List was known to his followers and admirers—had discovered the key to runic symbolism inherited from the original source, which stemmed from the antediluvian world of Atlantis. This esoteric approach was very reminiscent of the approach to religious symbolism exemplified by Theosophists, such as Helena Petrovna Blavatsky (1831–1891) in her two-volume magnum opus *The Secret Doctrine* (1888), which appeared in German translation as *Die Geheimlehre* in 1900. List also appears to have been greatly influenced by the writer Maximilian Ferdinand Sebaldt von Werth (1859–1916), who was also a member of List's society. But we should never underestimate the innovative and creative abilities of List himself in the formulation of his system.

Table 7.1 also provides some insight into the way in which the Listian system of runology worked. Based mostly on the phonology of Modern German, with some input from dialectal forms and the use of Old Norse cognates and so on, he built up an elaborate framework for the esoteric interpretation of language. List bases this on a quasi-systematic series of connections or correspondences that he discovers among words due to their similarities in sound. It may be likened to a sonic or phonic Kabbalah. Especially marked are words that begin with the same sound, followed by a vowel of any quality, and a consonant within the same natural class as other words; for example, classified under the *ka*-rune are: *kaun, kuna, kien* (as in Modern German *Kienholz,* "torch"), *kiel* (English "keel"), *kon, kühn* (bold), and *kein* (none). Thus, in an uncanny way, and not based on scientific principles of actual historical linguistics, he makes the connection between "ability" (Ger. *Können*), torch, boat, boldness, and Old Norse *kaun,* "sore." List's approach to language resonates with that of many poets of his day in both the German and French languages.

A review of this system shows that List had innovated or significantly modified several of the rune-names (*fa, rit, bar, eh, gibor*), and a shape similar to his *gibor*-rune (ᚷ) is only to be found among the manuscript runes (ᛁ). He also acknowledges the complexity of the rune-names in his presentation, a complexity that was radically simplified in later iterations of the Armanen tradition. Note, too, that he did not use the peculiar forms of the **f**- and **u**-runes that are found in the works of S. A. Kummer and which became so influential though the writings of Karl Spiesberger.

A deeper analysis of List's runology reveals some interesting results. List's supposed insights into the structure and meaning of the German language seem to have informed his interpretation of the runes as much as the runes—or any traditional runology—influenced his Armanen teachings. A few examples of this kind of thinking will demonstrate what is meant: *Ur* (aurochs, slag, drizzle) is firmly linked to the German prefix *ur-,* meaning "primeval, ancient, original"; *rit* (riding, wagon) is attached to Sanskrit *rita,* "cosmic order"; *hagal* (hail) is connected to the idea of enclosing or harboring (Ger. *hegen*); *sig* (sun) is linked to German *Sieg,* "victory"; *eh* (horse) is equated to German *Ehe,* "marriage." Such examples could be multiplied. But before we make too many smug assumptions, we should note the apparent similarities between some of List's ideas and those of Johan Bure, who also made the connection between *hagal* and "enclosure," despite the evidence of the rune poems to the contrary. The likely source for these similarities is not a traditional connection between the teachings of Bure and those of List but rather a case of two men with analogous underlying theories working on data with a similar structure: the Swedish and German languages, respectively. The marked difference between the approaches of Bure and List remains conditioned by the ages in which they lived. In Bure's time, a close association between what was understood as science and spiritual pursuits was possible, and even expected, whereas List lived at the dawn of the hypermodern age in which these two sisters in science, the esoteric and exoteric, were beginning to become woefully estranged.

One of the chief features of the Armanen tradition seems to be its relative disinterest in the use of runes as a mode of writing natural language. The runes are seen more in terms of individual symbols, or "hieroglyphs" in the Romantic sense, than as phonemic signs for the writing of an actual language. Each rune is mostly viewed with regard to its own isolated symbolic or magical content. This tendency was also present in the two sides of the runic philosophy first pioneered by Johan Bure, where he differentiated between *uppenbara runor* (ordinary runes) and *adulrunor* (noble-runes). This hieroglyphic approach to runic symbolism would continue to dominate the work of esoteric rune revivalists throughout the twentieth century. We might also note that the hieroglyphic approach makes the runes useful in an experiential way without involving the practitioner in the tedious task of having to write words and sentences with them—especially in archaic languages!

The ancient approach to the runes was one in which the symbolic content of a runic inscription was much more holistic in character. The runes could be seen as significant as isolated symbols, while they remained potent tools for composing formulaic words, such as **alu** or **laukaz**, or perhaps sound formulas such as **luwatuwa**, but it appears unlikely that the new emphasis on the symbolic content of the individual rune was the result of any decrease in the regular use of runes as a utilitarian script. In many respects, on a deep level, the twentieth-century hieroglyphic approach can be seen as a reflection of the ideology of the *modern,* whereby the *signifier* is distanced from the *signified.*

List's way of identifying the runes was, as we have seen, based on the idea that the "Rúnatals þáttr Óðins" is the key to an archaic runic system. List's system is basically the sixteen runes of the Younger Futhark with the two supplemental runes *eh* (**e**) and *gibor* (**g**). Noteworthy is the transposition of runes fourteen and fifteen from the younger order of **m–l** to **l–m**. The motive for this switch appears to have been an interest in getting the **m**- and **y**-runes to be directly juxtaposed to one another for symbolic reasons (since they were seen as the runes of man and woman, life and death, etc.) as well as for graphic symmetry.

THE ESOTERIC REVIVAL AFTER LIST
(Phase II: 1919–1935)

After the end of the First World War, Germany became increasingly fascinated with matters of the occult and other cultural diversions. Perhaps this was in part a way of coping with the disastrous effects of the Treaty of Versailles. In this second phase of the Armanen Movement, the ideas of now departed "Master" Guido von List continued to dominate, and this influence would persist in the esoteric world within Germany for many decades to come.

One of List's most unusual students was Philipp Stauff (1876–1923), an anti-Semitic journalist active in a number of nationalist organizations in Germany. In 1912 he published his most remarkable contribution to the history of runic esoterica, the book *Runenhäuser* (Runic Houses). Here Stauff theorized that the patterns made by the wooden beams used in the construction of half-timbered (*Fachwerk*) houses had a *runic* significance. If a person knew the secret code, then the hidden meaning of the house could actually be *read*. The "messages" built into these houses were rarely thought to be anything other than a series of abstract symbols, not actual texts in natural languages.

At this time there were several occult groups that used the runes and runic symbolism. Most of these were *völkisch,* or nationalistic, in character. Among them were the Germanen Orden (Germanic Order) and its offshoot Germanen-Orden Walvater (Germanic Order, Valfather), which published a periodical called *Runen* (Runes). This periodical often featured pieces on the runes both from a historical and an esoteric viewpoint. Articles promulgated the idea that the runes were the oldest script of humanity and that the Latin alphabet, for example, was derived from the runes, rather than the other way around. These articles were apparently the work of the editor of the publication, Hermann Pohl. The runes were sometimes presented in an alphabetic order and redesigned to be a suitable medium for the writing of New High German. This alphabet was presented in the pages of *Runen*

(1925, no. 1, pp. 13–14). It followed a translation of the Old Norse poem *Hávamál* (stanzas 138–65), which describe Óðinn's "taking up" of the runes. A pseudonymous author, "Tannhäuser," then presents a system of runic divination based upon this runic alphabet.

ᚠ· (ᛒ)· ᚼ ᛙ· ᚠ· (ᚷ) (ᚼ)· (ᛁ). (ᛡ)· ᚨ· ᛚ· ᛙ·
a   b   d   e   f   g   h   i   j   k   l   m

(ᚰ)· ᚭ· (ᚱ·) (ᛣ·) ᛋ· ᛐ· (ᚢ). (ᚹ)·(ᛉ)· ◇ (ᚦ)· ᛦ·
n   o   p   r   s   t   u   w   z   ng   th   ei

    Since the runes in parentheses are considered unfavorable, there are therefore twelve favorable and twelve unfavorable divine signs. Dear Order-siblings, learn and write the ancient runes of Odin.

    If you want to know how the ancestors inquired of the heavens by means of the runes in cases of distress or doubt, then you should properly cut small, approximately 3-centimeter-long, staves from the branches of a fruit (apple) tree and carve the divine signs illustrated above (without parentheses) into the bark using a sharp pointed instrument. Then take up position in a quiet, holy place and face south. Speak a devout prayer directed toward the heavenly realm and request knowledge and then randomly throw the staves onto the ground covered with a white linen cloth. Now reverently pick up three staves, one after the other, while keeping your mind as empty of intention as possible and interpret them as being favorable or unfavorable. If all three runestaves are unfavorable, then this particular inquiry must no longer come under consideration for the rest of the day. In you have in your environment a person (namely a virgin girl) who has talent as a medium, then let her choose the lots. In this procedure you may write your question in runic signs on a piece of paper and cast the staves onto this paper. What the individual runestaves have to say, you will gradually learn for yourself.

The favorable time for inquiring of the gods was, according to ancient Germanic experience, consistently the time of the full moon or the new moon.

Now what the individual runes mean in the deepest sense has been learned after years of experimentation: The rune ᚠ = sincere love, willingness to sacrifice, gold. ᛒ = curse, evil, sickness, bondage. ᛗ = recovery, health. ᛗ = harmony, sympathy, happy marriage, money. ᛈ = fire, power, sexual desire. ᚷ = agitation, ill humor, bad news. ᚺ = sickness, lack of health, hail. ᛁ = standstill. ᛋ = negation, destruction. ᚲ = child (open lodge); ᛚ = love, property, money. ᛗ = strength, spiritual power, health; ᛏ = need, nothing, no. ᛉ = woman, order. ᛅ = pain, sickness. ᚱ = brutality, meanness, injury. ᛋ = victory. ᛏ = masculine power, ability to reproduce. ᚾ = bad heath, ruin, decline. ᛈ = woe, pain, suffering. ᛉ = trouble, prayer. ◊ = Walburg, fruitfulness, femininity (closed lodge); ᚦ = pain, sickness, bodily aches; ᛋ = sunshine, becoming, ascent, money.

Tannhäuser

Readers of *Runes* were thus encouraged to use runes for *magical* purposes. Metal runic rings were sold in the pages of the journal, and in general the tenor of the texts was both esoteric and political, with frequent attacks on the Jews.

As for the Armanen tradition more narrowly, it received its most comprehensive and wide-ranging ideological presentation in the roughly six-hundred-page 1930 work of Rudolf John Gorsleben (1883–1930) titled *Die Hoch-Zeit der Menschheit* (The Zenith of Humanity). The runology followed by Gorsleben is essentially that of List, with additional ideas of his own and others taken from other contemporary rune-esotericists. This book has, perhaps rightly, sometimes been called the "bible" of Armanic runology.

Like List before him, and as was the case with most Ariosophists of the day, Gorsleben was heavily influenced by the doctrines of Theosophy. In contrast to the latter, Ariosophy often emphasized the idea that Aryan mankind was at one time a pure and noble race, which has devolved over time due to interbreeding with subhuman species. This worldview was heavily promoted by an eccentric Austrian ex-monk, Lanz von Liebenfels, who was a member of the some of the same circles as Guido von List. Theosophy, on the other hand, saw the human race more in terms of a progressive line of evolution through various so-called Root Races, or stages of human evolution. Theosophy was more orthodox in its Darwinistic views than was Ariosophy. Theosophy did have teachings about the "Lost Continent of Atlantis," where the beings who inhabited this lost civilization had certain occult powers that modern man has otherwise lost. Gorsleben, as was the case with many contemporary German esotericists, believed that the noble characteristics of the original Aryan god-men could be remanifested though eugenics and the development of occult powers. The runes were thought to form an essential part of this development.

For the most part, rune-occultists followed the lead of Guido von List, but one writer, Friedrich Bernhard Marby (1882–1966), charted a bit of a different course. He was an astrologer and a student of various forms of alternative spirituality. He was the earliest writer to publish widely about innovative practical applications of the runes in magical work. The beginning of the twentieth century in Germany was a time very much obsessed with the human body, its beauty, and its meaning in motion. Marby combined this German predilection with the runes and created a system of what he called *Runengymnastik* (runic gymnastics). In this system, the runes were imitated by bodily postures and in these postures the practicing magician was said to be able to manipulate the powers inherent in the runes, as if they were some sort of dynamistic force. Influenced by Marby was another occultist of the day, Siegfried Adolf Kummer (1899–1977) of Dresden, who developed similar practices that he called *Runenyoga* (runic yoga). Kummer's runology was more strictly in keeping with the Armanen teachings of Guido von List, and he mixed this with elements drawn from the practices and symbolism of more standard Western occultism.

Despite his considerable written output, Marby never explained his full runology. It generally seems that he took the Anglo-Frisian Futhorc as the oldest and most original system because it was the most extensive, with the most signs. For Marby the runes were signifiers for sounds, which bore a special power. Although he rejected the use of the term "rune yoga," which was used by his occult competitor, Kummer, it seems that Marby had a runic ideology that was very similar to the esoteric study of letters in Indian tantric schools wherein the letters of the Devanagari alphabet are more or less arbitrary signs for the sounds of language, which are sacred and magically powerful.

Marby remained active during the first few years of the National Socialist regime in Germany. He had been a supporter of the Nazis politically, but he also continued to publish books and organize runic groups independent of the official Party line on the subject. For this he was arrested in 1936 and would spend the next eight years or so in concentration camps.

Siegfried Adolf Kummer was intensely active between the years 1932 and 1935 when he published a series of books, led off by his main work, titled *Heilige Runenmacht: Wiedergeburt des Armanentums durch Runenübungen und Tänze* (Holy Rune Might: Rebirth of Armanism through Runic Exercises and Dances), and then other texts supporting his school for runic yoga. His runology was firmly based on that of List, but his method of utilizing them through physical exercises and mantras is closely linked to the work of Marby. An unfortunate convergence of difficulties—charges of plagiarism being leveled by Marby and the crackdown on runic esotericism by the National Socialists around 1935—seem to have forced Kummer out of the runic field. He appears to have worked as a bureaucrat and part-time artist in and around Dresden during both the period of the Third Reich and the postwar (East) German Democratic Republic. Many of Kummer's exercises are shown in the book *Rune Might* (Thorsson 2018, 107–12) and two of his works, *Rune-Magic* (Kummer 1993) and *Holy Rune Might* (Woodharrow Gild, 2019), have been translated into English.

In the high tide of the runic renaissance there were dozens of writers and private occultists dealing with the runes. Every sort of magical school, it seemed, had to come to terms with them. It was during this time that the most influential eclectic magical lodge in Germany, the Fraternitas Saturni (Brotherhood of Saturn), began to incorporate runic occultism into its magical curriculum. For a review of the teachings of this magical order, see my book *The Fraternitas Saturni* (Flowers 2018).

As a general comment, from an esoteric point of view, what appears to be occurring with movements such as the Gothicism of Sweden, which persisted over several centuries, or the Armanism of Guido von List and his followers in Central Europe, is that a latter-day *synthesis* is being *projected back* and posited as an original, all-encompassing archetype or paradigm. Such synthesized "back-projections" can be insightful to the degree to which the materials and methods used to create the synthesis are accurate. But it is important to realize, too, that claims of this sort are not restricted to the theories being considered in this book—the same type of thinking is displayed by Christians, Marxists, and many other ideologues when considering interpretations of the past. For human beings who dream of a better future and are inspired to create a model for it, this kind of thinking allows them to project their model back into the mythic past—*in illo tempore,* as Mircea Eliade put it—so as to fortify it in the minds of present-day people. This is just one of the many ways in which *myth* works.

All in all, during the 1920s and early 1930s the runes had found a broad and powerful field of activity, in the exoteric sphere as well as in the esoteric one. But during this era a bitter edge was also being ground on the runic sword, so to speak, and this development, perhaps coupled with the lack of a wise leader to wield that sword magically, effectively laid down the law, leading to woeful *wyrd* . . .

CHAPTER EIGHT

RUNOLOGY IN THE AGE OF THE THIRD REICH

(1933–1945)

RUNOLOGY IN GERMANY

It would be a huge error to assume that all runology pursued in the time of the National Socialist regime in Germany was somehow "Nazi runology." There was something—or there were some things—that might be characterized as National Socialist runology, as we shall see, but it bears little resemblance to what most sensationalists would have us believe. For example, speculation has run wild over the supposed connections between the runic occultism and National Socialism. This speculation comes from those who are fearful of it, as well as from those who actually promote the idea. When dealing with the possibilities residing in the world of occult/esoteric orders and groups, and the people who formed them, there is an inherent difficulty in sorting out fact from fiction, history from propaganda.

The best sources for becoming familiar with the general context of these ideas are *The Occult Roots of Nazism* by Nicholas Goodrick-Clarke (1985) and *The Secret King* by Flowers and Moynihan (2007).

The former book is comprehensive but a bit tainted by its own Marxist roots, while the latter book is specifically focused on the person and writings of Karl Maria Wiligut and also contains an introductory section that provides a critical overview of the idea of "Nazi occultism." When attempting to analyze the phenomenon of Nazi occultism, it is useful to understand that the generation of men responsible for National Socialism in Germany was by and large a product of the broad Neo-Romantic cultural *Reformbewegung* (Reform Movement), which, as we have noted, began as early as 1880. For this movement—which was also the deep-root of what we call the Green Movement today—the ideas of *indigenous* qualities and features of culture, land, flora and fauna, and so forth were consistently evaluated as superior to those imported from the outside—simply because they were indigenous. Things from the outside were seen in terms of being "invasive species." Such ideas extended themselves to the runes, as these were seen as the indigenous Germanic way of writing.

With regard to the whole study of the Nazis and the occult, a great deal of misinformation and sensationalism, as well as obsessive interpretations, have been pumped out over the years. I try to present a comprehensive view of this topic in my forthcoming detailed study of the subject of Nazi occultism, which will appear sometime after 2021. In *The Secret King* we offered a first glimpse of a rational approach to the study of this topic. The key to understanding the history of these ideas is to recognize that the facts, history, myths, and legends actually stem from quite disparate sources: (1) the prehistory of ideas that formed a basis for National Socialist ideology; (2) actual contemporaneous activity with within Nazi Germany; (3) contemporaneous anti-German propaganda; (4) postwar pro-Nazi interpretations, often fantastical in tone; and (5) postwar anti-Nazi interpretations, often likewise fantastical in tone.

These sources, and how they intermingle with one another in the popular imagination of today, make for some fairly sensationalistic mythologizing. The runes have sometimes been caught up in this intellectual tangle.

Strictly within the confines of documented Third Reich history, runology can be seen as a complex topic. It basically existed on three different levels: (1) the purely academic-scientific, (2) the lay-scientific, and (3) the esoteric.

When considering the involvement of the Nazis with matters of esoteric or alternative interpretations of history and symbolism, it is always valuable to keep in mind that the generation of 1914 (those old enough to have fought in the Great War) grew up amid the cultural current of the Life-Reform Movement, which was also a time marked by certain popular ideas about *Germanentum* ("Germanicness," loosely translated) and runes.

Certainly, runological scholars involved in academic studies at universities, such as Wolfgang Krause, received more attention than ever before, but they were largely left unencumbered by politics to pursue their scientific ends. This fact shows that on one level the Nazis realized these studies had some validity. However, the Party also virtually installed men who had formerly been what we might call lay investigators (self-appointed, self-taught, experts who were without academic credentials) in academic posts. A detailed history of this phase of the work of the infamous Ahnenerbe (Ancestral Heritage) office of the SS and of the Institut für Runenforschung (Institute for Runic Research) are to be found in Ulrich Hunger's 1984 dissertation *Die Runenkunde im Dritten Reich* (Runology in the Third Reich). The third, or esoteric, level of study appears to have been restricted and highly sensitive, even within the confines of Party politics, and therefore quite secret.

During the period of the National Socialist regime in Germany there was certainly a great proliferation of written works, many of them by leading scholars, designed to popularize awareness of the runes and runic history. These included Wolfgang Krause's 1935 *Was man in Runen ritzte* (What Was Carved in Runes), Helmut Arntz's 1938 *Die Runenschrift* (Runic Writing), Wilhelm Weber's 1941 *Kleine*

Runenkunde (A Brief Runology), Schilling's 1937 *Kleine Runenkunde* (A Brief Runology), and Konstantin Reichhardt's 1936 *Runenkunde* (Runology). Notable about these works is that they have no excessive esoteric dimensions but usually do not deny the spiritual dimension of the runes, either.

One of the most significant and general misunderstandings of runology in the period of the Third Reich is the claim that it essentially represents a direct continuation of the esoteric school of thought founded by Guido von List. To be sure, List instilled in a whole generation a newfound enthusiasm for the secrets of the runes, but an actual examination of all materials developed just prior to and during the time of the Nazi regime in Germany shows that the Armanen tradition of List was influential but not determinative. Nazi runology is not the same as Listian runology, either in aim or form. As a general assessment, I think it would be fair to say that List's ideas and methods were far too mystical to be suited to the kind of ideas being pursued by National Socialism as a political movement. By the same token, however, a number of List's ideas and terms did find their way into the jargon of the National Socialist German Workers' Party (NSDAP), albeit in a rather piecemeal way (Lenthe 2018, 222–38).

The runes constitute a cultural feature that was treated on two distinctly different levels during the time of the Third Reich: (1) for public consumption and for purposes of education in the ideology of the movement and (2) as a private, inner, pursuit of the elite of the Party, such as the SS under Heinrich Himmler.

Actual magical or esoteric applications of the runes and rune magic as such seems to have been a minor obsession of Reichsführer-SS Heinrich Himmler. For a time, his chief adviser in this pursuit was the mysterious Karl Maria Wiligut (1866–1946). Wiligut also wrote under the names Jarl Widar, Weisthor, and Lobesam.

But who was this Wiligut, and where did he come from? This information was obscured at the time and intentionally so. Following his retirement from the Austrian army in 1919, he was a participant in esoteric runic circles in Germany and Austria. But Wiligut's career in the world of mysticism had started much earlier with the publication of his book titled *Seyfrids Runen* (1903), which appears to have been influenced by the earlier writings of Guido von List. He started his own esoteric study circle in Salzburg in the first years of the 1920s. His unorthodox teachings, coupled with marital problems, resulted in him being involuntarily committed to a mental institution from 1924 to 1927. After his release, he went to Munich, where one of his students was Richard Anders, a member of the SS who introduced Wiligut to Heinrich Himmler. Wiligut himself was inducted into the SS in 1933, and he became an adviser to Himmler on matters relating to runic symbolism, ritual, and esoteric history. For the next six years Wiligut was Himmler's mentor concerning these areas, and he designed the "death's head" ring (*Totenkopfring*) of the SS. But he was also an influence for the suppression of rival runic esotericists, such as Siegfried Kummer and Friedrich Marby, as well as for the protection of the members of the Edda Gesellschaft (Edda Society), a study group founded by Rudolf Gorsleben and with which Wiligut was affiliated.* Wiligut's past caught up with him when Karl Wolff, chief of Himmler's personal staff, made others aware of Wiligut's record with regard to mental illness. The old man had to leave Himmler's service. The story of Wiligut and translations of his esoteric work are all contained in the aforementioned book *The Secret King.*

The most systematic presentation of anything that approaches a coherent runology by Wiligut was published in his 1934 article "Whispering of Gotos—Rune Knowledge." This appeared in *Hagal* 11 and is translated

---

*It is interesting to note that Werner von Bülow, the editor of *Hagal,* the official organ of the Edda Society (and a publication to which Wiligut himself had contributed), continued to publish the journal until 1939 and the outbreak of the Second World War. In general, however, it was the case for alternative "neo-Germanic" groups like this to be suppressed far earlier, as we outlined in the previous chapter with the story of F. B. Marby.

in the pages of *The Secret King* (Flowers and Moynihan 2007, 92–94). Wiligut reveals a decidedly hieroglyphic approach to the runes, which emphasizes the idea that they represent a development of natural and metaphysical forces in an evolutionary pattern of unfoldment. It is evident here that Wiligut was greatly influenced by the runology of Guido von List but had his own unique interpretation of the organization of the runic symbols.

Obviously, as we have learned over the course of this book, the Nazis did not invent interest in the runes. This had been growing of its own accord for centuries. They did, however, exploit the already existing popularity of runic signs and designs among a certain segment of the German population, and they did so for propagandistic purposes. It must be acknowledged that the Nazis themselves were also to a great extent the products of the general cultural atmosphere of the earlier part of the twentieth century when runes had reached a high level of popularity in the hands of rune-esotericists such as Guido von List and many others.

This popularity of runes, especially in the area of general interest and quasi-academic presentations, enjoyed a great upswing in the early years of the Nazi regime. The three levels of interest in runes—the academic, lay-academic, and popular/esoteric—were all well represented during this period. The most influential academic figures of the time were Helmut Arntz (in Giessen) and Wolfgang Krause (in Göttingen). For the most part the studies completed by these academic figures still hold up in the light of scientific scrutiny today, and both remain respected figures in the history of runology. Arntz suffered significant setbacks in his career during these years as it was suspected that he was an *Achteljude* (one-eighth Jewish); in other words, one of his great-grandparents was Jewish. Krause headed the Institut für Runenforschung (Institute for Runic Research) at the University of Göttingen and was himself actually inducted into the Ahnenerbe early in 1943 (Hunger 1984, 224), but his membership was entirely within his role as a scholar. Both Krause and Arntz were open-minded as to the possible magico-mythic significance of runes and runic inscriptions, and both emphasized the idea that the individual runes conveyed (through the power of their names) mythic or ideographic content.

The National Socialists made sweeping and sudden changes to the structures of all cultural institutions, and the universities were no exception. Academic departments were politicized and "purified" racially: Jewish professors were expelled, and often in their place were appointed lay enthusiasts, marked more by their ideological fervor than their academic qualifications. Among these were men such as Karl Theodor Weigel (SS-Hauptsturmbannführer), who headed the Lehr-und Forschungsstätte für Runen- und Sinnbildkunde (Instructional and Research Institute for Runology and Symbology). Weigel had no higher academic degree, but he was a dedicated lay-folklorist who collected images of medieval folk art supposedly connected with the ancient Germanic past. The collection of his images (drawings and photographs) is still housed at the University of Göttingen as the Weigel-Archiv im Seminar für Volkskunde (Weigel Archive in the Department for Folklore).

The politicizing of science is a trend and drift that is in no way unique to the Nazis. The same phenomenon, albeit with a different orientation, was at work in Soviet Russia: Stalin and certain Soviet linguists tried to implement the systematic instrumentalization of everything, and language was a key component. Similar tendencies can even be discerned in today's Western academic world, which has also become an environment obsessed with political outcomes and matters of race, ethnicity, and biological identity—although in a manner entirely inverse to the aims of National Socialism. Stalin's admirers in the Anglo-American academy used these ideas in the past, and we can see them being used today in our politics (and in our universities). Language is used to frame political realities and define the debates by defining (or redefining) the words and phrases used in those debates.

✦ ✦ ✦

Groups dedicated to the pursuit of the esoteric qualities of the runes were actually severely curtailed during the Nazi regime. Publications by members of these circles also became rare. There were two kinds of runic esotericism: that which was approved by the government and that which was rejected by officials. Independently minded men such as Marby and Kummer fell into the latter category. Things that were tinged with the overtly magical were the most singled out for disapproval—apparently on the theory that they were dangerous to the order and direction of the collectivist philosophy and agenda of the Party. Widespread magical and mystical ideas only encourage individualized experience and subjective understandings, both of which were antithetical to the program of the Party.

The serious advocates of totalitarian philosophies tend to encourage wild and subjective approaches to reality in years prior to their actual assumption of absolute control, as such trends are useful in creating cultural chaos, which makes the host culture weak and full of self-doubt. Then, when absolute power is obtained, such features are systematically bought under ideological control or eliminated. The same process occurred in the Bolshevik Revolution in Russia, where all sorts of avant-garde ideas were supported in the years of Lenin, only to be crushed under Stalin. These trends can be seen as a sobering warning from history.

Runes were generally popular in Germany during the Nazi era. An example of one of the popularizers was Heinar Schilling (1894–1955), who constitutes an interesting case study for the period. Schilling began his writing career in 1908. All in all, his output would equal approximately one hundred works. He served in the First World War and was later sympathetic toward pacifistic ideas in Expressionistic circles in Dresden. He was a friend of the artist Otto Dix, who painted a portrait of Schilling. Politically, he was involved in socialistic and even communistic ideas at that time. But from 1920 onward he drifted away from this political sphere and in the direction of nationalistic ideology. He began writing in earnest about ancient Germanic history and culture beginning in 1922. By 1930 he had gravitated toward the National Socialist movement, but he did not formally join the Party until after Hitler's assumption of power in 1933. He wrote a column for the SS magazine *Das Schwarze Korps*. Interestingly, Schilling rejected Nazi racist ideology! He was eventually sentenced to a prison term for intellectual sabotage. His main offense was his support for the idea of monarchy. He was stripped of his membership in the Party in 1942 but also given the title of "professor" for his work on German prehistory. After the war, as his property was in the Soviet occupation zone, his real estate was seized and his archive was plundered. He escaped to the West and lived out his days as a librarian at the Glücksburg palace in Schleswig-Holstein. One of Schilling's most obvious contributions to the popularization of runes is his 1937 work *Kleine Runenkunde*. An introductory paragraph from his seventy-seven–page book is representative of the general tenor of this kind of literature of the time.

Rune—the word alone, through its similarity of sound with the anciently related "rown" (whisper), fills us with trembling feelings of awe and mystery. Yet these were the austere letters of our own forefathers, with their strict signs so characteristically corresponding to the temperament of Nordic man that made up the script used by the Germanic folk before we adopted the Judeo-classical culture. These truly original "letters"—for our German word *Buchstabe* (letter) also originates from the time when the runes were being used, since according to holy practice, the individual signs were carved onto staves of beech (Ger. *Buche*) wood—and the not all too numerous inscriptions in this alphabet are therefore the oldest evidence for our own particular form of writing. Therefore, it is more necessary than ever before not to remain ignorant of these mysterious signs, especially since they belong to the most valuable and authentic inheritance of our race.

This book was originally intended as a sort of official runology of the Ahnenerbe, but it was ultimately rejected for this role because

Schilling's views regarding the runes did not correspond exactly with those of Himmler (Kater 1997, 72).

PARTISAN RUNOLOGY WITHIN THE NSDAP

The National Socialists had a general interest in popularizing runes and runic symbolism as an instrument of propaganda. The purpose of this propaganda was to emphasize the distinction of German(ic) culture from other cultures and to suggest that it was, in fact, superior to all other cultures. The runes were useful in this regard for implying that the Germanic people were literate with their own form of writing and that this form of writing was perhaps older than the other writing systems of the world. In this general idea, the propagandists found antecedents in earlier scholarship. But by the early twentieth century, when these notions were being put forward in propaganda, academic runology had already determined the approximate time of runic origins and had some idea about the origin of the runes based on older Mediterranean scripts. Therefore, claims of an indigenous origin for the runes, or that the runes first arose many thousands of years before any known runic inscription, clearly fall under the label of "occultism" or belong to the realm of the esoteric.

Runes found official interest mainly in two institutions of the NSDAP itself: the Rosenberg Office (Amt Rosenberg) under Alfred Rosenberg (1893–1946) and the SS under Reichsführer-SS Heinrich Himmler (1900–1945). Rosenberg, who had become prominent in the Party due to his authorship of the popular 1930 book *Der Mythus des Zwanzigsten Jahrhunderts* (The Myth of the Twentieth Century)—an ideological survey of human history from a National Socialist viewpoint—headed up a rather symbolic office in the Party apparatus called the Dienststelle des Beauftragten des Führers für die gesamte geistige und weltanschauliche Schulung und Erziehung der NSDAP (Station of the Deputy to the Führer for General Intellectual and Philosophical Schooling and Education of the NSDAP), commonly referred to as simply "Amt Rosenberg" (the Rosenberg Office). Within this was the Amt für Volkskunde und Feiergestaltung (Office for Folklore and Ceremonial Design).

Publications produced by and for members of the SS, such as *Das Schwarze Korps* (The Black Corps) or *Der Schulungsbrief* (The Educational Letter), frequently published articles about runes. The specific part of the National Socialist governmental operations that was most involved with anything runic was the so-called Ahnenerbe, which was part of the SS.

THE AHNENERBE

The official designation of this office was originally the Studiengesellschaft für Geistesgeschichte "Deutsches Ahnenerbe" (Society for the Study of Humanities "German Ancestral Heritage"). It was a quasi-independent department, more akin to a think tank, which operated within the SS. The scientific purview of the Ahnenerbe encompassed all of what we call the humanities (including history, folklore, religious studies, symbology, musicology, etc.) as well as racial and ecological studies. In postwar sensationalistic literature it has been falsely referred to as the "occult bureau." The history and wide scope of this organization is substantially outlined in Michael Kater's 1974 book (second edition, 1997), while the runological dimension is delineated in Ulrich Hunger's *Die Runenkunde im Dritten Reich* (1984, 171–289). In general, it appears that Himmler's vision was a broad one that included many mysterious areas of interest— and ones that also interested lay-investigators of dubious qualifications. Himmler recruited these latter types, but he planned to replace them once qualified academics could be developed to investigate these areas more scientifically and reliably. Men such as Wiligut clearly fell into this unscientific category. Some of the older spirit of the Listian enthusiasm for the supposed runic aspects of heraldry could be found in work done by Karl Konrad Ruppel for the Ahnenerbe, such as *Die Hausmarke, das Symbol der germanischen Sippe* (The House-Mark, the Symbol of the

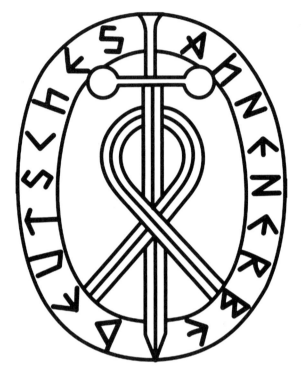

Figure 8.1. The quasi-runic colophon of the Ahnenerbe

Germanic Clan) in 1939. Franz Altheim, who was primarily a classicist, also wrote *Vom Ursprung der Runen* (On the Origin of the Runes) for the Ahnenerbe in 1939, a work that bolstered the theory of a North Etruscan origin for the runes.

Of course, the leading force behind the Ahnenerbe was Reichsführer-SS Heinrich Himmler. He was someone whose talents lay in the fields of organization and management rather than original creativity or research. He apparently applied the same organizational skills to ancestral research as he did to mass murder. Himmler was primarily a political activist, but he also had deep and longstanding interests in alternative philosophies and sciences. He was active in the Artamanen Gesellschaft (Artaman League), founded by Willibald Hentschel, which advocated the colonization of territory through the settlement of polygamous agrarian communities, as outlined in Hentschel's book

Mittgart (1904). The Artamanen Gesellschaft was later absorbed into the Hitler Youth of the NSDAP in 1934.

The most conspicuous example of runic esotericism to be found within the official operations of the Nazi Party itself is found in the case of Karl Maria Wiligut, already outlined above. His case is very unique in that he is clearly a representative of the earlier twentieth-century school of visionary or poetic interpretation of the runic (or pseudo-runic) "tradition" who serendipitously found his way into official circles.

Although the Nazis never developed an official and established system of National Socialist runology, many uses of the runes are to be found in official documents and publications.

The *Sig*-rune was seen as the rune of victory (Ger. *Sieg*), the *Tyr*-rune was the rune of the struggle (Ger. *Kampf*), the *Othil*-rune was the symbol of blood and soil, and the *Hagal*-rune was that of salvation (and/or racial purity). The name of the **s**-rune (ᚼ) actually means "sun," but because of the spelling of the Old English rune-name (*sigel*, pron. [SEE-yell]) the association between the German word *Sieg* (victory) and this rune was made long before the Nazis.

Fig. 8.2. Design of the runic death's head ring by Wiligut

Wiligut explained the meaning of the symbols on the *Totenkopfring* of the SS in a manuscript (see Hunger 1984, 149–51) as follows:

ᛋᛋ = "The creative spirit must be victorious."

ᛉ = "Man, be one with God, with the Eternal."

ᛝ = "Enclose the All in yourself and you will command the All."

ᛋᛋ + t/a = [victory] *tyr* = *os* = "Be guileless, brave and true." "The power of your spirit makes you free."

In his article "Unsere Stellung zu den Runen" (Our Attitude toward the Runes), Karl Theodor Weigel applied the following meanings to certain runes.

ᛋᛋ = In the meaning of victorious power.

ᛝ = "For the protection of the wearer against an enemy."

ᛋᛋ [misinterpreted as a single rune, *gibor*] = "victorious power of the personality."

↑/f = ↑ = Preparedness for self-sacrifice unto death + f = well-being, riches. (Weigel 1936, 57)

Among the most popular conclusions reached within the National Socialist understanding of the runes was that they were primarily to be connected with prehistoric ideograms. This idea is rooted in the work of Herman Wirth as outlined in his monumental 1931 to 1936 *Die heilige Urschrift der Menschheit* (The Holy Primordial Script of Mankind). Wirth was among the founders of the Ahnenerbe in 1935 and headed that organization until 1938, when he was forced out due to his unorthodox beliefs—as far as the National Socialist ideology was concerned—regarding ancient Germanic matriarchy and pacifism. Wirth's methodology had the underlying rationale and function of opening his line of reasoning to a widely comparative approach focused on the physical shapes of the symbols. This allowed him to reach conclusions relatively free of the constraints of rigorous rules of philology.

This allowed for a freer range of ideas to be applied to the symbols. Wirth's influence was not entirely responsible for the interest of both Arntz and Krause in the concept of *Begriffsrunen* (the use of individual runes to stand for the meaning of their names or for related formulaic words), though such an interpretation certainly became highly regarded during these times. The idea of runes as ideograms standing for their names is an undeniable part of scientific runology; however, the idea that they are based on older, pre-runic ideograms of rather subjective value is a different matter.

From the standpoint of the use of runes for purposes of what might be called overt propaganda, or simply the branding of NS programs and concepts, the runes constituted a ready-made set of symbols that were both meaningful and attractive to the eye. Some of the most common runic symbols used during the Nazi era were:

ᛋᛋ *Schutzstaffel* (Protection Division)
ᛏ = Hitler-Jugend leadership badge
ᛉ = Life
ᛦ = Death (origin of the Peace Sign; see appendix)
ᛟ = Homeland
ᛡ = *Lebensborn*

The *Lebensborn* (Life's Wellspring) was an SS program designed to raise the birthrate of Aryan children. Unwed motherhood was encouraged through sexual liaisons with SS-men, and babies were supplied to SS families for adoption.

Here are a number of other runic explanations from Fritz Weitzel's 1939 small tract *Die Gestaltung der Feste im Jahres- und Lebenslauf in der ᛋᛋ-Familie* (The Planning of Ceremonies in the Course of the Year and of Life in the SS Family):

> ᛡ Hagal-rune means: "The All-surrounding." Hagal (Germanic) literally means "I destroy." Through the destruction of the enemy, all-surrounding peace is ensured.

ᛋ Sig-rune means "Victorious sun" and signifies the indwelling strength that assures victory. "The two Sig-runes on the banners of the ᛋᛋ express the old formula '*sig und sal,*' which is the salvation that lies implicitly in the certainty of the sun's victory." (K. Th. Weigel)

ᚼ Gibor-rune is made up from the Sig-rune and the Is-rune. It is therefore a combined rune. The Is (ice)-rune is the north–south line of the circle of the year and symbolizes "life"; in human terms: the living personality. The Gibor-rune therefore stands for the victory-assuring strength of the personality.

ᛏ Tyr-rune: It symbolizes the Germanic god of war, Tyr (= Ziu = Zeus) and signifies preparedness to sacrifice oneself unto death for the redemption of honor.

ᚠ Fa-(Fe-)-rune: "Fe" is contained in the Germanic word *feod* = farm animals. It symbolizes all movable farming goods, livestock, wealth. The Fa- and Tyr-runes together mean: self-sacrifice unto death, despite any cherished material goods.

ᛉ Man-rune: With its up-stretched arms, it shows the birth of a living creature. (Cf. the heraldic symbol of the Lily.)

ᛦ Yr-rune: With its downward-pointing arms, it indicates the death of a creature. Man- and Yr-runes are taken from the six-spoked wheel of the year. (Cf. the Is- and Hagal-runes.)

ᛜ Ing-rune: Ing means "to be born," "to stem from," and can still be found in this meaning as a suffix to hundreds of words in today's German language. The rune shows the interconnection of two life-bearers and is therefore used as a wedding-rune.

ᛟ Odal-rune: Odal or Alod is the Germanic word for the allodium of the clan. It also stands for this meaning. It encompasses everything that we understand in the concepts allodium, soil, homeland. (Weitzel 1939, 41–43)

Obviously, many of these interpretations will rightly strike the scientific runologist as fanciful and subjective. The Nazi rune-symbolists were not concerned with accuracy but rather only *effectiveness* in their efforts to convey subtle messages to the viewer. The runes and various runelike symbols became iconic slogans that spoke directly to the unconscious minds of the individuals viewing them. It is also clear that the meanings of the runes and runic symbolism varied among National Socialist writers and that there was no overriding orthodoxy with regard to runic symbolism.

By the same token, it can also be seen that the *esoteric* use of the runes by the Nazis was far more sophisticated and subtle than most people normally think, but it was also of a distinctive nature. The main use of runes did not involve sitting around casting runic spells, doing runic yoga, or chanting runic mantras in any organized way. The spell was a much larger operation. It was virtually identical to what we call "branding" in the advertising world today. Runes and runelike aesthetics were used to attract an already Germanophilic population to the cause and repel those who were not attuned to this aesthetic. The symbol of the swastika (Ger. *Hakenkreuz*), which the National Socialist Movement adopted at the suggestion of Hitler himself in 1920, became its chief logo. Certain circles, cells, or offices within organizations such as the Ahnenerbe may or may not have explored the esoteric side of the runes further. But if they did it was most likely just a holdover from their previous interests in such things stemming from their younger days.

The role of the Nazis in the Germanic revival and the revival of the runes was often a damaging one. These things were evolving naturally and broadly in Germany in the early twentieth century. They were highjacked by the National Socialist ideology (with its preconceived and often erroneous doctrines about race, religion, myth, and history) and many enthusiasts of the Germanic revival were co-opted by this political wave, although not all of them were accepted or promoted (as we have seen in the examples of figures like F. B. Marby and Heinar Schilling). Certainly, opponents of the legitimate and independent Germanic and runic revival have enthusiastically attempted to use the black mark of Nazism to stain our cause in more recent years as well. The only positive way forward is through understanding the real truth of these matters in context.

RUNOLOGY OUTSIDE NAZI GERMANY

On one level, in the 1930s and early 1940s runology continued to develop outside the borders of Germany as if the Nazis did not exist. The subsequent events of the Second World War, however, did seriously impact the lives of many scholars and disrupted normal affairs in every European country. But runological studies tend to grind on very slowly, and from the historical perspective of the whole field of study, the National Socialist episode in Germany was a short-lived phase. What makes it a major interest is both the enduring (often sensationalistic) fascination it holds for people and the ways in which the Nazi interest in runic symbolism is "hyped up" in our present day by both enthusiasts and fearmongers alike. These factors do lead to significant disruptions in the objective pursuit of knowledge in runology, whether academic or esoteric.

Runology in Scandinavia during the Nazi years was affected somewhat by the occupation of Denmark and Norway by Germany from 1940 to 1945. However, it must be noted that runological work continued in occupied Denmark with the production of the standard edition of the Danish inscriptions by Jacobsen and Moltke in 1941/42 as well as the edition of the Icelandic inscriptions by Anders Bæksted in 1942. Similarly, the standard edition of the Younger Futhark inscriptions in Norway by Magnus Olsen began to be published in the occupied country in 1941. Sweden maintained its neutrality throughout the war.

An amusing story once recounted to me personally by the great American linguist Winfried Lehmann involved the adventures of the famous Norwegian linguist, runologist, and Celticist Carl Marstrander, whom we met earlier. He was active in the Norwegian resistance to the

Nazi occupation of his country. The philologist was imprisoned on several occasions, but in one instance Marstrander devised a plan to foil his Nazi captors. He carved some ogham-inscriptions on sticks and secretly threw them over the fence of the camp where he was being detained. These were discovered by guards patrolling the perimeter and, as everyone was ordered to report any strange antiquities to the Ahnenerbe, word quickly got back to Berlin about these unusual finds. Intelligence about experts in Norway determined that there was only *one* man in the country who could possibly decipher these strange inscriptions—none other than Marstrander! The Norwegian Celticist was at once moved from the camp and put to work in more comfortable surroundings to interpret these cryptic texts, a task that, for some strange reason, he was able to do with relative ease!

CHAPTER NINE

THE RUNIC RENEWAL

(1945–1975)

In May of 1945 the Third Reich underwent its final death throes. Germany was in ruins, but the spirit to rebuild the country in a new way was strong. Those who survived the war would take some years to reorient themselves before they could again take up their old interests. In the case of the runes themselves, they had become closely associated with the National Socialist regime simply because runic images were so widely used in Nazi insignia. Few people had any awareness of Himmler's private obsessions or the quasi-esoteric studies of the Ahnenerbe. But the runes did have to be reenvisioned in much of the public eye in order to separate them from their conspicuous association with National Socialism.

No one did more in this effort to "rehabilitate" the runes in Germany's esoteric and occult subculture than Karl Spiesberger (1904–1992). Spiesberger trained as an actor in Vienna. In 1932 he made his way to Berlin, which at the time was the center of world filmmaking. He was a student of hypnosis and other occult arts when he arrived. In Berlin, he became friends with the Grand Master of an occult order known as the Fraternitas Saturni (Brotherhood of

Saturn) named Gregor A. Gregorius (= Eugen Grosche). In 1948 Spiesberger was finally initiated into the order, taking the lodge-name of Frater Eratus.

In the 1950s Spiesberger wrote two important contributions to the esoteric runic traditions: *Runenmagie* (Rune Magic) in 1955 and *Runenexerzitien für Jedermann* (Rune Excercises for Everyone) in 1958. In these works, he presented the esoteric Armanen tradition as founded by Guido von List, but he incorporated ideas and practices developed by Marby, Kummer, and others. He also tried to purge the tradition of what was perceived to be racialist aspects and position what he was teaching within what might be termed a "pansophical," or eclectic, context.

A comparison between the contents of table 7.1 in chapter 7 (see p. 122) and table 9.1 on page 154 will show the dynamism of the Armanen rune meanings and how these meanings evolved over just a few decades. Although List founded and shaped the original Armanen system, it did not remain simply a replication of his ideas; rather, several other writers contributed to its character and content. The main influence for the evolution of the runic symbolic values stems from the world of practical occultism and esoteric physics as expressed in the works of F. B. Marby, S. A. Kummer, Friedrich Teltscher, Emil Rüdiger, and Karl Spiesberger.

Another exponent of the new runic revival was Roland Dionys Jossé (birth and death dates unknown), who published a work, also in 1955, called *Die Tala der Raunen: Runo-astrologische Kabbalistik* (The Numeric Interpretation of the Runes: Runo-astrological Kabbalism). In this work he made use of the sixteen-rune futhark, which was a major historical departure for the practice of runic esotericism in Germany. Jossé rightly assumed that the seventeeth and eighteenth runes of the *Hávamál* (taken up by List as gospel) were actually additional runes lying outside the numerological system. Jossé presented a complex but highly workable numerology and a system of astrology based on the formula of sixteen.

TABLE 9.1. THE ARMANEN FUTHORK AS DESCRIBED BY KARL SPIESBERGER

No.	Shape	Name	Meaning
1	ᚨ	Fa	Primal fire, change, re-shaping, banishing of distress, sending generative principle, primal spirit
2	ᚢ	Ur	Eternity, consistency, physician's rune, luck, telluric magnetism, primal soul
3	ᚦ	Thorn	Action, will to action, evolutionary power, goal-setting, rune of Od-magnetic transference
4	ᚩ	Os	Breath, spiritual well-being, word, radiating Od-magnetic power
	ᛜ	Othil	Arising, the power of the word, receptive power
5	ᚱ	Rit	Primal law, rightness, advice, rescue, rhythm
6	ᚲ	Ka	Generation, power, art, ability, propagation
7	ᚼ	Hagal	All-enclosure, spiritual leadership, protectiveness, harmony, cosmic order, the midpoint of order
8	ᚾ	Not	The unavoidable, karma, compulsion of fate
9	ᛁ	Is	Ego, will, activity, personal power, banishing, consciousness of spiritual power, control of self and others
10	ᛁ	Ar	Sun, wisdom, beauty, virtue, fame, well-being, protection from specters, leadership
11	ᛋ	Sig	Solar power, victory, success, knowledge, realization, power to actualize
12	ᛏ	Tyr	Power, success, wisdom, generation, awakening, rebirth in the spirit, spiraling development
13	ᛒ	Bar	Becoming, birth, the third birth in the spirit, concealment, song
14	ᛚ	Laf	Primal law, life, experience of life, love, primal water, water and ocean rune
15	ᛉ	Man	Man-rune, increase, fullness, health, magic, spirit, god-man, the masculine principle in the cosmos, day-consciousness
16	ᛦ	Yr	Woman-rune, instinct, greed, passion, matter, delusion, confusion, death, destruction, the negative feminine principle in the cosmos, night-consciousness
17	ᛇ	Eh	Marriage, lasting love, law, justice, hope, duration, rune of trust and of the dual (twin) souls
18	ᚸ	Gibor	God-rune, god-all, cosmic consciousness, wedding together of powers, the generative and receptive, sacred marriage, giver and the gift, fulfillment

Jossé presented a system for transliterating names into the sixteen runes of the futhark in the following way. This table accounts for sounds in Norse, German, and English.

TABLE 9.2. JOSSÉ'S TABLE OF RUNIC TRANSCRIPTION

Number	Rune	Sounds	Letters	Double-Letters
1	ᚠ	f	f v	
2	ᚢ	u v w	u v w	au uo ou
3	ᚦ	th d	th d ð þ	
4	ᚭ	o å	o aa a	
5	ᚱ	r	r	
6	ᚴ	k g ch ng	k ck g ch kj ng nk	
7	ᚼ	h (soft) ch	h ch kj	
8	ᚾ	n	n	
9	ᛁ	i	i j y e ie	ei ai ey ay
10	ᛆ	a ä e	a ä æ e	
11	ᛋ	s sch	s ss sch sh sk skj sj	
12	ᛏ	t	t d dt	z
13	ᛒ	b p	b p	pf
14	ᛚ	l	l	
15	ᛘ	m	m	
16	ᛦ	ö ü	ö ü ø y	eu oi äu øy øi œ ue ui iu eo

Jossé's numerology involves first transliterating a person's name into the sixteen runes of the Younger Futhark, then reducing it to a key number by units of 16, and finally adding the remainder until a number below 16 (or 18) is reached. For example, the name Aelfric Avery would be treated in the following manner:

ᛃᛒᛚᚱᛁᚠ   ᛏᛒᛁᚱᛉ

10.14.1.5.9.6   4.2.9.5.16

$$= 81 = 16 \times 5 + 1 = 6$$

That is, there are five units of 16 in the sum of the numerical values of the name (16 × 5), with one left over. These are added to the number of units to arrive at the key number of the name, which is 6. Therefore, the key-rune for this individual, according to this system, would be the Kaun-rune, which Jossé interprets with the Listian motto: "Your blood, your highest possession." This rune, or *Raune*,* as Jossé called it, is also connected with the idea of *artistry* and a deep concern with *beauty*.

As far as the great number of personalities involved in esoteric runology in the pre-Nazi period are concerned, only one seems to have weathered the storms of war: F. B. Marby. Although he had been persecuted by the Nazis and even imprisoned in Dachau, he was given no compensation for his losses by the Allies, as he was judged to have been a Nazi supporter. At least he was not re-imprisoned by the new authorities! Marby began to republish his material from the early 1930s and reestablished himself as a figure in postwar esoteric circles in Germany. In 1957 he came out with what is perhaps his greatest work, *Die drei Schwäne* (The Three Swans), which had been completed before his arrest by the Nazis in 1936. This book is a kind of mystical autobiography, and, as published in 1957, it contains copious notes and commentaries by the author that make it invaluable for understanding the Marbyan system.

POSTWAR SCIENTIFIC RUNOLOGY

Of course, scientific runology continued along its way with little to no regard for any of these purely occult ideas. Most of the credentialed

---

*Through his terminology Jossé is evoking the sense of a rune as a "whisper" (cf. Ger. *raunen,* and the archaic English verb *to round,* both meaning "to whisper").

and legitimate runologists in Germany continued to work after the war regardless of their attitudes or positions during the Nazi regime. However, Helmut Arntz seems to have been so embittered by his treatment during those dark days that he devoted himself to other academic and writing pursuits after 1945.

In 1966, Wolfgang Krause published his important compendium *Die Runeninschriften im älteren Futhark* (The Runic Inscriptions in the Older Futhark) with archaeological contributions by Herbert Jankuhn. Both of these men had been involved with the Ahnenerbe during the war, but these past events were allowed to fade into the background as life went on. Krause's edition of this body of inscriptions remains the standard today.

Scandinavian runology continued to develop and became better represented as an academic discipline in the major universities and museums of all of the Nordic countries.

In 1952 the Danish runologist Anders Bæksted (1906–1968) wrote a rather scathing critique of the widespread assumptions concerning the magical nature of the runes in his landmark work *Målruner og Troldruner* (Speech Runes and Magic Runes). Most scholars from the beginning had taken for granted that the runes had something to do with magic and mysteries given the constant reference to them in this regard in medieval literature as well as the contents of many inscriptions that seemed to corroborate this idea. Bæksted inaugurated the school of "skeptical" scientific runologists and called upon all runologists to be more careful and questioning in their approaches to runic evidence.

Despite a new wave of skepticism, the school of runic interpretation that took possible numerical symbolism into account would find its grandest and last great expression in the work of the Freiburg professor Heinz Klingenberg (b. 1934) titled *Runenschrift—Schriftdenken—Runeninschriften* (Runic Writing—The Ideology of Writing and Runic Inscriptions) published in 1973. He used the idea of gematria to its full effect. His interpretation of the inscription on the runic horn of Gallehus even brings into consideration the *phi*-ratio and the iconography on the elaborately decorated horn. The horn was made of gold and was obviously used as a drinking vessel for religious or cultic purposes. As regards the runic inscription on the horn, which is executed around the rim of the horn in a circular arrangement, Klingenberg notes certain numerical patterns that seem to defy random chance. The inscription reads:

ᛖᚲᚺᛚᛖᚹᚨᚷᚨᛋᛏᛁ᛬ᛁᚺᛟᛚᛏᛁᛃᛁᚱᛁᚺᛟᚱᚾᚨ᛬ᛏᚨᚹᛁᛞᛟ

ekhlewagastiR ⦙ holtijaR ⦙ horna ⦙ tawido
The values of these runes given as numerals would be:
19.6.9.21.19.8.4.7.4.
ek HlewigastiR HoltijaR horna tawido
"I, Hlewagast Holt ('man of the grove,' or 'descendant of Holt'), made the horn."

The division between words by four vertical dots is reckoned as being important, and they are given the numerical value of 4.

ekhlewigastiR	⦙ holtijaR	= 273 or 21 × 13
holtijaR	⦙ horna	= 169 or 13 × 13
horna	⦙ tawido	= 143 or 11 × 13
tawido	⦙ ekhlewagastiR	= 247 or 19 × 13

Note that the number of runes in the sections marked off by the word dividers also indicates the number with the multiplier of thirteen in the formulas above. According to Klingenberg, these formulas are recurring references to the number thirteen, the numeric equivalent of the rune *eihwaz* (ᛇ), which he logically connects to the World Tree from Germanic mythology. This simple presentation of Klingenberg's theories only barely scratches the surface of what he does in his erudite analysis. Many have dismissed such analysis as "too speculative," yet when we look at the inscription in question and the object upon which it was executed, and couple this with the fact that the inscription refers to the making of the *horn,* not the inscription—a horn that is covered with arcane symbols of obviously mythic or religious importance—one must pause before dismissing an interpretation such as that of Klingenberg out of hand.

Another important speculative field of runology that has continued to enjoy some energy focuses on the mythic and cosmological meanings and contexts of the rune-names themselves. As we know, these names are well attested for in the Old English and Old Norse traditions of the Anglo-Saxon and Younger Futhark, respectively, but for the Older Futhark period we must rely on reconstructions of the names. Both Krause and Arntz had been enthusiasts for this mythic line of thinking, while others such as Friedrich von der Leyen, Wolfgang Jungandreas, and Karl Schneider devoted special, and sometimes extensive, studies to the topic. Karl Schneider (1912–1998) was a professor of Old English philology at the University of Münster whose 1951 dissertation, *Die germanischen Ruenennamen: Versuch einer Gesamtdeutung* (The Germanic Rune-Names: Attempt at a Comprehensive Interpretation), was published in book form in 1956. In this study, he speculates that the rune-names are reflective of deep Germanic and even Indo-European cultural and religious concepts. In this he is not original, but he does take the structural relationships of these concepts to a new level. He presents runic pairs arranged by means of a series of twelve concentric circles by which the first and last rune (ᚠ:ᛟ) belong to the outermost circle, and so on. The resulting pairs are analyzed as belonging to certain circles of meaning, from the inside out, as follows:

1 = The circle of destiny: ᛋ:ᚲ
2 = Circle of primeval being (circle of the αρχη of life): ᚺ:ᛃ
3 = Circle of cold (or death): ᛁ:ᛇ
4 = Circle of warmth: ᛏ:ᚻ
5 = Circle of the warrior clan: ᚹ:ᛏ
6 = Circle of giving: ᚷ:ᛒ
7 = Circle of the luminous conception of the beyond: ᚲ:ᛗ
8 = Circle of light: ᚱ:ᛗ

9 = Circle of the dark conception of the beyond: ᚠ:ᛁ
10 = Circle of fertility in the human sphere: ᚦ:◊
11 = Circle of fertility in the animal-vegetable sphere: ᚢ:ᛗ
12 = Circle of ownership: ᚹ:ᛉ

It should be noted that Schneider considered the order of the thirteenth and fourteenth runes to be ordered ᛤ–ᛁ, which is a reversal of how are typically assumed to be sequenced.

Beyond these perceived runic dyads, Schneider also proposed a more elaborated view of the dyadic relationship between adjacent runes in the futhark order. Jungandreas and others had recognized the special relationship between neighboring runes such as ᚹ:ᚢ, ᚦ:ᚠ, and so forth, but Schneider took this a step further and noted how these dyads related to the next dyad in an almost interweaving, or interlocking, pattern. He counts nineteen dyads as relevant in this analysis (it is only with certain dyads that he sees the interweaving of one set with the next). They are as follows:

ᚹ–ᚢ: Livestock (including bull and ram)—fructifying moisture of the primeval essence conceived of as a bull or ram.

ᚢ–ᚦ: Fructifying moisture (*semen virile*)—Thunar as god of matrimonial generation.

ᚦ–ᚠ: Thunar as god of thunder—Wodan as the storm god; both rulers within the atmospheric realm.

ᚱ–ᚲ: Solar wagon—cremation (with the luminous heaven as the beyond); unifying idea: realm of light.

ᚷ–ᛈ: Hospitality—clan; the former is the obligatory law of the latter.

ᛈ–ᛏ: Clan—*membrum virile;* context given by the idea of generation: ᛈ the work of ᛏ.

ᛁ–ᚺ: The primeval material (ice)—the primeval essence (born out of ice, cf. Yrmin-myth).

ᚺ–ᛃ: Primeval material—harvest; the First as originator of the Second.

ᛛ–ᚳ: Yield of the harvest (agricultural destiny)—religious destiny.

ᚳ–ᛇ: The power of destiny (*uurðiz*)—world yew; notice that the well of Urð according to ON tradition lies beneath the World Tree.

ᛇ–ᛦ: World yew—Valkyries; note the well of the swans beneath the World Tree and the Valkyries who determine destiny as swans.

ᚺ–ᛏ: Sun—Sky God as the god of radiant light.

ᛏ–ᛒ: Sky God—Mother Earth as bride of the Sky God (for the generation of one of the divine brothers).

ᛒ–ᛗ: Mother Earth—Father Sky; between the two: the Sacred Marriage.

ᛗ–ᛖ: Father Sky—the youthful divine brothers (grandfather—grandson, according to the family tree of the gods) who are the Morning and Evening Stars.

ᛖ–ᛚ: The youthful divine brothers—sea; conceptual connection: the youthful divine brothers as rescuers in distress at sea.

ᛚ–ᛜ: Sea—Earth God; the latter simultaneously a god of the sea.

ᛜ–ᛝ: Earth God—Day-star (with the symbolic value "youthful divine brothers"); connection: Earth God is the father of one of the brothers.

ᛝ–ᛟ: Day-star (= youthful divine brothers as the protective gods in the form of the gable horses on the hall)—the seat of the clan.

This basic idea is appealing on an indigenous aesthetic level, as it would reflect a particularly Germanic idea of patterning of words and images.

Such theories usually depend on the idea that the names of the runes, or the words that were attached to the signs, formed an underlying cosmological or mythic system of meaning. Speaking against this theory is the fact that the evidence for these names comes along at a fairly late date when we consider the entire historical span of the Older Futhark and that we have to depend not on direct evidence for the names but on reconstructions of them for the Older Futhark period. As testimony in favor of the validity of such an exploration are the internal structural patterns that emerge when the meanings of the names are considered and the fact that most of the names that are well known and well established seem to refer to matters of mythology and concepts of deep cultural significance.

CHAPTER TEN

THE RISE OF CONTEMPORARY SCIENTIFIC RUNOLOGY AND THE RE-EMERGENCE OF THE RUNE-GILD

(Phase VI: 1975 to Present)

The revival of contemporary Germanic spirituality has often been linked to publicity surrounding the rebirth of Norse paganism in Iceland under the leadership of the Icelandic poet Sveinbjörn Beinteinsson. This occurred in 1972 and was widely covered in the press throughout the world. As there was a general "occult revival"—which ranged from Wicca to Anton LaVey's Satanism and from Aleister Crowley to Scientology—going on in Western culture during the end of the 1960s and the beginning of the 1970s, the news of the renewal of Norse paganism in Iceland fell on receptive ears wherever it was heard.

In this same period the academic world found itself in the midst of a new golden age of philology as well as comparative linguistics, mythology, and religion. Many American universities had healthy programs in Germanic and Indo-European studies like never before. But the seeds of their destruction were already being planted in those very same universities as such areas of study increasingly came to be seen as the bastions of "dead white European males." So instead of this being the beginning of a new and brighter phase, it was a time when it was as good as it would ever be. The history of how this deterioration in academia took place has yet to be written, but its epicenter appears to have been the universities of the United States where the schools of the social and behavioral sciences and humanities were inundated with the 1960s generation (many of them staying in school for prolonged periods of time to avoid military service in the Vietnam War). As this generation gained footholds of power in various departments—and eventually in the administrations—of the universities, the die was cast.

EDRED THORSSON AND
THE ROOTS OF THE RUNE-GILD

One of the problems in writing this book has been that its subject matter is one in which the author is so intimately involved on all levels. I have taken great pains to remain as objective as possible, while at the same time not hesitating to make use of what I think is a unique and empathetic perspective on the whole story. But it is at this point that I must insinuate myself in a virtually autobiographical manner. For those who want even more of the details on this phase of the runic revival, there is no better source than my book *History of the Rune-Gild* (Thorsson 2019).*

In the summer of 1974, while I was an undergraduate student at the University of Texas at Austin, I heard the word *runa* (pron. ROO-nah) in my mind's ear. Research at the university library resulted in my finding, along with many academic runological books, Karl Spiesberger's book *Runenmagie*. This was the needed link for me to connect scientific runology with practical or experiential magical work. I privately translated his book and began to work with it in the context of other

---

*Published under my pen name, Edred Thorsson.

Armanen material that I had been able to locate written by Gorsleben, Kummer, and others. Daily work and magical training—which would become the prototype for the curriculum in *The Nine Doors of Midgard*—undertaken in 1974 and 1975 led to the completion of a book-length manuscript called *A Primer of Runic Magic* in the summer of that year. This work was still within the Armanen tradition. I sent the manuscript around to various publishers in the United States and in England, and it found interest with the well-known acquisitions editor Tam Mossman of Prentice-Hall. I was promised a contract before the Yuletide of 1975. But then word came back that Mossman had gotten a report from the marketing department of the company saying that they did not think runes would "sell." This sent me back to the proverbial drawing board.

For some reason or another I had remained unaware of the activity of the Ásatrúarfélag (Fellowship of Ásatrúar) in Iceland until well after I had begun to engage in the work of a reawakening of runic esotericism in 1974. I was alerted to the activity of such groups as the Ásatúarmenn and John Yeowell's Odinic Rite in England by a friendly Swedish professor at the University of Texas who knew something of what I was already doing at the time.

Stephen A. McNallen founded a religious organization originally called the Viking Brotherhood in the USA in 1969/70, independent of the Icelandic movement. He published a newsletter called *The Runestone*. News of the developments in Iceland and elsewhere would be instrumental in transforming McNallen's organization into the Ásatrú Free Assembly (AFA) in 1976. The AFA had a general interest in runes, but it was not a main focus of that religious organization. Many years later, Stephen McNallen would become a Master in the Rune-Gild.

An apparent early rival to the AFA was the Runic Society led by N. J. Templin. It, too, had little to do with runic practice or ideology. A leaflet produced by this organization (although no one really knows if this group had any members) presented a single sheet of idiosyncratic information about the runes, not worth repeating here.

This group was highly political and racialist, demanding that Denmark turn over Greenland to the group to form a Nation of Odin and exhorting subscribers to "Return to the Religion of Our Race." Ideas were drawn from German groups such as the Ludendorff Society and the Artgemeinschaft (Community of Our Kind). Happily, the Runic Society faded away fairly quickly.

In the late 1970s many of the ideas that would become the foundation of the Rune-Gild were being established. My great disadvantage—or possible gift—was that I had no living informant or teacher who knew anything about the esoteric dimensions of the runes. I worked almost entirely from books, which directed me back to an immediate connection with the ultimate teacher, Woden himself. The only exception to this circumstance came in the person of David Bragwin James (1937–2014), a deeply learned poet and scholar, whom I met at his home in New Haven, Connecticut, together with his young student, Alice Karlsdottir, around 1978. He was full of great ideas, about which we corresponded extensively afterward. It is regrettable that not more of his work has come to light.

A curious publication appeared in 1978 titled *Rune Magic* by Carlyle A. Pushong. This book was full of the author's other specialties, I Ching and yoga. The runic sections appear to have been taken directly from Spiesberger, although Spiesberger is not acknowledged. It is also possible that this material came his way from my 1975 manuscript, which had circulated in England at that time. Another book from 1982 was *Rune Games* by Marijane Osborn and Stella Longland, which has recently fallen into obscurity. Osborn was a professor (she is now emerita) at the University of California, Davis, and a specialist in Old English and Old Norse. The book is a serious attempt at runic reawakening with an unfortunately frivolous-sounding title. The fatal flaw is, however, its combination of the runes of the Anglo-Saxon Futhorc with the Kabbalistic Tree of Life cosmology. This was apparently done on the rationale that the Anglo-Saxon runes were often carved in a Christian context, and since the Christians might plausibly be familiar with Jewish learning, the combination of Kabbalistic cosmology with the Anglo-Saxon runes becomes a possibility. As the studies of Gershom Scholem have shown, however, the Kabbalistic cosmology as we know it today is not of archaic origin; it is a medieval phenomenon. In any event, the chance to combine the runes with a genuine Germanic cosmology was missed.

This particular period of the modern runic revival—characterized as it was by the work of Pushong, Blum, and Osborn—lacked the authenticity of an autochthonous understanding of archaic Germanic myth. This element of authenticity would only come about with the publication of my book *Futhark* in 1984. It remains regrettable that this book was not made available at the time of its actual completion in 1979. As flawed as *Futhark* may be in some respects, its accomplishment is that it combined, for the first time, an authentic runology with actual Germanic myth, cosmology, and psychology—a reunion of elements reforged after a thousand years.

My academic work soon demonstrated to me that the Armanen tradition was a modern Listian innovation, and I wanted to go deeper. By 1979, I had competed a new manuscript based on the Older Futhark. This was *Futhark: A Handbook of Rune Magic.* After sending this manuscript around to publishers, I received a contract with Llewellyn Publications, which at the time was going through some difficult financial straits. The book languished there, unpublished, for three years. In 1981, I got the rights to the book back from them. Throughout these years, I had been continuing my own studies and exercises, and during the Yuletide of 1979, shortly after finishing the manuscript for *Futhark,* I founded the Rune-Gild and the Institute for Runic Studies, Ásatrú (I.R.S.A.) in a ritual conducted in a remote area of Zilker Park in Austin, Texas. The Gild began publishing booklets called the *Lore-Books.* On the eve of my time of studying in Göttingen (1981–1982), I negotiated a contract with the publisher Samuel Weiser for *Futhark* to be published under my pen name Edred Thorsson, which I have generally reserved for my more esoterically oriented works. It would not actually appear in print until May of 1984—the same month I formally received my Ph.D. from the University of Texas. It would be a nine-year process from the summer of 1975 to this moment of fruition. After *Futhark* appeared and met with a positive reception, a second book of mine was published two years later: *Runelore* (1986). Its contents were based on the collected *Lore-Books* writings that had circulated within the Rune-Gild, together with additional material. My third work in this initial series of Thorsson books was *At the Well of Wyrd* (1988; it was later reissued in 1999 as *Runecaster's Handbook*).

In Germany, I attended events of the Armanen Orden and continued to study esoteric runology. But mainly I was deeply initiated into the world of academic and scientific runology by my mentor, Prof. Dr. Klaus Düwel. At that time I also had an office in the Scandinavian Department. The office I was given had been Wolfgang Krause's personal study—a small room filled with runic knowledge on all levels.

On my return to Texas in 1982, I was soon confronted by the appearance of Ralph Blum's *The Book of Runes* in October of that year. Blum tells the story of how he discovered the runes, but there is another story here as well. Blum ran in circles of publishers, editors, and book packagers. His project was generated as an idea for an ideal Christmas gift package for the year 1982, not only a book but also including a set of cast-resin "rune cookies" (mimicking those that Blum had claimed to have found in England when researching runic divination) as well. It was a huge financial success, and over time it would sell more than two million units worldwide. (Apparently, runes did "sell" after all!) The fact that Blum popularized the runes could have been a great development. But because he used an ordering principle that was based on a single reading he did for himself one night, his work gave readers the impression that the ancient tradition of our ancestors was unimportant or, worse yet, never existed. Great numbers of potential runic enthusiasts were given the wrong impression that the runes were not a venerable and well-established tradition but rather part of some New Age, "do-your-own-thing"–kind of invention. In this way, the burgeoning runic revival in the English-speaking world during the late twentieth century was dealt a serious blow. When what it needed was for all the stars to align just right to succeed quickly, what it got was a major roadblock.

Blum describes in his book (pp. 28–31) how he discovered the runes. His system stems from a reading he did, reportedly on a summer solstice, in which he asked the runes: "In what order do you wish to be arranged?" This was done after he had invoked "the Holy Spirit, the Tao, my Higher Self, and all my Unseen Guides and Helpers." The result was the following:

$$ᚢᛏᚲᚢᛤᛃᚷᛤ$$
$$ᛒᛧ<ᛩᛈᛃᛏᛌ$$
$$□ᛋᛁᛗᛒᛤᚺᛃᛧ$$

As Blum reports, his reading was done with a set of commercially produced rune cookies that he had purchased in England, so the peculiar mixture of rune-shapes and the presence of the "blank rune" cannot be ascribed to him. Blum decided to read this sequence from right to left, starting with the top row. If the reading of inverse runes as a negative or problematic indication had been heeded,* he would have stopped right there. In any event, Blum's biography would indicate that he subsequently took a course at San Diego State University with Dr. Allan W. Anderson, who taught in the subject areas of religion and spirituality; this and other studies provided the framework to interpret the runes independent of other evidence. He later ascribed the following meanings to the runes in the order of his "revelatory" reading.

---

*In Blum's interpretative system, reversed runes are taken as a sign of blockage and represent a "call for caution in the runic vocabulary" (cf. Blum 1983, 37).

TABLE 10.1. BLUM'S INTERPRETATION OF RUNES

No.	Shape	Meaning	No.	Shape	Meaning
1	ᛗ	The Self	14	ᚲ	Opening
2	ᚷ	Partnership	15	ᛏ	Warrior
3	ᚨ	Signals	16	ᛒ	Growth
4	ᛟ	Retreat	17	ᛖ	Movement
5	ᚢ	Strength	18	ᛚ	Flow
6	ᛈ	Initiation	19	ᚺ	Disruption
7	ᚾ	Constraint	20	ᚱ	Journey
8	ᛝ	Fertility	21	ᚦ	Gateway
9	ᛇ	Defense	22	ᛞ	Breakthrough
10	ᛉ	Protection	23	ᛁ	Standstill
11	ᚠ	Protection	24	ᛊ	Wholeness
12	ᚹ	Joy	25	□	The Unknowable
13	ᛃ	Harvest			

I could spend a good deal of time analyzing and criticizing the writings of Blum, but that would be pointless in this work. In the final analysis, I will just say that his results could have been a whole lot better if he had done some more research on the runes before writing his book. It appears that material he refers to and his bibliography were all added after *The Book of Runes* and its approach were already a finished product.

One may contrast my path with that of Blum. I used an untraditional system—the Armanen tradition—to create my first project. That project was thwarted, in my view, by the spiritual influence of Woden with the intention of "sending me back to school" to do better next time—and the experience opened me to the possibilities of reawakening a traditional and integral runology. Blum, on the other hand, was given a free ride to success and prosperity with his first effort. But the results of that will be but a footnote in the history of runology, and a blighted one at that.

THE RUNES IN GERMANY TODAY

No other land is more esoterically bound up with the runes in modern times than Germany has been. Since the dawn of the occult revival there, the runes have been playing a significant part in that process. Therefore, when we look at the ways in which the runes are used in magical circles in Germany today, we see a deep-level network of interconnections that is much richer, but also more diffuse, than that which we might expect to find in England or the United States. There is at least one German order based on what are essentially runic ideas: the Armanen Orden (Armanen Order). This is a direct continuation of the legacy of Guido von List and is also connected to the Guido von List Society. The magical order Fraternitas Saturni, which maintains an eclectic magical curriculum, probably also continues to have instruction in the art of rune magic as a part of that curriculum.

Ralph Tegtmeier is an important figure in the world of esoterica in Germany. In 1988 he published a book, *Runen: Alphabet der Erkenntis* (Runes: Alphabet of Knowledge), which made use of the twenty-four-rune futhark system. This appears to have been influenced by Rune-Gild research and it was dedicated to Edred Thorsson, *"Runenmeister sans pareil."* Tegtmeier was also the translator of the German version of my book *Runelore*.

The Armanen Orden was, for all intents and purposes, a moribund institution before it was revived by Adolf Schleipfer in 1968. He received the charter of the order from the then aged president of the Guido von List Society, Hanns Bierbach, and proceeded to rebuild it based on what seems to be a syncretization of not only List's ideas but also those of the other rune mystics and magicians of the German past (Marby, Kummer, Gorsleben, etc.) as well as the traditions of the Order of the New Templars and the Fraternitas Saturni. The rune magic of the Armanen continues to be taught mostly within the confines of the Armanen Orden itself.

A review of chapters 7 through 10 of this book will clearly show the dynamic and ever-changing nature of the Armanen tradition. It had various phases and faces over the course of the twentieth century. The first phase was that defined by the works of List himself. The next phase was characterized by the practicalizing of the runes in occult exercises as presented by Marby and Kummer. The third phase, quite distinct from the first two, was a politicizing of the runes under the Nazi regime. In the next phase, which came in the postwar period, the runes were universalized by writers such as Spiesberger and brought, in Germany at least, into the mainstream of Western occultism. Following this, the runes and the Armanen tradition were situated more firmly into an overtly heathen context by Adolf and Sigrun Schleipfer from the end of the 1960s forward. Toward the end of the twentieth century, the Armanen system was brought to the attention of the English-speaking world by my translation of List's *The Secret of the Runes* (1988) and the first edition of *Rune Might* (1989).* Subsequently, the various phases of the history of the Armanen Movement have been *synthesized* in ways that are not necessarily reflective of any one of the actual individual phases of Armanen history. Gone, for example, is List's respectful tone toward Christianity and now present are the occult practices of Kummer, Marby, and Spiesberger, which are quite foreign to the spirit of List's original presentation.

Another almost exclusively rune-based system is that of Rune Gymnastics. This magical system continued to be promoted through the works of F. B. Marby, as published by the Rudolf Arnold Spieth Verlag. In the 1980s another latter-day runic school gathered around Werner Kosbab, essentially based on the runic divinatory system elaborated in his 1982 book *Das Runen-Orakel* (The Oracle of the Runes).

During the 1990s the Germanic religious revival experienced a new upswing in Germany. Not all of these groups and organizations were in any way allied with the political right. But since the time of the reunification of Germany, runes and runelike signs and symbols have increasingly been the object of legal persecution in Germany as the federal authorities seek to ban and prohibit what they have determined to be symbols dan-

---

*A third revised and expanded edition was published in 2018 by Inner Traditions.

gerous to the constitution of the Federal Republic of Germany.

There really has not been a new explosion of interest in the runes in Germany; the original explosion already took place back in the beginning of the twentieth century. What is taking place there now is a slow and steady, and not always smooth, readjustment to the indigenous national esoteric traditions of the German people. In this instance there is a good deal of influence from the Anglo-American schools, such as the Rune-Gild. This is perhaps because the pioneering Germanic spirit appears especially strong in cultural outposts, and hence the vitality of what seems to be a "new" idea is full of a special energy there. This vitality can expand from its epicenter to the rest of the world. In the beginning of the twenty-first century, the Rune-Gild itself began the process of expanding into Germany and the rest of German-speaking Central Europe, and beyond.

KARL HANS WELZ AND
THE KNIGHTS OF RUNES

Back in the United States, many others began to follow in the wake of the success of the Blum phenomenon. Among these was an Austrian named Karl Hans Welz, who says he studied runes in Berlin. In 1984, Welz organized the Knights of Runes (KOR) based on the Armanen system. Welz took pains, as Spiesberger had done, to rid the Armanen tradition of its *völkisch* elements. Following much in the footsteps of Spiesberger, who also lived in Berlin in the 1980s, Welz sees the runes in terms of energy fields and forces. Clearly, this sort of view was also heavily developed and promoted by Marby, who must be seen as the true father of runes interpreted as quasi-physical forces: orgone, odic force, and so on. Welz has invented and markets machines and devices meant to generate and manipulate this sort of vital energy. Welz describes himself in KOR literature from the 1980s in the following way:

KARL HANS WELZ was born in Innsbruck, Austria. He attended the University of Innsbruck and obtained his bachelor's degree at the age of nineteen. He went on to study theology, and later psychology and mathematics there in graduate study.

Karl Hans Welz was interested in metaphysics from the age of fourteen. During the course of time and during his extensive traveling, he explored and practiced nearly all fields of metaphysics.

Karl Hans Welz became a Rune Master as a member of the Sacred Brotherhood of the Golden Ray, West Germany.

He is the author of several books and essays on the spiritual and occult sciences, and he has appeared on many TV shows. He considers the Runic system to be one of the most powerful spiritual tools known to mankind and that it can bring about rapid advancement in and mastership of psychic skills.

It is unfortunate but true that there is no book in English which describes the symbolism of the 18 Sacred Futhork Runes, even though the Runic system was extensively used in the Anglo-Saxon, Nordic, and Keltic countries before it was mercilessly exterminated by the followers of the Christian religion in the eleventh century CE.

Fig. 10.1. The emblem of the Knights of Runes

Karl Hans Welz sees it as his mission to make this powerful Runic system accessible to as many people as possible and to train more Rune Masters in this country.

It will be well worth your effort to practice Runes until your initiation as Knight of Runes, after four months, and Rune Master, after approximately one year of practice.

Welz apparently taught bodily and manual rune postures in the tradition of Marby and Kummer as ways to channel runic forces.

In brief, he presents his Armanen runology as follows:

ᛕ Fa (to help)   ᛏ Ar (to reframe)

ᚱ Ur (to heal)   ᛌ Sig (to win)

ᚦ Thorn (to project)   ↑ Tyr (to sacrifice)

ᚯ Os (to accept)   ᛒ Bar (to rest)

ᚱ Rit (ceremonial)   ᚱ Laf (comic law)

ᚴ Ka (capability)   ᛃ Man (spirituality)

✳ Hagal (universe)   ᛉ Yr (roots)

✝ Nod (karma)   ✝ Eh (cosmic union)

| Is (true ego)   ᚷ Gibor (self, oneness)

These values can be compared to those of Guido von List given in table 7.1 (see p. 122).

In 2000, Welz relinquished the charter of the KOR for a period of time to a man named Larry Camp (Dietrich) of Sandusky, Ohio. Camp tried to return the Armanen tradition to a more Listian mythic vision. This did not always sit well with Herr Welz, who secretly dissolved the KOR about 2008 and then reconstituted his own version of the KOR as an almost rival organization called the Great Timeless Brotherhood of Runemasters. Both organizations became moribund in the ensuing years, but periodically efforts to reactivate this school in a unified form have surfaced.

MIGUEL SERRANO

Miguel Joaquín Diego del Carmen Serrano Fernández (1917–2009) was a proponent of National Socialism in his native Chile as a young man during the Second World War, a war in which his country remained neutral. Serrano was initiated into a *völkisch* esoteric stream of thought by a "mysterious" German immigrant during these years. Later he would enter the diplomatic service of Chile in a career that would last from 1953 to 1970, when the Marxist regime of Salvador Allende took power in Chile. With the ouster of Allende, Serrano returned to Chile and undertook his work in articulating the idea of "Esoteric Hitlerism." It is clear that he was interested in esoteric matters his whole life, he was versed in German culture, and he had been an adherent of National Socialist ideology since the 1930s. However, it also appears that his esoteric Nazism stems from himself and was the product of the times in which he began to write the works that supported these ideas; that is, from the late 1970s onward. He, too, picked up on what was in the air during those years. Perhaps because of his ties with a respectable establishment, his ideas became influential in certain circles. (Due to some shady dealings, his books were only translated into English late and in a haphazard way, or they probably would have been even more influential.)

In 1984, Serrano published the best-known work in his "Esoteric Hitlerism" trilogy: *Adolf Hitler, el Último Avatāra* (Adolf Hitler: The Last Avatar). In this book he provides an almost hundred-page outline of runic symbolism based on the eighteen runes of the Armanen Futhork. His runology is fitted out with elaborate illustrations by the German artist Wolfgang von Schlemm (1920–2003), some of which were inspired by the work of the German esotericist Peryt Shou (1873–1953) as found in his 1920 book *Die "Edda" als Schlüssel des kommenden Weltalters* (The *Edda* as the Key to the Coming Age). Shou was not particularly involved with runic symbolism himself, nor was he a *völkisch* philosopher. In the final analysis, Serrano's work is poetic, mystical, inspired (by something), but is not coherent from a runological perspective. His is a very unique take on the runes. He draws on material from the Armanen and other German rune-esotericists and couples it freely with Indian mysticism and Gnoticism, synthesizing these elements and other elements in a "Pan-Aryanist" crucible.

Fig. 10.2. Diagram from Serrano's *El Último Avatāra* that is referred to as the "Rune Zodiac" and characterized as the "Secret Platform" or plane of combat against the extraterrestrial enemy, the Demiurge

The following passage from the English translation of *El Último Avatāra* (Serrano 2014, 223) is instructive with respect to his attitudes and ideas concerning the use of the runes.

Runes appeared to Wotan as sound-signs, number-letters. They are the exterior form that now carries the *Vril* and are sent to *viras* as weapons in the Great War they undertake against the Demiurge Jehovah, within his corrupted Universe. They deliver us the necessary schematic knowledge of the Science of Return, keys with which to open doors. Only they can give us the possibility of *escape*, of the *leap* into *Sunya*, the Void of the Black Sun, beyond this diabolical Creation. So the Jew will never use them. They do not serve him. Only Aryans. Yet the Jew has falsified the Hagal Rune, using it as the "Star of David." The Rune symbols are the only ones among magic alphabets with sharp symmetric shapes that resemble the bodies of *divyas* alone and no others. Rune exercises, Runic Yoga of the body, impregnate their matter with magic vibrations. [The one who] knows his Runes acquires the power of material dissolution and reintegration, of voluntary death and resurrection. He will be able to make his Note vibrate in the highest pitch. *To escape,* thereby, from the Circle of Returns.

The mixture of runic ideas with Hindu religious concepts and elements of the postwar myths of Nazi occultism (Vril, the Black Sun) coupled with overt Anti-Semitic verbiage are characteristic of Serrano's writings. His world-denying (Hindu/Gnostic) ideology is a clearly non-Germanic trait. Serrano's overall approach and style is similar to that found in Trevor Ravenscroft's 1973 *The Spear of Destiny* or Pauwels's and Bergier's 1960 *Le Matin des magiciens* (The Morning of the Magicians), both of which seem to have exerted some influence on him. Serrano's text is an evocative spell in its own right, but one that is restricted to a "poetic truth" at best.

THE FIRST RUNIC WAVE

In general, there was a tidal wave of rune books in the wake of the economic success of Ralph Blum's *Book of Runes* and the establishment of a more authentic runology with Thorsson's *Futhark*. It now seemed that every sort of publisher had to have a rune book of one kind or another. Because so many people had received their first impressions about the runic tradition from the book by Blum, there was for a long time much confusion even among supposed authors and lay "authorities" on the runes. The shoddy level of scholarship in these books raised the animosity of the scholarly runologists even more than had been the case in the old days of Guido von List and others. It might be said that from the early 1980s forward, there developed two schools of esoteric runology: the Blumian and the Edredian. The motto of the Blumian school would be: "Do your own thing" or "If it feels good, it's right." On the other hand, the motto of the Edredian school would be: "Verified tradition activated by experience leads to inner truth."

As time went on, many books were produced in both streams of thought. In the Blumian stream we find books with titles such as *Lady of the Northern Light, Runes for Today's Woman,* and many others. Although Blum did not invent the "blank rune" idea, it is certainly a hallmark of his influence. One of the worst offenders against tradition in the pseudo-runic "revival" was the British author Michael Howard, who actually published three books using the Etruscan alphabet and calling them "runes." At one point (on page 20 of his 1980 book, *The Magic of the Runes*) he admits that he has made an error previously but rationalizes continuing in the error "so as not to confuse the reader." That was just one overt sign of a pervasive trend in the spate of rune books that came out in this period. That trend was characterized by authors who did not know their subject matter being confused about things that were actually quite clear to those who had done their homework, and then those authors spread their confusion to the general public. Often the very names of the runes would be butchered, all because the author apparently thought the names they had invented sounded better than the actual ones. The enormous number of basic inaccuracies found in books produced in this period did a great disservice to the public and to the cause of the runic revival. Several of these books are reviewed in some detail in my anthology *Mainstays* (Thorsson 2006).

Some other examples from the first runic wave are Donald Tyson's *Rune Magic* (1988) and Lisa Peschel's *A Practical Guide to the Runes* (1989). It is difficult to take Tyson as a sincere proponent of runic esotericism, as he wrote the following in another book, *The New Magus,* which appear that same year with the same publisher: "The gods of the Germanic peoples . . . are dangerous. There is no more polite way to phrase it. By modern standards, many would be classified as demons. They represent the crudest of elemental forces" (Tyson 1988a, 268). I suspect that this confession of bad faith is indicative of a trend in many—but thankfully, not all—of the books that made up this first wave of the runic revival of the 1980s.

A notable publication that came toward the end of the first runic wave was Jan Fries's *Helrunar: A Manual of Rune Magick* (1993). His system is based on the Anglo-Frisian inventory of signs, and the book is heavily jazzed up with dark and primitive illustrations and admixed with techniques and symbols drawn from a variety of Western magical traditions including the Armanic rune yoga of Kummer (by way of Spiesberger), Aleister Crowley, neo-shamanism, and so forth.

One of the most persistent and erroneous notions abroad is that the *Celts* had anything to do with runes. One regularly sees the phrase "Celtic runes." No such thing exists. I originally wrote my book on the Irish ogham in 1992 to clarify what the Celtic tradition, which is somewhat analogous to the runes, actually was.* No runic inscription exists in a Celtic dialect. But all this seems to have had little effect on the most stubbornly ignorant among us. Really the list of such books, blogs, and websites appears endless and growing as the forces of chaos

---

*This was *The Book of Ogham* (1992), which I have since let another author, Michael Kelly from the Isle of Man, rework into a revised and expanded edition, issued under his name in 2010.

and misinformation continue to attack our venerable tree of runic tradition from every angle.

On the other hand, in the wake of *Futhark* and *Runelore* there also developed a more traditional school of runic esotericism. To qualify to be a member of the traditional school simply means that (1) the author minimally adheres to one of the established ancient runic traditions: the Older Futhark, Younger Futhark, or Anglo-Frisian Futhorc as a basis for what is written; (2) the names of the runes are presented in a reasonably accurate form (as based on academic references); and (3) the cosmology or mythic framework in which the runes are understood is historically part of the Germanic world. That may seem like a fairly low bar, but this is only a testimony to just how bad some writing about runes had become in the 1980s and beyond. In this early period, there was a handful of authors who belonged to one degree or another to some traditional school. These authors include Nigel Pennick, James M. Peterson, Kveldulf Gundarsson, and Freya Aswynn.

Nigel Pennick is a very prolific writer from Cambridge, England. He has well over thirty books to his credit, most of them having to do with esoteric Germanic or Celtic studies. He first started out in the 1970s publishing small pamphlets on geomantic and folkloric topics, including one on the swastika. Over the years, he has published books with several major publishers. His books are like encyclopedic manuals to the Germanic folk tradition, which include a good deal of runic and other esoteric knowledge. Nigel was named an honorary member of the Rune-Gild in 2016.

Following in many ways directly in the wake of the tradition of the Rune-Gild is the scholar and novelist Kveldulf Gundarsson (= Stephan Grundy). Kveldulf wrote books for Llewellyn and also penned several successful works of fiction: *Rhinegold* (1994) and *Attila's Treasure* (1996). He received a Ph.D. degree from Cambridge with a dissertation on Óðinn as a "god of death." Subsequently, he served as a leader in the religious organization called the Troth (formerly: the Ring of Troth).

Freya Aswynn became the first major female writer in the field of esoteric runelore with her book *The Leaves of Yggdrasil,* which she first published in London in 1988. It was later reissued in the United States under the title *Northern Mysteries and Magick* (1998) and has since reached a much larger readership. She, too, became involved with the Ring of Troth, until she was expelled from the organization for making politically incorrect remarks on social media.

One of the most extreme exercises in speculative esoteric runology in the past few decades is the French work by Jean-Yves Guillaume published in 1992 and titled *Les Runes et l'écriture des étoiles* (The Runes and the Script of the Stars). The French have specialized in the world of the imagination when it comes to the esoteric for a long time, so this comes as no surprise. Guillaume reconfigures the heavens with new runically based constellations and traces such a view of the sky back to the time of Atlantis!

There is no way a complete and *annotated* bibliography of these "New Age" books on runes published after 1975 can be included here; however, such a project would be an interesting endeavor for someone to undertake.

This runic new wave was not just limited to "New Age"–type applications and esoteric literature; it entered the popular culture generally and found its way into all sorts of other subcultures. Among these was the Neo-Nazi, Skinhead, White Nationalist faction. Groups and individuals in this subculture also began to use runes in their symbolism to a degree far beyond that of the original Nazis. At first these groups used the runic symbolism that had been prevalent in National Socialist Germany (1920–1945) as seen in chapter 8 of this book. But in the wake of the runic wave of the 1980s, the use of runes expanded in a more general way within popular culture and began to be used in tattoo art and other ways, especially beginning in the early 1990s. The motivation for the use of runes appears mainly as an attempt to project a sinister or terrifying image to "outsiders," as well as to act as a code of solidarity within the group(s) using them. In that sense, it can be counted a revival of one of the functions of the runes in ancient times—to appear scary to the non-initiate and express a specific identity among initiates themselves. As a rule, the use of runic symbolism by White Nationalists has to be assessed as a setback for the broader runic revival because of its *profaning* tendencies. It has become popular to say, about the Nazis (paleo- or neo-), that they "misuse" the runes. This criticism is only legitimate once one has posited the actual sacred, tribal, and initiatory character of the Germanic runes. If, by contrast, the runes are to be understood merely as arbitrary and alternative phonetic signs used for writing natural language, then Nazis and New Agers cannot really be said to be misusing them, as they are merely employing them for a new purpose. To say they are being misused is to presuppose that they are endowed with a certain *sacred* sense that is being violated. It is ironic that those who are quick to charge others with misusing the runes also tend to be the very ones who claim that runes actually have no intrinsic, sacred meaning. But certainly, if we realize a deeper, archaic, and authentic symbolism inherent in their history and mythology, then all efforts to use them contrary to their original and culturally specific purpose may be considered a misuse. Just because Nazis and New Agers hit upon the runes after the runic wave of the 1980s should not deter sincere seekers of the mysteries from pursuing their eternal meanings.

Another manifestation of the concept of runes in popular culture came along in their use in various role-playing games (RPGs) that became increasingly popular in the 1980s. Not infrequently, the idea of a "rune" in these games is a sort of hidden power to shape events rather than a symbol or sign. As such, this reflects an archaic conceptualization of the runes as well. The subculture involved in RPGs also tended to be fans of the fiction of J. R. R. Tolkien, the Oxford professor of Anglo-Saxon from 1925 to 1945 and author of various works of fantasy, for which he created pseudo-runes as part of the backstory of the cosmos he called Middle Earth.

ANOTHER REVIVAL OF THE RUNES
IN SWEDEN

Here we may consider another example of how the spirit of *Wōðanaz moves in the world in entirely mysterious ways. At the exact same moment in time that I was doing intense workings to reestablish the runes in North American culture, another wave of runic revival was taking place in Sweden. In that same summer of 1975, the association called Yggdrasil was founded by Mikael W. Gejel and Karin Norberg, and in 1976 they began to publish the periodical *Gimle*. Participants in this group also included Mikael Hedlund (Bodvar Bjarke), Jörgen I. Eriksson (Atrid Grimsson), and Marie Ericsson. The goal of the Yggdrasil group was the study of magical or esoteric dimensions of the Nordic tradition, which included *seið, galdr,* rune magic, and the practice of *útiseti* (sitting out), a sort of Norse version of a vision quest. Runelore was always important in the work of the Yggdrasil group and was first presented in a 1976 article in *Gimle* by Mikael Gejel titled "Talmystiken i den äldsta runraden" (The Number-Mysticism in the Oldest Rune Row). This text was subsequently adapted for a chapter in the Swedish book *Seid* (1985), collectively authored by various members of the Yggdrasil group, which included more material on rune magic. The esoteric model for much of the Swedish runic revivalism of the 1970s and 1980s was rooted in the discovery by a new generation of the work of the Swedish philologist Sigurd Agrell and his Uthark-theory (see chap. 7). This theory and the context of the ideas that Agrell presented in his books were tailor-made for a new generation schooled in the Kabbalah and the Western magical revival. Agrell's original books were also readily available at the time in the antiquarian bookstores of Sweden. The Uthark-theory was generally accepted by every Swedish revivalist of the day. Other important contributions stemming from this group include Atrid Grimsson's 1988 *Runmagi och Shamanism* (Rune Magic and Shamanism) and Bodvar Bjarke's 1988 ᚱᚢᚾᛏᚠ: *En kortfattad introduktion till Runorakel &*

Runmagi (Runa: A Concise Introduction to Rune Divination and Rune Magic).

This map of the four directions amply demonstrates the breadth of the vison encompassed by the work of the Yggdrasil group.

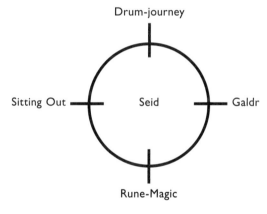

North
Night
Water
Growth
Winter
Night, darkness
Dark-Moon
Death/Rebirth
Freyja

Drum-journey

West
Earth
Minerals
Autumn
ening, twilight
Vaning Moon
Old Age
rigg/Grandma

Sitting Out

Seid

Galdr

East
Air
Animals
Spring
Morning, dawn
New Moon
Childhood
Odin

Rune-Magic

South
Fire
Humans
Summer
Day, light
Full Moon
Adulthood
Thor

Fig. 10.3. The Four-Directions Map of
the Yggdrasil group

No discussion of the runic revival in the current climate can go without giving kudos to the Swedish scholar and esotericist Thomas Karlsson. He is the founder of a major magical order called the Dragon Rouge and the author of several books that touch on the runes, especially in a practical way in connection with the runology of Agrell. Thomas was a young guest during the early phase of the Yggdrasil group but was not a member of that organization. In 2002 he published the book *Uthark—Nightside of the Runes.* But Karlsson's shining contribution lies in his scholarly work with the legacy of Johannes Bureus. A good primer of his contributions is provided by his composite book *Nightside of the Runes* (2019), which contains a complete translation of his 2005 book *Adulrunan och den götiska kabbalan* (Adulruna and the Gothic Kabbalah) on the work of Bureus. Karlsson received a Ph.D. from the University of Stockholm in 2010 with a dissertation titled *Götisk kabbala och runisk alkemi* (Gothic Kabbalah and Runic Alchemy).

THE SECOND RUNIC WAVE

After the first wave of runic revivalism that began in the early 1980s, higher-quality books on runelore began to be written and published, as the basic traditions were increasingly better understood. The rising use of the Internet and the generally more widespread availability of higher-quality research materials for esoteric rune-enthusiasts made this possible. It seems that after about the year 2000, a second wave of more solidly written esoteric rune books began to be published. These were marked by the tendency to use actual runic traditions, and the names of the runes and so on were increasingly accurate. The best examples from this second wave include Paul Rhys Mountfort's *Nordic Runes* (2003), Leon D. Wild's *The Runes Workbook* (2004), Diana Paxson's *Taking Up the Runes* (2005), and Kaedrich Olsen's *Runes for Transformation* (2008). Each of these books contains elements that make it worthy of recommendation. We can now only hope for a third wave, in which the full promise of integral runology will be met.

THE AGE OF THE INTERNET AND
THE REVIVAL OF THE ARMANEN RUNES

With regard to the Armanen tradition and the work of Guido von List, it had been my original plan (dating back to the early 1980s) to contribute a few works to the legacy of this chapter of the runic revival from the early part of the twentieth century connected to and derived from the ideas of Guido von List. My efforts were aimed at satisfying the curiosity of those who were interested in this historical phase of the movement. Thus, over the years I have translated List's *Das Geheimnis der Runen* (The Secret of the Runes), *Der Unbesiegbare* (The Invincible), *Die Religion der Ario-Germanen* (The Religion of the Aryo-Germanic Folk), and *Der Übergang vom Wuotanismus zum Christentum* (The Transition from Wuotanism to Christianity). I devoted a whole book to the study of some of the history and practices of the early twentieth-century German rune-magicians in the form of the book *Rune Might,* first published by Llewellyn in 1989, and subsequently reissued by Inner Traditions in a revised and expanded edition in 2018. This effort to inform people about an interesting past phase of the movement actually ended up stimulating a wider and deeper interest in this alternative runic tradition.

In the age of the internet, the Armanen tradition enjoyed a renewed level of enthusiasm, especially in the English-speaking world. This interest is largely unexpected because the vast German-language literature from within that tradition has never been published in English translation. Some of this renewed interest seems to have been fueled by polarized political feelings. The Armanen ideology of Guido von List has wrongly been condemned as somehow identical with that of National Socialism. Those drawn to the Armanen tradition today seem to find it attractive that it is so taboo and "politically incorrect." This world, like so much of our society today, is driven by the unseen laws of value-polarization: sides are drawn, identities are reinforced or exaggerated through verbal and symbolic echo chambers, and as one side goes on the attack, the opposite side that feels hostility is only further entrenched in ever more radical versions of its own ideology. In this way, individuals and groups allow themselves to be defined by their opponents. The whole process is largely driven by perceptions gained through the media and compounded by experiences on social media. An honest appraisal of events tends to show that traditionalists and those proposing authentic and autochthonous values are first attacked by the forces of political correctness and targeted as "racists." This then baits the conservative wing into overreacting, pushing both sides into ever more extreme corners.

But beyond any merely "political" dimension, the Listian tradition—with the contributions of men such as Marby, Kummer, and Spiesberger—also expresses ideas and developed practices that are highly accessible to the contemporary Western mind. This stream of thought remains compelling for some. For this reason, in 2018 I re-released my long-forgotten text written in 1975 as *The Runic Magic of the Armanen*.

In reality some of the best minds in the reawakening movement, such as Stefn Thorsman and especially Aelfric Avery, have devoted themselves to this Armanic branch of the revival. Avery published a translation of Kummer's major runic text, *Heilige Runenmacht* (Holy Rune Might) in 2019 as well as a three-volume study, *Armanen Runes and the Black Sun* in 2018.

THE REAWAKENING OF THE RUNE-GILD

Since its genesis in the mid-1970s, its establishment and growth between 1980 and 2011, and its organizational transformation following 2011, the Rune-Gild has been a remanifestation of the guild of runemasters of old. The Gild counts among its ranks an accomplished array of individuals meant to rival the Florentine academy of the Medicis. This evolution can be experienced in many of its nuances in the volume titled *History of the Rune Gild* (Thorsson 2019), so I do not need to delve too deeply into it here.

Most importantly, the *myth*—the esoteric level of self-understanding—of the Gild is that the organization itself, and the individuals within it, represent, in essence, the reawakening of the ancient network of rune-masters. The material contained in the present volume and in *History of the Rune Gild* constitute a record, as brief and incomplete as it might be, of the long process of this reawakening. Recalling the methodological lens used in my book *The Northern Dawn,* for reawakenings of older paradigms to occur, we need to have four factors present: motivation, freedom, sources, and methods.

Motivation is the *desire* of individuals or groups to undertake the work of reawakening slumbering paradigms. This volition is the primary factor; without it, any "study" or "contemplation" of archaic patterns is sterile antiquarianism.

Freedom is a factor that has two edges: inner freedom (the psychological freedom to seek the reawakening) and outer freedom (a political or cultural condition that allows individuals and groups the engage in such pursuits). Today this freedom, which in the recent past was taken for granted, is once more facing challenges.

Sources constitute the concrete data (written or traditional) necessary to effect a reawakening. In the case of the runes, this factor required centuries of hard work by scholars to once more bring to light the contents of runic inscriptions and the literary material that supplemented and expanded this knowledge base.

Methods are the intellectual resources necessary to interpret the source data. These are refined and improved over time, but it is not always the case that the most recent methods or approaches are the best. The humanities are especially susceptible to prejudices—be they religious, philosophical, or political. For this reason, methods can be rapidly corrupted by external considerations. The traditionalist wants to uncover the mysteries of how our predecessors thought and conceived of the runes in order to be informed by these ideas today. We do not seek to make use of these ideas to further an agenda external to the prime directive of seeking the mysteries.

All of these factors must be present and cultivated to assure a true reawakening. A review of the contents of this book shows how the presence of these factors guided and aided the process of the runic revival and how their absence or corruption disrupted that process.

Essential to the reawakening of the Gild and of the power of the runes was the development of the esoteric workbook titled *The Nine Doors of Midgard*. This was first published in 1991 and went through several additional editions over the years. This is the best and most complete guide to runic studies on an esoteric level, and its program has even been adapted to other traditions as well.

In some corners the runic revival is increasing in its quality and velocity as we enter more fully into the twenty-first century. In other corners is it just as off-base as it ever was. This revival, or reawakening, faces many challenges, both from within regarding the enhancement and growth of the quality of the ideas and works related to it, and from without as runes and the Germanic are frequently targeted by the thursic forces of "political correctness." These two challenges are inexorably linked. The attacks from the outside cannot be allowed to affect the authentic and inner-driven qualities of the ancestral runic spirit. Most objective observers would have to agree that it is within the Rune-Gild that this spirit lives and where it is cultivated. The impeccable scholar of Western esoteric traditions, Prof. Joscelyn Godwin, Ph.D., writing in his book *The Golden Thread,* refers to Edred Thorsson as the most "active and erudite spokesman" of the philosophically based neo-Germanic movement (Godwin 2007, 165). The Rune-Gild transcends the polarized mundane world of contemporary politics, with its often-superficial conflicts, and reflects the original intertribal network of the runemasters who freely and authentically sought the mysteries.

CHAPTER ELEVEN

AN INTEGRAL RUNOLOGY FOR THE FUTURE

The runes have been studied and pursued on many levels since the beginning of the modern age. The growth of scientific or academic runology at first developed only slowly and was always shadowed by what can be described variously as mystical, magical, and esoteric ideas connected to the runic system. This connection is seen by some to have been with the tradition from the beginning, whereas others see it to be a fantastic misinterpretation of the simple and practical purpose of the system.

After reviewing the history of the pursuit of the runes and critiquing the current state of runology—both exoteric and esoteric—our main purpose here is to suggest ways the study of runes can be made to be a more integral form of study for individuals and groups of individuals working together to understand this unique feature of European culture in a more synthetic way.

The objective, logical, and rational study of the artifacts left behind from the pre-1500 runic record is a noble pursuit and one that should be protected from *all* forms of outside interference, ranging from the subjective fantasies of individuals to the imposition of agendas from political ideologies. At the same time, based on the track record of the past five hundred years, it has to be recognized that the runes will continue to be a source of fascination in people's minds, just as they did during the earlier phases of the runic revival. There will always be those who let their imaginations run wild over this body of evidence and those who simply focus on the most mundane dimensions of runic writing. But these two opposing trends should not be allowed to destroy the middle ground. Between such extremes of fire and ice lies a way that requires attention and thought so that it might be better developed. This is the pathway of integral runology.

When we review the history of the runic revival, we must first recognize that the ancient and medieval periods (pre-1500) of runic practice were filled with phases of innovation, decay, and renewal. The use of runes was in constant flux, with the major stabilizing influences remaining in the human institution of the oral tradition, which supported and transmitted knowledge of the runes apart from literature and books. This is the institution of rune-learning, which passed from teacher to student over the centuries during the times of preliteracy and highly restricted literacy. This is what we could refer to as the ancient guild of runemasters. The dawn of the Modern Age brought with it more widespread literacy and the printing press. With these developments, the first printed references to the runes appeared and the revival phase can be said to have truly begun. As our review of the scientific study of the runes shows, it took approximately three hundred years for scholars to develop the knowledge base and methodological tools to unravel the basic history and development of the runic tradition. The impediments to these discoveries were mainly a lack of a coherent picture of the runic record itself (due to the dearth of major editions of enough inscriptions for scholars to study) and the prevalence of erroneous concepts (such as the belief that the sixteen-rune system was older than the twenty-four-rune system).

In the world of esoteric runology, several strong currents emerged in the twentieth century. The revolutionary impact of the writings of Guido von List was remarkable. From the first decade of the twentieth century, List's influence is felt in a continuous fashion right up to the present through the agency of the printed word. Even if the particulars of his theories have been increasingly superseded by an expanded knowledge base and ever more traditional ideologies and awareness of mythic patterns, the power of his poetic vision cannot be denied. The twentieth century concluded with the foundation of the Rune-Gild as a more comprehensive and integral view of runology and the transmission of runic knowledge, and the next century saw the maturation of that institution.

Of course, it must be realized that the Modern Age generally brought about the demise of traditional modes of knowledge transmission that were based on lineages of oral teaching. But it has compensated for this loss with an expansion of the possibilities of recording the ideas of people from the past in ways that allow for knowledge to be transmitted over time and space in a discontinuous fashion. This reality is central to the real mystery of writing itself, which is only intensified and expanded by the ability to reproduce the written word more broadly through the printing press—and now the Internet!

Some would argue that this expansion in the possibilities of the *quantity* or volume of such communication inevitably causes a reduction in the *quality* of the content of such transmissions. Realizing this tendency is the first step in taking measures to prevent the decay of intrinsic quality.

An observable trend in the history of science and scholarship has been the shift from more general and overarching approaches to ones dominated by highly specialized studies. This is true in the field of natural sciences as well as in the humanities. Early in the development of scholarly interest in the runes, this trend toward specialization worked in favor of runology. The study of either biblical or classical topics, being seen as things that provided general or global perspectives on knowledge, were challenged by the growth of interest in specialized national topics that were given new focus and interest in the early modern period. Previously dismissed as "pagan" or "barbaric," topics relating to Germanic or Celtic antiquities attracted rapidly increasing levels of interest and respect from a new breed of scholars. The repercussions of this development on runology were dramatic.

The effects of these new approaches to knowledge led to the loss of an integral understanding of the topics being studied, but by the same token it also facilitated deeper levels of precision in the analysis of particular parts of the data. In other words, the discipline fell into the same conundrum as the rest of the world as regards the effects of *modernism* comprehensive knowledge is lost to the particulars, and in the particulars people soon lose sight of the meaning of what it is that they are endeavoring to understand.

In general, modernism as an ideology is held to be suspect in many corners today. It is seen as being overspecialized and saddled with erroneous conceptions of inevitable progress based on a purely rational mode of "problem-solving." The utility of this approach cannot and should not be denied, but ultimately it may not be best equipped to answer many of the most enduring riddles of human existence. In the field of runology, one of the most significant intrusions of hypermodernistic thinking was introduced by the highly respected and influential English runologist R. I. Page (1924–2012), who posited the existence of what he called "skeptical" and "imaginative" runologists. While his analysis was undoubtedly correct in many respects, the labeling of these "schools" served to polarize the discipline in a way that was perhaps unnecessary and counterproductive. His observation had the effect of exacerbating the division. Of course, his intent may have been akin to that of one or another of the early Church Fathers, who were anxious to label ideas as "orthodox" or "heretical" in an attempt to purify doctrine.

In many ways, Page's imaginary division led to increasingly real divisions in the science of runology. The academic community, as it drifted more and more into the cult of political correctness, often considered the study of runes to be suspect in itself. This suspicion was supported by the supposed connection between the Nazis and the runes, but in fact it was more a matter of attempting to eliminate any sort of interest in pre-1500 European intellectual life, as such interests would inevitably lead to the discovery of the quality of the values of ancient Indo-European culture. This was something that had been targeted for elimination by ideological opponents of Western culture and civilization. The only refuge for many runologists was simply to immerse themselves ever deeper into the more quantifiable aspects of their study. The decidedly "unimaginative" school of runology has a death grip on the discipline in academia, and one that will not be soon broken. Most recently, another English runologist, Michael P. Barnes, wrote in an article attempting to define runology: "A meaningful definition of runology must, I think, be narrow. If it is to include archaeology, mythology and all kinds of history there might as well be no definition at all" (Barnes 2013, 27). Simplifying and narrowing one's focus is a classic method of ensuring accuracy and thoroughness in academic work, but if one's assumed task is the discovery of the actual *meaning* of the data, rather than merely an attempt to appear clever in front of one's peers or not to risk losing face before them, then this narrow path will surely lead into a dark crevasse.

Despite the fact that the hyperspecialization of any discipline will inevitably lead its practitioners further away from a global and general understanding of the topic, if these specializations can be harnessed in a more integral way, the contributions of these particular studies are invaluable. Specialists devoted to the fields of diachronic linguistics, art history, archaeology (and specifically the data relating to the construction of runic artifacts), codicology (regarding the manuscript tradition of the runic record), and a dozen other such fields only deepen and expand the possibilities for greater understanding.

But it might also be seen that the recent history of the discipline we know and love as runology is slipping into the paradigm familiar to all as the parable of the "Blind Men and the Elephant," which originated on the Indian subcontinent in ancient times and tells of six learned men who were blind and who came to study an elephant: each concluded, based on his own experience depending upon what part of the elephant he examined, that the object of their study was akin to a wall, a snake, a spear, a tree, a fan, or a rope. This formed the basis of a clever poem written by John Godfrey Saxe in 1872, which includes the lines:

> *And so these men of Indostan*
> *Disputed loud and long,*
> *Each in his own opinion*
> *Exceeding stiff and strong,*
> *Though each was partly in the right*
> *And all were in the wrong!*

The poem concludes:

> *So, oft in theologic wars,*
> *The disputants, I ween,*
> *Rail on in utter ignorance*
> *Of what each other mean,*
> *And prate about an Elephant*
> *Not one of them has seen!*

The challenge of integral runology is to bring a global understanding of the field back into the picture without sacrificing the precision of specialized studies. The object of our study must be seen in its entirety while maintaining the possibility of analyzing its constituent parts with precision. If, indeed, we are all blind as we deal with an object as mysterious and elusive as the runes represent, then some imagination must be exercised so that, even in our blindness and by honestly comparing notes of our understandings, we can construct a model of what the whole elephant must look like—even if we can only conceive of it in our *imaginations*.

To put it another way, as an obscure character in imaginative fiction named "A. Square" discovered when, living in his two-dimensional world of Flatland, he had an encounter with a certain "A. Sphere," whom to A. Square only appears to be a series of progressively larger, then smaller, circles. What A. Square has encountered is a being from a three-dimensional world as it passes through his two-dimensional homeland. A. Square is able to reason out what he has experienced, but not without a dose of imagination, as he can never directly perceive a sphere in his two-dimensional universe. Thus, the writer Edwin Abbott shows us in his little book *Flatland* (1884) that even A. Square can realize the truth, but not without the application of some imagination. The formula should probably be something like nine-tenths logical analysis and objective study coupled with one-tenth imagination.

As we have seen over the course of the history presented in this book, academic runology has regularly succumbed to various intellectual and ideological trends of the day. In the Storgöticism of the early modern age as well as in the National Socialism of the early twentieth century, such pressures were obvious. Today it is no different. The ideological climate of academic institutions in the West has become dominated by positivistic and quantitative methodologies that are often tinged to one degree or another with the assumptions of Marxist critical theory from the humanities. In general, topics drawn from pre-1500 (pre-Modern) fields are denigrated. Studies that focus on the symbolic and mythic content of pre-Modern European cultures are especially singled out for elimination in favor of multicultural and global approaches that focus on agendas of social injustice, and so on. Instead of the natural trend that could be observed from the early 1980s when interest in runes and runic writing was exploding in the popular culture and should have been reflected in the *expansion* of such studies in the world of academia, they were increasingly and severely curtailed, if not totally eliminated. Generally speaking, in the instances where runology does continue to be studied in academic contexts, the trend in recent years has been toward increased study of runic evidence in connection with purely linguistic data analysis and other more quantifiable and thus "safe" aspects.

One of the reasons I wrote this book was to examine the history of runology on all levels and thereby give current students and professionals a better view of the historical context of the pursuit of the meaning and interpretation of the runes and runic writing. It is my hope that in the future runology can be increasingly returned to its roots as an integral contextual study of Germanic culture. Runes are certainly best understood as a part of a larger cultural context. By the same token, within the study of runes, all individual artifacts and every group of related artifacts have to be seen as multidimensional cultural phenomena—a nexus of linguistics, art, ideology, and ethnology.

GENERAL CHARACTERISTICS OF AN INTEGRAL RUNOLOGY

First of all, it should be realized that runology will always have various branches and specialties and that those who study the runes will understand and misunderstand them to varying degrees. From a reading of this study it should now be apparent that this has always been the case, and recent history only amplifies that conclusion. What I propose as integral runology is a specialty unto itself, and one that involves a number of other kinds of study in a balanced synthesis. One of the main things that the integral runologist will realize is that there are several ways of approaching runology. They run along a spectrum from the highly objective and quantified to the exceedingly subjective and even "personal." On the one hand, the objective type of studies is invaluable as the nuts and bolts of the discipline. Without this basis, the resulting writing or research about runes can only be considered *poetry* or an exercise in fantasy. On the other hand, the individual who pursues a hyper-quantifiable form of study certainly runs the risk of falling into the same trap as those in the parable of "The Blind Men and the Elephant." The integral runologist takes the objective findings of science into account as much as possible and only uses imagination and educated guesswork as a way to hermeneutically bridge the gap between the objective analysis of the data and a holistic interpretation of what it really means, which includes a consideration of who the original creators of these artifacts and texts may have been. Essential to the approach of the integral runologist is also the acquisition of scientific knowledge from adjunct fields, such as comparative religion, history of religion, comparative mythology, anthropology, folklore, and so on, to broaden and focus his or her perspective and analytical tools.

It would appear that the aims of runologists over the most recent years have become ever narrower and limited with regard to what they hope to learn or discover. The integral runologist seeks to broaden those aims and to attempt to uncover something more about the character and nature of the individuals who wrote the runic texts over the centuries and to learn something of the culture in which they lived and worked. The hopeless skeptic will argue that we can never know anything certain about these matters, and so we should cease trying, but the ever-hopeful Romantic will try to persuade us that we should try harder, in ever more refined and comprehensive ways, and with a mind open to great possibilities. What is needed is an imaginative skepticism when it comes to runic evidence.

If, as most etymologists agree, the Proto-Germanic word *rūnō originally signified a "mystery"—that is, an awe-inspiring thing of unknown qualities deriving from some cosmic source—then the ramifications of the meaning of this word should be taken into account in any approach to an integral runology. Additionally, if the use of this word by the ancients as a designator of written characters is any indicator, the understanding of this word is an essential part of the pursuit. A mystery exhorts the observer to *solve* it. Assuming the cosmic level of awe ascribed to the runes by the ancients, it may be that runes can never be completely understood, that our knowledge of them, no matter how close we come to apprehending them, will remain eternally just beyond our reach. This circumstance then requires of us to develop ever more comprehensive methods of investigating them. We can make progress toward such knowledge, but the nature of their mystery is really such that it can never be fully grasped, understood, or defined by the finite intellect of humanity. In any event, such an attitude, if adopted by the world-be integral runologists, will always instill a healthy dose of humility—as well as respect—toward the ways the ancient runemasters thought and expressed themselves.

In the end, the situation revolves around answering to the sort of questions that arise when confronting the runic inscription on the Noleby stone (Vätergötland, Sweden, ca. sixth century) that we invoked at the beginning of this book:

ᚱᚢᚿᚮᚠᚨᚺᛁᚱᚨᚷᛁᚿᚨᚲᚢᛗᛟ [. . .]

runofahiraginaku(n)do [. . .]

rūnō fahi raginakundo . . .

"(A) rune I color, one stemming from the gods . . ."

Was the man who carved these runes more concerned with communicating with unseen beings and levels of reality, or was he more focused on representing his language in a grammatically correct manner to make himself clear to a human reader? Was he more a magician or a linguist? If we knew him personally, would he be more like a priest or a grammar teacher? How to discover greater knowledge about this man and the thread of those previous generations who taught him, and the thread of his future descendants in the craft of runecarving, is the most fascinating central question of integral runology. All components of the runic tradition are important and ideally none should be neglected in favor of another. The big picture is this: We have lost a great deal, especially in the humanities, in an era of overspecialization. There is a great role to be played by the generalist in all fields—someone who can weave all of the cords together into a coherent and meaningful pattern.

Historically, the runic tradition has been torn between the two beasts of timid intellect and raging emotion. An authentic *inner* approach to the tradition would have to go beyond the hyper-objectivity of diehard skeptics who—usually for reasons of career preservation—

reject any sort of imaginative insight. In equal measure, such an approach would have to be able to resist the hyper-subjective spells cast by modern political agendas of whatever stripe. The traditional runic system seems clear. The mythic context of runic understanding is also clear in that it most closely belongs to the Odinic and heroic (for example, the lineage of the Volsungs) paradigm.* Runes are most authentically understood from within this mythic paradigm. Other models of approach are secondary.

In one regard, however, I would agree with the modernistic approach as it concerns the health and well-being of the future discipline of integral runology: the scholarly approach must be kept strictly apart from the esoteric application of knowledge concerning the runes. The integration of these two aspects is only possible and productive on an individual basis and within the confines of a specialized school of thought. This is rather akin to the Platonic separation between two distinct forms of knowledge: *dianoia* (rational thought) and *noesis* (rational intuition). In the Academy of Plato both were necessary; and *dianoia* was the precursor to, and basis of, *noesis*. This seems a wise course of thought. For myself, and for the future school of integral runology, attention should continue to be paid to both branches of knowledge to best understand the ever-mysterious objects of our study.

---

*Both the Old Norwegian and Old Icelandic rune poems contain a half dozen clearly recognizable references to material from the *Saga of the Volsungs*. There may be further such references that are too obscure to identify easily.

CHRONOLOGY OF
THE RUNIC REVIVAL

1554 *Historia de Omnibus Gothorum Sueonumque Regibus* by Johannes Magnus

1555 *Historia de Gentibus Septentrionalibus* by Olaus Magnus

1557 *De gentium aliquot migrationibus, . . .* by Wolfgang Lazius (1514–1565) makes known the treatise *De inventione litterarum* (usually attributed to Hrabanus Maurus)

1597 *De literis et lingua Getarum, siue Gothorum, . . .* by Bonaventura Vulcanius (1538–1614) (*runica manuscripta*)

1599 *Runkänslans lärospån* by Johannes Bureus

1600 Letter from Granius to Vulcanius with Swedish rune poem

1603 *Runaräfst* by Johannes Bureus

1605 *Adulruna* by Johannes Bureus completed in its first version

1606 *De inventione litterarum* published in *Rerum Alamannicarum scriptores aliquot vetusti, . . .* edited by Melchior Goldast von Haiminsfeld (1578–1635)

1611 *Runa ABC-boken* by Johannes Bureus

1626 *Fasti Danici* by Olaus Wormius

1630 Office of *Riksantikvariet* created by King Gustav Adolf in Sweden

1636 ᚱᚢᚺᛁᛆ, *seu Danica literatura antiquissima* by Olaus Wormius

1642 Last version of the *Adulruna* completed by Johannes Bureus

1643 *Danicorum Monumentorum* by Olaus Wormius

1643 *Codex Regius* discovered in Iceland

1651 Second edition published of ᚱᚢᚺᛁᛆ, *seu Danica literatura antiquissima* by Wormius

1675 *Manuductio ad runographiam* by Olaus Verelius; Magnus Celsius delivers a lecture in which he deciphers the runes of Hälsingaland

1689 *Atlantica (Atland eller Manheim)* by Olof Rudbeck

1699 *Vita Theodorici regis Osrogothorum et Italiae, auctore Joanne Cochalaeo, . . .* edited by Johan Perinskiöld

1705 *Linguarum veterum septentrionalium Thesaurus, . . .* by George Hickes, in which he edits the Old English Rune Poem

1732 *Runologia* by Jón Ólafsson of Grunnavík

1734 Runic horn of Gallehus discovered

1747 *Is Atlinga* by Johan Göransson

1750 *Bautil, det är Svea ok Götha rikens runstenar* by Johan Göransson

1811 Götiska Förbund (Gothic Society) founded in Sweden

1815 Manhemsförbund (Manheim's Society) formed in Sweden

1821 *Ueber deutsche Runen* by Wilhelm Grimm

1832 *Run-Lära* by Johan G. Liljegren

1825 *Svea rikes häfder* by Erik Gustaf Geijer

1833 *Run-Urkunder* by Johan G. Liljegren

1866–1901 *The Old-Northern Runic Monuments of Scandinavia and England* (4 vols.) by George Stephens

1856–1859 *Die Urreligion, oder das endeckte Uralphabet* (2 vols.) by Jakob Laurents Studach

1874 *Runeskriftens Oprindelse og Udvikling i Norden* by Ludvig Wimmer

1884 *Handbook of Old-Northern Runic Monuments of Scandinavia and England* by George Stephens

1885 *Die älteren nordischen Runeninschriften* by Fritz Burg

1887 *Die Runenschrift*, new edition and translation of Wimmer's 1874 work

1889 *Die deutschen Runendenkmäler* by Rudolf Henning

1891–1924 *Norges Indskrifter med de ældre Runer* (3 vols.) by Sophus Bugge and Magnus Olsen

1900 *Ölands Runinskifter*, first volume of the ongoing series *Sveriges Runinskrifter: Ursprung der Buchstaben Gutenbergs* by Friedrich Fischbach

1908 *Das Geheimnis der Runen* by Guido von List

1916 "Om Troldruner" by Magnus Olsen

1927 *Runornas Talmystik och dess antika Förbild* by Sigurd Agrell

1930 *Die Hochzeit der Menschheit* by Rudolf John Gorsleben

1931–1935 Marby Rune book series (8 vols.) by Friedrich Bernard Marby

1932 *Heilige Runenmacht* by Siegfried Adolf Kummer

1939 *Die einheimischen Runendenkmäler des Festlandes* by Helmut Arntz and Hans Zeiss

1941/42 *Danmarks Runindskrifter* (3 vols.) by Erik Moltke and Lis Jacobsen

1942 *Islands Runeindskrifter* by Anders Bæksted

1952 *Målruner og Troldruner* by Anders Bæksted

1955 *Runenemagie* by Karl Spiesberger

1966 *Die Runeninscriften im älteren Futhark* by Wolfgang Krause and Herbert Jankuhn

1975 Manuscript of "A Primer of Runic Magic" by S. Edred Thorsson completed; Yggdrasil group founded in Sweden

1979 Manuscript of *Futhark: A Handbook of Rune Magic* by Edred Thorsson completed; Rune-Gild founded on December 20

1982 *The Book of Runes* by Ralph Blum

1984 Publication of *Futhark: A Handbook of Rune Magic* by Edred Thorsson

1985 *Nytt om Runer* first published

1993 The Rundata (Scandinavian Runic-text Data Base) project initiated

1997 First World-Moot of the Rune-Gild held in Austin, Texas

2010 *Futhark: An International Journal of Runic Studies* first appears

RUNIC ORIGINS OF THE "PEACE SIGN"

(Originally published in Runes *IV:5 [1986])*

In the early 1960s a curious sign, which until then had been unknown to most people, became prevalent. It could be seen on buttons, on the sides of microvans, and often painted or drawn on neighborhood buildings. Perhaps it was first noticed as a sign carried in various left-wing

demonstrations for peace and/or nuclear disarmament. It came to be known popularly as the "peace sign."

Among rune occultists it is popular to assume that anything that is runelike is in fact, on some level, actually runic; that is to say, mysterious or magical in character. While such forms of ascriptive magical thinking when kept under control can be made meaningful, it might be interesting first to find out whether a given runelike sign has factually runic roots. In the case of the "peace sign," this can be shown.

Some years ago, I read an account of this sign that was highly unsatisfactory. It stated that the sign was made up of a combination of two letters, N + D, from some obscure alphabet or another, and that these letters stood for "Nuclear Disarmament." Furthermore, it was reported that the sign was first developed and used by British anti-nuclear activists in the early 1960s. Later I was to discover that the "alphabet" in question was the semaphore signal system in which ⋀ stood for N and ⎮ stood for D. The resulting sign, ⊗, *was* in fact seen in protest groups, but it is distinctly *different* from the more familiar "peace sign." It seems beyond doubt that the latter sign was also used by such groups at that time, but was it their invention or did they borrow it from some previous source?

As it turns out, the use of this sign was not new to the Left in the 1960s. It had been used, for example, by the anti-Nazi Left in Germany itself and also by clever Russian propagandists on the eastern front. Actually, it is an example of the use of a group's internal symbolism against itself. In the esoteric runology of the early twentieth century, chiefly originated by Guido von List and his followers, the sign ⋏ indicated "death." This is in contrast to the sign ⋎, which meant "life." This symbolism quickly spread to popular use in early twentieth-century Germany, so that even certain newspapers began to print the dates of a person's birth and death prefixed by the signs ⋎ and ⋏, respectively—for example: Guido von List ⋎ 1848 – ⋏ 1919. Some papers continued the practice long after the war. It was well established that these symbols essentially stood for "life" and "death." (Perhaps it should be noted that far-right-wing organizations have also taken up the "life rune" as a symbol, for example, on the masthead of the *National Vanguard*.)

The Russians, as the Red Army advanced toward Berlin, distributed leaflets urging the Germans to give up the fight, telling them that the war was lost and that only death awaited them. These leaflets were decorated with the "peace sign"—in this case a sign of death. In the example below, we see a propaganda poster alerting the German Leftists that Heinrich Himmler (that is, the SS) was to assume responsibility for internal security in Germany as he had done in various lands the Germans had conquered—wherein massive genocide had been practiced. "Now it's OUR turn!!" the poster declares. Note the use of the "death rune."

It would seem that the sign was later taken up by Leftists. Doubtless, this was due as much to its mysterious allure (common to runic symbols in general) as to its associations with previous causes.

This can be taken as an example of the power of attraction possessed by certain signs, a kind of "command to look" (esoteric geometry),* and also as an example of the use of cultural associations with signs being used in a mode of psychological warfare. It may be a fact that if such signs have their roots in the deep psyche of the group being targeted, they will be far more effective than if they are arbitrary and wholly artificial. In this form of black magic, of course, Madison Avenue has far outstripped both Moscow and Berlin.

[*R.I.P.*]

---

*This concept is further discussed in my article "The Command to Look" (Flowers 2019b); for its original explication, see William Mortensen and George Dunham, *The Command to Look: A Master Photographer's Method for Controlling the Human Gaze* (Feral House, 2014).

BIBLIOGRAPHY

BOOKS

Abbott, Edwin Abbott ["A. Square"]. 1884. *Flatland: A Romance of Many Dimensions.* London: Seeley and Co.

Altheim, Franz. 1939. *Vom Ursprung der Runen.* Frankfurt/Main: Deutsches Ahnenerbe.

Andersson, Björn. 1997. *Runor, magi, ideologi.* Uppsala: Swedish Science Press.

Anttila, Tero. 2015. *The Power of Antiquity: The Hyperborean Research Tradition in Early Modern Swedish Research on National Antiquity.* Dissertation, University of Oulu.

Arntz, Helmut. 1938. *Die Runenschrift: Ihre Geschichte und ihre Denkmäler.* Halle/Saale: Niemeyer.

———. 1944. *Handbuch der Runenkunde.* Second edition. Halle/Saale: Niemeyer.

Arntz, Helmut, and Hans Zeiss. 1939. *Die einheimischen Runendenkmäler des Festlandes.* Leipzig: Harrassowitz.

Aswynn, Freya. 1988. *The Leaves of Yggdrasil.* London: Aswynn.

———. 1998. *Northern Mysteries and Magick: Runes, Gods, and Feminine Powers.* [Revised edition of *The Leaves of Yggdrasil.*] St. Paul, Minn.: Llewellyn.

Avery, Aelfric. 2018. *Armanen Runes and the Black Sun.* 3 vols. Vavenby, B.C.: Woodharrow Gild.

Bæksted, Anders. 1942. *Islands Runeindskrifter.* Copenhagen: Munksgaard.

———. 1952. *Målruner og Troldruner: Runemagiske Studier.* Copenhagen: Gyldendal.

Balzli, Johannes. 1917. *Guido von List: Der Wiederentdecker uralter arischer Weisheit.* Vienna: Guido-von-List-Gesellschaft.

Barnes, Michael P. 2012. *Runes: A Handbook.* Woodbridge, UK: Boydell.

———. 2013. "What Is Runology, and Where Does It Stand Today?" *Futhark* 4: 7–30.

Bienert, Josef. 1964. *Raunende Runen: Vergeistigung der Körperlichkeit.* Winnenden: Rubin.

Bjarke, Bodvar. 1988. ᚱᚢᚦᚠ: *En kortfattad introduktion till Runoralel & Runmagi.* [Stockholm]: Hedlund.

Blachetta, Walther. 1941. *Das Buch der deutschen Sinnzeichen.* Berlin-Lichterfelde: Widukind/Boss.

Blum, Ralph. 1983. *The Book of Runes.* New York: St. Martin's.

Brix, Hans. 1928. *Studier i nordisk Runemagi: Runemester-Kunsten, upplandske Runestene, Rökstenen, nogle nordiska Runetekster.* Copenhagen: Nordisk Forlag.

Bülow, Werner von. 1925. *Der Ewigkeitsgehalt der eddischen Runen und Zahlen: Grundriss arischer Weisheit und Jungbrunnen des deutschen Volkstums.* Munich: Siegeler.

Burnett, Charles S. F., and Marie Stoklund. 1983. "Scandinavian Runes in a Latin Magical Treatise." *Speculum* 58/2: 419–29.

Dillmann, Francois-Xavier. 1976. *Les runes dans la littérature islandaise ancienne.* 2 vols. Dissertation, University of Caen.

Cleary, Collin. [Forthcoming]. *Wagner's Ring and the Germanic Tradition.* Unpublished manuscript.

Düwel, Klaus. 1979. Review of W. Hartner, *Die Goldhörner von Gallehus,* and H. Klingenberg, *Runenschrift—Schriftdenken—Runeninschriften. Göttingische Gelehrte Anzeigen* 231: 224–50.

———. 2008. *Runenkunde.* Fourth revised and expanded edition. Stuttgart: Metzler.

Enoksen, Lars Magnar. 1998. *Runor: historia, tydning, tolkning.* Falun: Historiska Media.

Eriksson, Jörgen I., Marie Eriksson, Mikael W. Gejel, and Mikael Hedlund, eds. 1988. *Sejd—en vägledning i nordlig shamanism.* Stockholm: Vattumannen.

Faivre, Antoine. 1994. *Access to Western Esotericism.* Albany: State University of New York Press.

Fischbach, Friedrich. 1900. *Ursprung der Buchstaben Gutenbergs: Beitrag zur Runenkunde.* Mainz: Mainzer Verlagsanstalt.

Flowers, Stephen E. 2006. "How to Do Things with Runes: A Semiotic

Approach to Operative Communication." In *Runes and Their Secrets,* edited by Marie Stoklund, M. L. Nielsen, et al. Copenhagen: Museum Tusculanum. Pp. 65–81.

———. 2008. *Runes and Magic: Magical Formulaic Elements in the Older Runic Tradition.* Third edition. Bastrop, Tex.: Lodestar.

———. 2018. *The Fraternitas Saturni: History, Doctrine, and Rituals of the Magical Order of the Brotherhood of Saturn.* Rochester, Vt.: Inner Traditions.

———. 2019a. *Anglo-Frisian Runes: A Concise Edition of Old English and Frisian Runic Inscriptions.* Bastrop, Tex.: Runestar.

———. 2019b. "The Command to Look." In *Dark Rûna: Containing the Complete Essays Originally Published in* Black Rûna *(1995).* Bastrop, Tex.: Runestar. Pp. 17–21.

———. 2019c. *The Rune-Poems, vol. I: Introduction, Texts, Translations and Glossary.* Second edition. Bastrop, Tex.: Runestar.

———. 2020. *Runes and Runology: An Introduction to the Study of Runes and Runic Inscriptions.* Smithville, Tex.: Lodestar.

Flowers, Stephen E., and Michael Moynihan, trans. and eds. 2007. *The Secret King: The Myth and Reality of Nazi Occultism.* Los Angeles and Waterbury Center, Vt.: Feral House/Dominion.

Fries, Jan. 1993. *Helrunar: A Manual of Rune Magick.* Oxford: Mandrake.

Godwin, Joscelyn. 2007. *The Golden Thread: The Ageless Wisdom of the Western Mystery Traditions.* Wheaton, Ill.: Quest.

Goodrick-Clarke, Nicholas. 1985. *The Occult Roots of Nazism: The Ariosophists of Austria and Germany 1890–1935.* Wellingborough, UK: Aquarian.

Göransson, Johan. 1747. *Is Atlinga; Det är De Forna Göters, här uti Svea Rike, Bokstafver ok Salighets Lära, Tvåtusend Tvåhundred år före Chistum, utspridd i all Land.* Stockholm: Salvius.

Gorsleben, Rudolf John. 1930. *Die Hoch-Zeit der Menschheit: Das Welt-Gesetz der Drei oder Entstehen–Sein–Vergehen in Ursprache-Urschrift-Urglaube, aus den Runen geschöpft.* Leipzig: Koehler & Amelang.

Gothart, Br. 1928. *Die ariosophische Runen-Magie: Das ario-germanische Runen-Weistum.* Pforzheim: Reichstein.

Grimm, Wilhelm Carl. 1821. *Ueber deutschen Runen.* Göttingen: Dieterich.

Grimsson, Atrid. 1988. *Runmagi och Shamanism.* Stockholm: Vattumannen.

Guillaume, Jean-Yves. 1992. *Les runes et l'écriture des étoiles.* Paris: Dervy.

Håkansson, Håkan. 2012. "Alchemy of the Ancient Goths: Johannes Bureus'

Search for the Lost Wisdom of Scandinavia." *Early Science and Medicine* 17/5: 500–522.

Hauck, Karl, et al. 1983–1989. *Die Goldbrakteaten der Völkerwanderungszeit: Ikonographischer Katalog.* 7 vols. Berlin: De Gruyter. [Cited as IK]

Heinz, Ulrich Jürgen. 1987. *Die Runen: Ursprung, Bedeutung, Wirkung, Weissagung.* Freiburg/Breisgau: Bauer.

Hildebrand, Hans. 1910. "Minne af riksantikvarien Johannes Bureus." [= *Svenska Akademiens Handlingar* 23 (1908): 55–435]. Stockholm: Norstedt & Söner.

Hollander, Lee M. 1962. *The Poetic Edda.* 2nd edition. Austin: University of Texas Press.

Howard, Michael. 1980. *The Magic of the Runes: Their Origins and Occult Power.* Northamptonshire, UK: Aquarian.

Hunger, Ulrich. 1984. *Die Runenkunde im Dritten Reich: Ein Beitrag zur Wissenschafts- und Ideologiegeschichte des Nationalsozialismus.* Bern: Lang.

Jacobsen, Lis, and Moltke, Erik. 1941–1942. *Danmarks Runindskrifter.* 4 vols. Copenhagen: Munksgaard.

Jensen, Hans. 1969. *Sign, Symbol and Script: An Account of Man's Efforts To Write.* New York: Putnam.

Jossé, Roland Dionys. 1955. *Die Tala der Raunen (Runo-astrologische Kabbalistik): Handbuch der Deutung des Wesens und Weges eines Menschen auf Grund der in seinem Namen verborgenen Schicksalsraunen.* Freiburg/Breisgau: Bauer.

Jungandreas, Wolfgang. 1974. "Die Namen der Runen. Futhark und Kosmologie." *Onoma* 18: 365–90.

Karlsson, Thomas. 2002. *Uthark: The Nightside of the Runes.* Seattle: Ouroboros.

———. 2005. *Adulrunan och den götiska kabbalan.* Syndbyberg: Ouroboros.

———. 2009. *Götisk kabbala och runisk alkemi: Johannes Bureus och den götiska esoterismen.* Dissertation, University of Stockholm.

———. 2019. *Nightside of the Runes: Uthark, Adulruna, and the Gothic Cabbala.* Translated by Stephen E. Flowers, et al. Rochester, Vt.: Inner Traditions.

Kater, Michael. 1997. *Das 'Ahnenerbe' der SS 1935–1945: Ein Beitrag zur Kulturpolitik des Dritten Reiches.* Second edition. Stuttgart: Deutsche Verlags Anstalt.

Kelly, Michael. *The Book of Ogham.* Creative Space Publishing Platform, 2010.

Kennedy, Gordon. 1998. *The Children of the Sun: A Pictorial Anthology, from Germany to California 1883–1949.* Ojai: Nivaria.

King, David. 2005. *Finding Atlantis: A True Story of Genius, Madness, and an Extraordinary Quest for a Lost World*. New York: Three Rivers Press.

Klingenberg, Heinz. 1973. *Runenschrift—Schriftdenken—Runeninschriften*. Heidelberg: Winter.

Kosbab, Werner. 1982. *Das Runen-Orakel: Einweihung in die Praxis der Runen-Weissagung*. Freiburg/Breisgau: Bauer.

Krause, Wolfgang. *Was man in Runen ritzte*. Halle/Saale: Niemeyer, 1935.

Krause, Wolfgang, with contributions from Herbert Jankuhn. 1966. *Die Runeninschriften im älteren Futhark*. 2 vols. Göttingen: Vandenhoeck & Ruprecht.

Kummer, Siegfried Adolf. 1932. *Heilige Runenmacht*. Hamburg: Uranus.

———. 1933. *Runen-Magie*. Dresden: Hartmann.

———. 1934a. *Runen-Raunen: Eine Sammlung eingesandter Berichte nach den Runenkunden von S. A. Kummer*. Dresden: Self-published.

———. 1934b. *Walhall: Hand- und Bilderschrift für Runenkunde, Mystik und Vorgeschichte. Briefe an Runenfreunde zum persönlichen Gebrauch*. Dresden: Self-published.

———. *Rune-Magic*. 1993. Smithville: Rûna-Raven.

———. *Holy Rune Might*. 2019. Translated by Aelfric Avery. Vavenby, B.C.: Woodharrow Gild.

Kurtzahn, E. Tristan. *Die Runen als Heilszeichen und Schicksalslose*. Bad Oldesloe: Uranus, 1924.

Lange, Hans-Jürgen. 1998. *Weisthor: Karl Maria Willigut: Himmlers Rasputin und seine Erben*. Engerda: Arun.

Lauth, Franz Joseph. 1857. *Das germanische Runen-Fudark, aus den Quellen kritisch erschlossen und nebst einigen Denkmälern zum ersten Male erklärt*. Munich: n.p.

Lenthe, Eckehard. 2018. *Wotan's Awakening: The Life and Times of Guido von List, 1848–1919*. Translated by Annabel Lee. Waterbury Center, Vt.: Dominion.

Liljegren, Johan Gustaf. 1832. *Run-Lära*. Stockholm: Norsted & Söner.

Lindroth, Sten. 1943. *Paracelsismen i Sverige till 1600-talets mitt*. Stockholm: Almqvist and Wiksell.

List, Guido von. 1891. *Deutsch-mythologische Landschaftsbilder*. 2 vols. Berlin: Lustenoder.

———. 1908. *Das Geheimnis der Runen*. Gross-Lichterfelde: Zillmann.

———. 1910. *Die Bilderschrift der Ario-Germanen*. Vienna: Guido-von-List-Gesellschaft.

———. 1914. *Die Ursprache der Ario-Germanen und ihre Mysteriensprache*. Vienna: Guido-von-List-Gesellschaft.

———. 1988. *The Secret of the Runes*. Translated by Stephen E. Flowers. Rochester, Vt.: Destiny.

———. 2005. *The Religion of the Aryo-Germanic Folk: Esoteric and Exoteric*. Translated by Stephen E. Flowers. Smithville, Tex.: Rûna-Raven.

———. 2011. *The Invincible*. Translated by Stephen E. Flowers. Bastrop, Tex.: Lodestar.

Lomer, Georg. 1927. *Die Götter der Heimat: Grundzüge einer germanischen Astrologie*. Bad Schmiedeberg and Leipzig: Baumann.

Malm, Mats. 1996. *Minervas äpple: Om diktsyn, tolkning och bildspråk inom nordisk göticism*. Dissertation, University of Gothenburg.

Marby, Friedrich Bernhard. 1931. *Runenschrift, Runenwort, Runengymnastik*. Stuttgart: Marby.

———. 1932. *Marby-Runen-Gymnastik*. Stuttgart: Marby.

———. 1935. *Rassische Gymnastik als Aufrassungsweg*. Stuttgart: Marby.

———. 1935. *Die Rosengärten und das ewige Land der Rasse*. Stuttgart: Marby.

———. 1957. *Die Drei Schwäne*. Stuttgart: Marby.

———. 1977 [1957]. *Der Weg zu den Müttern*. Stuttgart: Spieth.

McKinnell, John, and Rudolf Simek, with Klaus Düwel. 2004. *Runes, Magic and Religion: A Sourcebook*. Vienna: Fassbinder.

Mercer, A. D. 2016. *Runen: Wisdom of the Runes*. Amsterdam: Aeon Sophia.

Mortensen, William, and George Dunham. 2014. *The Command to Look: A Master Photographer's Method for Controlling the Human Gaze*. Edited by Michael Moynihan and Larry Lytle. Port Towsend, Wash.: Feral House.

Mountfort, Paul Rhys. 2003. *Nordic Runes: Understanding, Casting, and Interpreting the Ancient Viking Oracle*. Rochester, Vt.: Destiny.

Mund, Rudolf J. 1982. *Der Rasputin Himmlers: Die Wiligut Saga*. Vienna: Volkstum.

Murphy, G. Ronald. 1989. *The Saxon Savior: The Transformation of the Gospel in the Ninth-Century Heliand*. Oxford: Oxford University Press.

Neckel, Gustav, and Hans Kuhn, eds. 1962. *Edda: Die Lieder des Codex Regius nebst verwandten Denkmälern*. Second edition. Heidelberg: Winter.

Olsen, Kaedrich. 2008. *Runes for Transformation: Using Ancient Symbols to Change Your Life.* York Beach, Me.: Weiser.

Osborn, Marijane, and Stella Longland. 1982. *Rune Games.* London: Routledge and Kegan Paul.

Paxson, Diana. 2005. *Taking Up the Runes: A Complete Guide to Using Runes in Spells, Rituals, Divination, and Magic.* York Beach, Me.: Weiser.

Pennick, Nigel. 1981. *Hitler's Secret Sciences.* Sudbury, UK: Spearman.

Peterson, James M. 1988. *The Enchanted Alphabet: A Guide to Authentic Rune Magic and Divination.* Wellingborough: Aquarian.

Peschel, Lisa. 1989. *A Practical Guide to the Runes: Their Uses in Divination and Magick.* St. Paul: Llewellyn.

Pushong, Carlyle A. 1978. *Rune Magic.* London: Regency.

Reichardt, Konstantin. 1936. *Runenkunde.* Jena: Diederichs.

Rudbeck, Olof. 1937–1950. *Atland eller Manheim.* 5 vols. Uppsala: Almqvist & Wiksell.

Ruppel, Karl Konrad. 1939. *Die Hausmarke, das Symbol der germanischen Sippe.* Berlin: Metzner.

Russell, James C. 1994. *The Germanization of Early Medieval Christianity: A Sociohistorical Approach to Religious Approach to Religious Transformation.* Oxford: Oxford University Press.

Rüsten, Rudolf. 1914. *Was tut not? Ein Führer durch die gesamte Literatur der Deutschbewegung.* Leipzig: Hedeler.

Schilling, Heinar. 1937. *Kleine Runenkunde.* Magdeburg: Nordland.

Schneider, Karl. 1956. *Die germanischen Runennamen: Versuch einer Gesamtdeutung.* Meisenheim: Hain.

Scholem, Gershom. 1987. *Origins of the Kabbalah.* Princeton: Princeton University Press.

Schöttler, Wolfgang. 1948. *Die Runenstrophen der Edda: Runenkundliche Untersuchungen über den Quellenwert der eddischen Runenstrophen.* Dissertation, University of Göttingen.

Schück, Adolf. 1930. "Kulturminnesvård genom tre Sekler." In *Svensk Kulturminnesvård: Ett 300-årsminne,* edited by Henrik Schück. Stockholm: Centralkommittén för Gustav-Adolfs-Fonden.

Sebottendorff, Rudolf von. 2013. *Secret Practices of the Sufi Freemasons: The Islamic Teachings at the Heart of Alchemy.* Translated by Stephen E. Flowers. Rochester, Vt.: Inner Traditions.

Serrano, Miguel. 1986. *Adolf Hitler, el Último Avatāra*. Bogota: Editorial Solar.

———. 2014. *Adolf Hitler: The Ultimate Avatar*. Translated by Franz Berg. N.p.: Heritage Helm Corpus. [English translation online at: https://blacksun -sole-nero.net/libri-pdf-ebooks/adolf-hitler-the-ultimate-avatar-miguel -serrano-english-pdf-ebook.pdf (accessed August 11, 2020)]

Seznec, Jean. 1961. *The Survival of the Pagan Gods*. Translated by Barbara Sessions. New York: Harper and Row.

Shou, Peryt [= Albert C. G. Schultz]. [1920]. *Die "Edda" als Schlüssel des kommenden Weltalters!* Berlin-Pankow: Linser.

———. 2017. *The Edda as the Key to the Coming Age*. Translated by Stephen E. Flowers. Bastrop, Tex.: Lodestar.

Spiesberger, Karl. 1955. *Runenmagie*. Berlin: Schikowski.

———. 1958. *Runenexerzitien für Jedermann: Die Erhaltung der Gesundheit, die Erlangung von Erfolg und magischer Kräfte durch die Macht der Runen*. Freiburg/Breisgau: Bauer.

Stauff, Philipp. 1913. *Runenhäuser*. Berlin-Lichterfelde: Scheffer.

Stephens, George. 1866–1901. *The Old-Northern Runic Monuments of Scandinavia and England*. 4 vols. London: Smith.

———. 1884. *Handbook of the Old-Northern Runic Monuments of Scandinavia and England*. Edinburgh: Williams and Norgate.

Studach, Jakob Laurents. 1856–1859. *Die Urreligion, oder das endeckte Uralphabet*. 2 vols. Stockholm: Bonnier.

Svennung, Josef. 1967. *Zur Geschichte des Goticismus*. Stockholm: Almqvist & Wiksell.

Svärdström, Elisabeth. 1936. *Johannes Bureus' Arbeten om Svenska Runinskrifter*. Stockholm: Wahlström & Widstrand.

Tacitus, Cornelius. 1948. *The Agricola and the Germania*. Translated by H. Mattingly. Harmondsworth, UK: Penguin.

———. 1975. *The Histories*. Translated by K. Wellesley. Harmondsworth, UK: Penguin.

Tegtmeier, Ralph. 1988. *Runen: Alphabet der Erkenntis*. Freiburg/Breisgau: Urania.

Thorsson, Edred. 1984. *Futhark: A Handbook of Rune Magic*. York Beach, Me.: Weiser.

———. 1987. *Runelore: A Handbook of Esoteric Runology*. York Beach, Me.: Weiser.

———. 1988. *At the Well of Wyrd.* York Beach, Me.: Weiser.

———. 1989. *Rune Might: The Secret Practices of the German Rune Magicians.* St. Paul, Minn.: Llewellyn.

———. 1991. *The Nine Doors of Midgard: A Curriculum of Rune-work.* St. Paul, Minn.: Llewellyn.

———. 1992. *The Book of Ogham.* St. Paul, Minn.: Llewellyn.

———. 1992b. *Northern Magic: Mysteries of the Norse, Germans and English.* St. Paul, Minn.: Llewellyn.

———. 1996. *Green Rûna: The Runemaster's Notebook: Shorter Works of Edred Thorsson, Volume 1 (1978–1985).* Smithville, Tex.: Rûna-Raven.

———. 2006. *Mainstays from* Rune-Kevels, *Volume 1 (1993-1998).* Smithville, Tex.: Rune-Gild.

———. 2012. *Alu: An Advanced Guide to Operant Runology.* San Francisco: Weiser.

———. 2016. *The Nine Doors of Midgard: A Curriculum of Rune-work.* Fifth revised and expanded edition. South Burlington, Vt.: Rune-Gild.

———. 2018. *Rune Might: The Secret Practices of the German Rune Magicians.* Third revised and expanded edition. Rochester, Vt.: Inner Traditions.

———. 2019. *History of the Rune-Gild: The Reawakening of the Gild, 1980–2018.* North Augusta, S.C.: Gilded Books.

Thorsson, S. Edred. 2018. *The Runic Magic of the Armanen.* [Originally written in 1975.] Bastrop, Tex.: Runestar.

Tyson, Donald. 1988a. *Rune Magic.* St. Paul, Minn.: Llewellyn.

———. 1988b. *The New Magus: Ritual Magic as a Personal Process.* St. Paul, Minn.: Llewellyn.

Wawn, Andrew. 2002. *The Vikings and the Victorians: Inventing the Old North in Nineteenth-Century Britain.* Woodbridge: Brewer.

Weber, Edmund. 1941. *Kleine Runenkunde.* Berlin: Nordland.

Weigel, Karl Theodor. 1937. *Runen und Sinnbilder.* Berlin: Metzner.

———. 1943. *Beiträge zur Sinnbildforschung.* Berlin: Metzner.

———. 1936. "Unsere Stellung zu den Runen." *SS-Leitheft* 2: 56–58.

Weitzel, Fritz. 1939. *Die Gestaltung der Feste im Jahres- und Lebenslauf in der SS-Familie.* Wuppertal: Völkischer Verlag.

Wild, Leon D. 2004. *The Runes Workbook: A Step-By-Step Guide to Learning the Wisdom of the Staves.* San Diego: Thunder Bay.

Wiligut, Karl Maria [Lobesam]. 1903. *Seyfrids Runen.* Vienna: Schalk.

Willis, Tony. 1986. *The Runic Workbook: Understanding and Using the Power of Runes*. Wellingborough, UK: Aquarian.

Wilser, Ludwig. 1905. *Zur Runenkunde: Zwei Abhandlungen*. Leipzig: Akademischer Verlag.

Wimmer, Ludvig F. A. 1887. *Die Runenschrift*. Translated into German by F. Holthausen. Berlin: Weidmann.

Wirth, Herman. 1928. *Der Aufgang der Menschheit: Untersuchungen zur Geschichte der Religion, Symbolik und Schrift der atlantisch-nordischen Rasse*. Jena: Diederichs.

———. 1931–1936. *Die heilige Urschrift der Menschheit: Symbolgeschichtliche Untersuchungen diesseits und jenseits des Nordatlantik*. 2 vols. Leipzig: Koehler & Amelang.

Yates, Frances. 1978. *The Rosicrucian Enlightenment*. Boulder: Shambhala.

PERIODICALS

Academic Runology

Futhark: International Journal of Runic Studies, 2010–present.

Nytt om Runer: Meldingsblad om runeforskning, 1985–2008.

Esoteric Runology

Hagal: Ur-Sprache, Ur-Schrift, Ur-Sinn. Published by the Edda-Gesellschaft, Mittenwald, 1934, 1936–1938.

Hag All/All Hag: Zeitschrift für arische Freiheit. Published by the Edda-Gesellschaft, Mittenwald, 1933.

Runen: Zeitschrift für germanische Geistesoffenbarungen und Wissenschaften. Merkblatt für den Freundschaftsgrad des Germanen-Ordens Walvater. Magdeburg: Germanen-Orden Walvater, 1918–1929.

INDEX